Bulgaria

*Public Expenditure Issues and
Directions for Reform*

THE WORLD BANK
Washington, D.C.

ISBN: 0-8213-5400-0
eISBN: 0-8213-5401-9
ISSN: 0253-2123

Cover Photo by Radoslav Spassov.

Library of Congress Cataloging-in-Publication Data
World Bank.
   Bulgaria—public expenditure issues and directions for reform.
      p. cm. — (A World Bank country study)
   Text in English with summary in Bulgarian.
   The report was initiated by Leila Zlaoui and a team of World Bank staff and Bulgarian and international experts.
   Includes bibliographical references.
   ISBN 0-8213-5400-0
     1. Bulgaria—Appropriations and expenditures. 2. Government spending policy—Bulgaria. 3. Bulgaria—Economic policy—1989– I. Title: Bulgarian title in galley: Bulgariia—vuprosi na publichnite razkhodi i nasoki za reforma. II. Zlaoui, Leila. III. Title. IV. Series.

HJ7865.W67 2003
336.3′8′09499—dc21

2002044908

TABLE OF CONTENTS

TABLES

FIGURES

Boxes

ABSTRACT

This is the first-ever Public Expenditure and Institutional Review (PEIR) on Bulgaria by the World Bank. The objective of this country study is to outline policies and institutional issues to improve the efficiency and effectiveness of public expenditures in Bulgaria. To this end, it assesses fiscal sustainability—a fiscal stance that is sustainable in the medium-term—and analyzes efficiency and effectiveness of public expenditures and their institutional framework. The report is based on findings of several missions that visited Bulgaria in mid-2001 and in 2002.

Overall Bulgaria has made substantial progress toward long-term macroeconomic stability—an important step along the way to its ultimate goals of improving living standards and accession to the EU. Growth has been re-established, per capita income has improved, poverty has declined, inflation has remained low, and the external debt to GDP ratio is declining. The banking sector has been put on a more solid footing, the share of the private sector in the economy is increasing, major regulatory reform is underway, and energy pricing reforms are improving efficiency and reducing the fiscal burden. Bulgaria is also making important progress in its EU accession program. However, the Report notes that important challenges remain: Bulgaria must continue to maintain macroeconomic stability, move forward on structural reforms to sustain the growth momentum and achieve further reductions in poverty and meaningful reductions in unemployment. Fiscal policies, and public expenditure policies in particular will play a critical role in meeting these challenges.

The PEIR carried out an in-depth analysis of public expenditures in five sectors—education, health, social protection, the state railways, and energy sectors. It also analyzes the institutional challenges in public expenditure management. Key findings include:

Fiscal Position and Policy Going Forward.   Bulgaria's overall fiscal position is strong compared to other countries in the region and the EU Cohesion countries (Greece, Ireland, Portugal, and Spain). Tax revenues, however, are high—reduction of fiscal deficits since 1997 was achieved primarily by increasing revenues while public expenditures have remained nearly unchanged as ratio to GDP. Easing of the overall tax burden, especially payroll taxes, is highly desirable to boost employment and reduce tax evasion but this would require first a rationalization and restructuring of public expenditures to ensure macroeconomic stability. Fiscal strategy will also need to adjust to the decline in privatization revenues as the privatization program is completed.

Inter- and Intrasectoral Allocations.   Without prescribing an optimal level and composition of expenditures, public expenditure levels on economic affairs, particularly railways and energy, defense and security, and general services appear high and are candidates for rationalization. Health, education and the social protection system, require reallocation of public expenditures according to pressing intrasectoral priorities and to improve efficiency and effectiveness of public expenditures allocated to these sectors.

Education—Facing the Demographic Challenge and the Challenge of Improving Quality and Access, to Secure the Future.   Education expenditures to GDP of Bulgaria are comparable to the average in Central Eastern European countries. But, Bulgaria's negative population growth rate, aggravated by net out-migration, results in declining school-age population—a trend that is expected to continue at least through the middle of the next decade. The main reform priorities in the education sector, including universities, is to reallocate expenditures from surplus capacity in teaching staff and underused facilities toward modernization and upgrading of curricula, textbooks, teaching materials, and schools. There is also an urgent need to address quality and access challenges.

Health Care—Facing the Demographic Challenge, Improving Quality and Access, and Securing Financial Integrity of the Health Insurance System.   Bulgaria's health indicators are poor compared to those of other transition economies. Factors contributing to this weak health status include: (i) inefficient use of resources, as manifested through both excess capacity and low utilization rates of facilities, especially in the hospital system; and (ii) neglect of maintenance of facilities and equipment. Key reform priorities include addressing the concurrent problems of surplus capacity issues in health facilities, the deterioration in the quality of facilities, and the inadequate modernization of equipment; securing financial integrity of the NHIF; and addressing access issues of the disadvantaged.

Social Protection System—Facing the Challenge of Consolidation to Ensure Sustainability and Further Improvements in Effectiveness. Social protection programs have a wide coverage among the population. Over 80 percent of Bulgarians receive at least one type of benefit-however, only one-third of the population is of retirement age or poor. Some social assistance and benefit programs have become more pro-poor since the mid-1990s and are playing a major role in alleviating poverty. But, given the plethora of these programs, the complexity of program design in many cases, a challenge of the social protection system is to examine opportunities for consolidation and engage in systematic monitoring of the programs, their costs and their effectiveness.

Railways—Reducing the Drain of Public Resources and Increasing Productivity. The Bulgaria State Railway (BDZ) operates very inefficiently: its net income has been negative since the economic transition. BDZ receives a large contribution from the State to cover its deficit-an average of 0.8 percent of GDP in recent years. These large subsidies have not prevented the serious deterioration of railway assets. To stem the deterioration of the railway sector, key priority reforms include a drastic reduction in uneconomic services, initiated on the basis of a carefully prepared and properly discussed rationalization plan.

Energy—Improving Efficiency and Modernizing the Regulatory Framework. The report acknowledges that the Government has made important progress in energy sector reforms. At the same time, key priority reforms, however, remain: (i) enhancing the capacity of the State Energy Regulatory Commission; (ii) implementing the recently adopted electricity price adjustment schedule to bring prices to full cost recovery in 2002–04; and (iii) delaying costly investment in new power and heating generation capacity until regulatory reforms are more advanced and investors can assume a larger share of the market risk under a suitable regulatory framework.

Institutional Framework of Public Expenditures—Improving Management and Accountability in the Use of Public Resources. To ensure the fiscal discipline necessary to support the Currency Board Arrangement, the Government of Bulgaria has already initiated a number of institutional reforms. As a result, effective control over cash flows has been greatly improved. Despite this important progress there is need to continue and broaden the reform effort, especially in accounting and auditing—internal audit needs to be made operational across all first-level budget units; capital expenditure proposals should be prepared under hard budget constraints and as integral part of the medium-term budget framework; and there is a need to strengthen financial management at the local government level.

PREFACE

This study of Bulgaria's public expenditures follows on the extensive review of the Bulgarian economy undertaken in 2000, with a focus partly on European Community (EC) accession requirements.[1] The study was initiated in parallel with a Poverty Assessment Update, which is in progress. As documented in the country economic memorandum (CEM), Bulgaria has been implementing a program of far-reaching reforms, especially since the economic crisis of 1996/97, which has produced positive results; but considerably more needs to be done if Bulgaria is to meet its goal of equitable and sustained growth.

Key to achieving these objectives in any country, especially in one facing Bulgaria's constraints and aspiring to European Union (EU) accession, are the allocation and efficiency of public expenditures. For that reason, this public expenditure and institutional review (PEIR) was initiated with strong government support and has been endorsed by both the previous government and the current one, which came to power in July 2001.

As its title indicates, the PEIR focuses on public expenditure issues and policy directions; it stops short of suggesting the make-up of an optimal public expenditure program with specified expenditure levels or shares. Several factors have shaped the report's focus and coverage. These include the following:

- This is the first PEIR on Bulgaria; it was launched without the benefit of prior work in several crucial areas.
- The Government is committed to continue and broaden the reform effort—the analysis presented here is intended to inform policymakers and support implementation of structural reforms to improve the efficiency of public expenditures.
- The reform program has reached a crucial state; the first-generation reforms having been successfully completed, the second generation reforms are to be defined at this juncture—a task which requires stock-taking and broadening the internal dialogue on policy directions.
- Bulgaria faces a broad agenda, magnified by EU accession requirements, and many of whose elements are closely interlinked.

These factors alone have led to broadening the scope of the PEIR beyond the two or three sectors, such as education and health, which has been common practice. The broad coverage, extending to five sectors in this case, was specifically requested by the Government.

The primary audience of this Report is Bulgarian decisionmakers at both the central and the municipal levels. The objective is to facilitate decision making through better knowledge. Bulgaria has a knowledge deficit in a number of areas. While this (the problem with the supply of knowledge) constrains the identification of issues and priorities, the agenda tackled (the demand for knowledge) shapes the knowledge base that is developed. For example, one of the key knowledge deficits concerns capital expenditure requirement, for both maintenance and new investments, built on specific knowledge of the state of the infrastructure and physical facilities. One can argue that the neglect of investment planning, evaluation and financing has contributed to the non-development of the knowledge needed to change course. The same applies to the problem of human capacity.

The audience for this study also includes Bulgarian technicians, policymakers, and civil society—managers and staff charged with evaluating choices, proposing actions to decision makers, and implementing the decisions. Many of the technicians are quite capable, but most are overwhelmed by the problems they have to address simultaneously, and their daily duties limit the time and means they have to invest in the task. For these reasons, the PEIR also aims to share knowledge and analyses of this joint effort, which leveraged local and international expertise, to Bulgarian technicians, policy makers, and civil society.

---

[1] *Bulgaria: The Dual Challenge of Transition and Accession*, A World Bank Country Study, 2001.

The Report is in two parts. The first serves as the "main report" and is intended for policy-makers who need a broad perspective on overall reforms. It is self-contained and is a synthesis of the detailed sectoral analyses in the second part. Part One is made up of five chapters. Chapter 1 lays out the strategic setting, or challenges, against the backdrop of Bulgaria' performance, prospects, constraints, and opportunities. Chapter 2 examines the structure and trends of Bulgaria's public expenditures in a macroeconomic context. Chapter 3 outlines the main sectoral issues and discusses sectoral reform priorities in each area; it is a summary of the discussion in Part Two. Chapter 4 describes the main institutional and expenditure management challenges, which must be met to improve overall expenditure policies. The main report concludes with Chapter 5, which sets out some cross-cutting themes, overall priorities and some proposals for further research bearing on public expenditures, either directly or indirectly.

Part Two presents the more detailed sectoral analyses. These background papers provide detailed analyses and recommendations for line ministry and budget officials. Part Two examines in detail five sectors—Education, Health, Social Protection, Railway Transport, and Energy. At the Government's request, the sectoral chapters address sectoral issues and policies as a whole, going beyond the expenditure aspects, partly because of the knowledge deficit. The sectors were selected in close consultation with the Government. They cover the main areas where reforms are under-way and where important expenditure issues need to be addressed to complete the ongoing process of fiscal consolidation. Inevitably, the coverage is not exhaustive and some important reforms areas have been omitted. At the end of the Main Report, we have outlined the priorities for future work.

ACKNOWLEDGMENTS

This Public Expenditure and Institutional Review (PEIR) is based on the findings of several missions that visited Bulgaria between May 2001 and March 2002. A working draft was discussed with the Government, development partners, and civil society during a mission that visited Bulgaria in June 2002. The period of analysis covers from the mid-90s up to 2001 and early 2002.

The team that prepared the Report wishes to thank the Government of Bulgaria for the excellent cooperation received from many senior officials during the different missions and during the government discussions. The team wishes to express its special thanks to Mr. Kiril Ananiev, Deputy Minister of Finance and Leader of the PEIR Working Group, and Ms. Rossitsa Velkova, the Coordinator of the PEIR exercise in the Ministry of Finance for their substantive input and their help in organizational arrangements. Mr. Petyo Nikolov, Senior Advisor to the Executive Director of the World Bank, also provided important insights and invaluable assistance in preparing the document.

The Report was initiated by Leila Zlaoui and a team of World Bank staff and Bulgarian and international experts. The first phase involved the preparation of a number of background papers: "Fiscal Sustainability in Bulgaria" by A. Craig Burnside; "Health in Transition" by William G. Jack; "Education—The Demographic Challenge" by Michael Mertaugh; "Energy—A Complex Restructuring: Fiscal, Social and Market Interactions" by Salman Zaheer; "Is Bulgaria Ready for MTEF and Outcome Budgeting" by Daniel Tommasi; "Social Protection: Issues and Recommendations" by Dena Ringold and Esperanza Lasagabaster; "The State Railway—Fiscal Burden and Options for Reform" by Jean-Jacques Crochet. Anita Correa assisted the team in the first phase. A team comprising Kyle Peters, Stella Ilieva, Rosalinda Quintanilla, Kathryn Rivera, and Doreen J. Duff (ECSPE) and Ben Varon (Consultant) finalized the Report.

Throughout the preparation of this Report, the PEIR team benefited from its close collaboration with various ministries and agencies, as well as with NGOs and international institutions such as the European Commission and USAID. In particular, the PEIR benefited from extensive discussions with the Ministry of Finance. While the Ministry of Finance was the principal partner on the Bulgarian side, the collaboration with almost all line ministries and a large number of state agencies greatly improved our understanding of the real fiscal stance and the challenges that the Bulgarian authorities are facing and will face in the future.

The team benefited from the effective and very close collaboration with government officials, in particular with Deputy Minister of Finance Mr. Kiril Ananiev and Mr. Dimitar Radev, former Deputy Minister of Finance. Mission members had the opportunity to discuss the main findings of the different topics and sectors analyzed with government officials at the Council of Ministers, Bulgarian National Bank, Ministry of Finance, Ministry of Regional Development and Public Works, Ministry of Education and Science, Ministry of Defense, Ministry of Health, Ministry of Transport and Communications, Ministry of Labor and Social Policy, Ministry of Interior, Ministry of Environment, National Statistical Institute, Agency for Economic Analyses and Forecasting, National Health Insurance Fund, National Social Security Institute, Public Internal Financial Control Agency, BDZ, and the sub-national government officials in Sofia, Blagoevgrad, Pleven, and Elin Pelin.

The missions' members also had the opportunity to discuss key issues with representatives from the Local Government Initiative supported by USAID, the European Commission, International Monetary Fund, and NGOs: The National Association of Municipalities in the Republic of Bulgaria, Romani Baht, and Club Economika 2000.

The PEIR also benefited from valuable comments, suggestions and guidance received at different stages of preparation from: Andrew Vorkink (Country Director, ECC05), Oscar de Bruyn Kops (Country Manager, ECCBG), Julius Varallyay (Lead Country Officer, ECCA5), Peter Pojarski (Operations Officer, ECSHD), Doncho Barbalov (Operations Officer, ECSIE), Istvan

Dobozi (Lead Energy Economist, ECSIE), Henk Busz (ECSIE, Sector Manager), Maureen Lewis (Sector Manager, ECSHD), and Bernard Funck (Lead Economist for EU Accession, ECSPE). Special thanks to Boryana Gotcheva (ECSHD, Senior Operations Officer) for her participation in the missions and valuable comments and suggestions on the education and social protection chapters, and to Albena Samsonova who provided administrative support to the various missions. Excellent suggestions and comments were received from the peer reviewers, Philippe Le Houerou (Sector Manager, AFTP1) and Philip O'Keefe (Senior Economist, ECSHD).

The authors would like to express their sincere gratitude to various ministries, agencies and local authorities in Bulgaria for the time they spent with the team in open and friendly discussions and many valuable comments they made on the working draft of the Report. Their cooperation made this Report possible. In particular, special thanks are due to Lyubomir Datzov, Vladimir Petrov, and Iana Paliova, from the Ministry of Finance, for their effective support and contributions to the multiple mission agendas.

Vice President:	Johannes F. Linn
Country Director:	Andrew N. Vorkink
Sector Director:	Cheryl W. Gray
Sector Manager:	Kyle Peters
Task Team Leader:	Kyle Peters, Leila Zlaoui

ACRONYMS AND ABBREVIATIONS

ALMPs . . . . .Active Labor Market Programs
BDZ . . . . .Bulgaria State Railway
BIHS . . . . .Bulgarian Integrated Household Survey
BOP . . . . .Balance of Payments
CBA . . . . .Currency Board Arrangement
CEE . . . . .Central and Eastern Europe
CEM . . . . .Country Economic Memorandum
CIT . . . . .Corporate Income Tax
COM . . . . .Council of Ministers
DH . . . . .District Heating
EBRD . . . . .European Bank for Reconstruction and Development
EC . . . . .European Commission
ECA . . . . .Europe and Central Asia
EIB . . . . .European Investment Bank
eop . . . . .end of period
EU . . . . .European Union
FDI . . . . .Foreign Direct Investment
FMIS .Financial Management Information System
GDP . . . . .Gross Domestic Product
GMI . . . . .Guaranteed Minimum Income
GP . . . . .General Practitioner
IMF . . . . .International Monetary Fund
MSIC . . . . .Mandatory Social Insurance Code
MTBF . . . . .Medium-Term Budget Framework
MTEF . . . . .Medium-Term Expenditure Framework
MES . . . . .Ministry of Education and Sciences
MOD . . . . .Ministry of Defense
MOF . . . . .Ministry of Finance
MOH . . . . .Ministry of Health
MOLSP .Ministry of Labour and Social Policy
NAO . . . . .National Audit Office
NATO . . . . .North Atlantic Treaty Organization
NEK . . . . .National Electricity Company
nei . . . . .not elsewhere identified
NCRI .National Company Railway Infrastructure
NGO . . . . .Non-Governmental Organization
NHIF . . . . .National Health Insurance Fund
NSI . . . . .National Statistical Institute
NSSI . . . . .National Social Security Institute
OECD . . . . .Organization for Economic Cooperation and Development
o/w . . . . .of which
PAYG . . . . .Pay-As-You-Go
PEIR . . . . .Public Expenditure and Institutional Review
PIT . . . . .Personal Income Tax
PSO . . . . .Public Service Obligation
PTUF . . . . .Professional Training and Unemployment Fund
REER . . . . .Real Effective Exchange Rate
SISA . . . . .State Insurance Supervision Agency
SOEs . . . . .State-Owned Enterprises
TSA . . . . .Treasury Single Account
USAID . . . . .United States Agency for International Development

CURRENCY AND EQUIVALENT UNITS
Currency Unit = Bulgarian Leva (BGN)
US$1 = Leva 1.97
(on October 31, 2002)

FISCAL YEAR
January 1 – December 31

Документите на Световната банка от серията "Изследвания за страните" са част от докладите, които се изготвят първоначално за вътрешно ползване и разглеждат икономическите и други условия в страните-членки на Банката, както и подпомагат диалога й с правителствата. Повечето от тях се публикуват във вид на изследване във възможно най-кратък срок, за да се ползват от правителствата, академичните, бизнес и финансовите среди, както и от партньорите за развитие. Поради това тези документи не отговарят на правилата за отпечатване на текстове. Световната банка не носи отговорност за допуснати грешки в тези издания. Част от цитираните документи в този доклад може да са неофициални и не винаги са на разположение.

Мненията, тълкуванията и заключенията в този доклад са само на автора(ите) и не отразяват по никакъв начин становището на Световната банка, на сродни организации или членовете на Борда на директорите, нито пък на страните, които те представляват. Световната банка не гарантира точността на данните, включени в това издание, и не поема отговорност за последиците от тяхното използване.

ПРИЗНАТЕЛНОСТ ЗА СЪТРУДНИЧЕСТВОТО

Настоящият Преглед на публичните разходи и институциите (ППРИ) се основава на констатациите на няколко мисии на Световната банка, които посетиха България през периода от май 2001 г. до март 2002 г. Работен вариант на доклада беше обсъден с правителството, международните финансови институции и гражданското общество по време на мисията през юни 2002 г. в България. Анализът обхваща периода от средата на 90-те до 2001 г. и началото на 2002 г.

Екипът, изготвил доклада, би желал да изрази своята благодарност на правителството на България за отличното сътрудничество, предоставено от страна на голям брой висши служители по време на мисиите и обсъжданията. Екипът изразява специални благодарности на г-н Кирил Ананиев, заместник-министър на финансите и ръководител на работната група по ППРИ, и на г-жа Росица Велкова, координатор на ППРИ в Министерството на финансите (МФ), за техния значителен принос и съдействие при организацията и провеждането на проучването. Г-н Петьо Николов, главен съветник на Изпълнителния директор на Световната банка, също даде важни насоки и безценна помощ при подготовката на този документ.

Докладът беше инициииран от Лейла Злауи и екип от служители на Световната банка, български и международни експерти. Първият етап беше посветен на изготвянето на следните основни документи: “*Фискалната устойчивост в България*” от А. Крейг Бърнсайд; “*Здравеопазването в преход*” от Уилям Г. Джек; “*Образованието – демографското предизвикателство*” от Майкъл Мерто; “*Енергетиката – комплексно преструктуриране: фискални, социални и пазарни взаимодействия*” от Салман Захир; “*Готова ли е България за средносрочна рамка за разходите и бюджетиране на база резултати*” от Даниел Томаси; “*Социалната закрила: въпроси и препоръки*” от Дина Ринголд и Есперанца Лазагабастър; “*Държавните железници – фискална тежест и варианти за реформа*” от Жан-Жак Кроше. Анита Кореа помагаше на екипа в началния етап. Докладът беше финализиран от екип, състоящ се от Кайл Питърс, Стела Илиева, Розалинда Кинтания, Катрин Ривера, Дорийн Даф (ECSPE) и Бен Варон (консултант).

По време на подготовката на този доклад екипът на ППРИ работеше в тясно взаимодействие с различни министерства и агенции, както и с неправителствени организации (НПО) и международни институции като Европейската комисия и Американската агенция за международно развитие (ААМР). Особено полезни за екипа бяха разискванията по същество в МФ. Въпреки че главният партньор от българска страна беше МФ, сътрудничеството с почти всички ресорни министерства и държавни агенции допринесе съществено за подобряване на разбирането ни за действителното състояние на бюджета и предизвикателствата, пред които са изправени и ще бъдат изправени в бъдеще българските власти.

Полезно за работата на екипа се оказа също така ефективното сътрудничество с правителствени служители, по-специално заместник-министъра на финансите г-н Кирил Ананиев и г-н Димитър Радев, бивш заместник-министър на финансите. Членовете на мисиите имаха възможност да обсъдят основните констатации по различните теми и анализираните сектори със служители в Министерския съвет, Българската народна банка, Министерството на финансите, Министерството на регионалното развитие и благоустройството, Министерството на образованието и науката, Министерството на отбраната, Министерството на здравеопазването, Министерството на транспорта и съобщенията, Министерството на труда и социалната политика, Министерството на вътрешните работи, Министерството на околната среда и водите, Националния статистически институт, Агенцията за икономически анализи и прогнози, Националната здравноосигурителна каса, Националния осигурителен институт, Агенция за държавен вътрешен финансов контрол, БДЖ и служители от органите на местното самоуправление в София, Благоевград, Плевен и Елин Пелин.

Членовете на мисията имаха и възможността да обсъдят ключови въпроси с представители на Инициатива в местното самоуправление (LGI), подкрепяна от ААМР, Европейската комисия, Международния валутен фонд и НПО: Националното сдружение на общините в Република България, Романи Бахт и Клуб "Икономика 2000".

Ценни коментари, предложения и насоки на различни етапи от подготовката на ППРИ дадоха: Андрю Воркинк (Директор за България, Румъния и Хърватска, ECC05), Оскар де Брун Копс (Постоянен представител на СБ в България, ECCBG), Джулиъс Варалиай (Главен специалист за България, ECCA5), Петър Пожарски (Ръководител проекти, ECSHD), Дончо Барбалов (Ръководител проекти, ECSIE), Ищван Добози (Главен икономист - енергетика, ECSIE), Хенк Буш (Ръководител сектор, ECSIE), Морин Люис (Ръководител сектор, ECSHD) и Бернард Фънк (Главен икономист по присъединяването към ЕС, ECSPE). Специални благодарности на Боряна Гочева (Старши ръководител проекти, ECSHD) за нейното участие в мисиите и за ценните й коментари и предложения по главите за образованието и социалната защита; както и на Албена Самсонова, която осигуряваше административната подкрепа за работата на мисиите. Отлични предложения и коментари имаше и от страна на външните рецензенти, господата Филип льо Уеру (Ръководител сектор, AFTP1) и Филип О'Кийф (Старши икономист, ECSHD).

Авторите биха желали да изразят сърдечната си благодарност на министерствата, агенциите и местните власти в България за времето, посветено на открити и приятелски обсъждания с екипа, както и за ценните коментари върху работния вариант. Настоящият доклад е реализиран благодарение на тяхното сътрудничество. Специални благодарности на Любомир Дацов, Владимир Петров и Яна Пальова от МФ за ефективната им подкрепа и принос към разностранните аспекти на програмата на екипа.

РЕЗЮМЕ

Стратегическа обстановка

До 1997 г. България беше една от страните с най-слабо развиваща се икономика в Централна и Източна Европа (ЦИЕ). Десетилетието преди това се характеризираше с огромни външни заеми, неустойчива политика на стабилизация и бавни структурни реформи. Неспособността да се наложи пазарна дисциплина, широкоразпространеният стремеж към облагодетелстване и преобладаващите "меки" бюджетни ограничения за предприятията, банките и държавния бюджет доведоха до кулминация на проблемите в страната и до остра икономическа криза през 1996-1997 г., в резултат на която БВП спадна с почти 14%. След неколкомесечен хаос страната премина през хиперинфлация, срив в банковия сектор и тежка валутна криза. През юли 1997 г. България въведе паричен съвет. Режимът на паричния съвет беше съпроводен с консервативна фискална политика и значително ускоряване на структурните реформи. Широкообхватната структурна програма включваше реформи в социалния сектор, селското стопанство, енергетиката, приватизацията, преструктурирането и финансовата дисциплина в реалния и банковия сектор, както и либерализация на цените и търговията. Стабилното макроикономическо управление и ускоряването на структурните реформи доведоха до постепенно възстановяване на растежа, овладяване на инфлацията и укрепване доверието на обществеността и инвеститорите.

Като цяло България постигна значителен напредък по отношение на дългосрочната макроикономическа стабилност – важна стъпка по пътя към крайната цел за по-добър стандарт на живот и присъединяване към ЕС. Възстановен е икономическият растеж, положени са основите за ускорен растеж. Според средносрочната правителствена програма, подкрепена от МВФ, Световната банка и други донори, през следващите четири години реалният БВП на България се очаква да нараства с около 5% годишно, а БВП на глава от населението с около 6%. Предвижда се поддържане на почти балансирани вътрешни сметки и по-нататъшно намаляване на външната задлъжнялост. Фискалното управление е един от крайъгълните камъни в средносрочната програма на България. Правителството си поставя амбициозни и консервативни цели за постигане на фискална дисциплина, за да укрепи макроикономическата стабилност и да създаде благоприятна среда за развитие на частния сектор.

Икономическата програма на правителството е изпълнима. В дългосрочен аспект дори може да надхвърли заплануваното, ако досегашните реформи и политика, които са служили добре на България, бъдат продължени и изпълнени в бързи срокове. България обаче е изправена пред редица предизвикателства:

- **Бедността**. Доходът на глава от населението в България (1 560 щ.д. за 2001 г.) е нисък. Той представлява само 31% от средния за ЕС (прогнозирано въз основа на паритета на покупателната способност). Въпреки забележителното подобрение, наблюдавано от 1997 г. насам, бедността остава на равнище два пъти по-високо от това през 1995 г. Освен това подобрението не е разпределено равномерно нито в географски план, нито по групи от населението.

- **Безработицата**. Безработицата в България, която е 17,5% през 2001 г., е сред най-високите в региона. Освен това 49,3% от безработните са безработни повече от една година и се смятат за "продължително безработни".

- **Демографският проблем**. В България прирастът на населението е отрицателен–средно – 0,7% през 90-те години. Допълнително отрицателно влияние върху броя на населението оказва нетната емиграция през последните две десетилетия.

- **Инвестициите**. Дълго време инвестициите в България бяха пренебрегвани. Едва напоследък започнаха да се възстановяват. Инвестициите като процент от БВП са доста под равнищата за страните от ЦИЕ, където са близо 30%.

- **Управлението**. Според резултати от независими проучвания, България е сред страните, в които слабото институционално управление е довело до ограничаване на инвестициите и влошаване на стопанската среда. Правителството предприе сериозни стъпки за подобряване на управлението. Необходими са обаче по-нататъшни усилия особено за преодоляване на слабостите в капацитета на администрацията при повечето равнища на управление и в редица сектори.

- **Поддържане на макроикономическата стабилност**. Въпреки че България отбеляза забележителен напредък в постигането на макроикономическа стабилност, през следващите години страната почти сигурно ще се изправи пред големи дефицити по текущата сметка на платежния баланс. Успешното привличане на необходимите капиталови потоци, заедно с намаляването на бремето на дълга, изискват значителен приток на чуждестранни инвестиции, което е възможно само в условията на стабилна макроикономическа среда.

Фискалната политика и политиката на разходите ще играят възлова роля за преодоляване на горните предизвикателства през следващите години. Фискалната политика е главният инструмент за поддържане на макроикономическа стабилност в условията на паричен съвет. За целите на настоящия доклад беше извършено моделиране на условията за фискална устойчивост. То показва, че фискалната програма на правителството, чийто акцент е постигането на балансиран бюджет в средносрочен план, отговаря на изискването за поддържане на макроикономическа стабилност, намаляване на съотношението дълг/БВП и адаптиране към намаляващите приходи от приватизация в резултат на приключване на програмата за приватизация. Разбира се, всичко това е в сила при положение, че правителството продължи да изпълнява своята програма за структурни реформи и при отсъствие на външни шокове.

Като се има предвид тежкото данъчно бреме и намеренията на правителството за намаляване на данъците в икономиката, политиката на разходите ще трябва да понесе главната тежест от усилията да се достигнат фискалните цели и да се компенсира всеки спад в приходите, свързан с данъчната реформа. За да се постигнат заложените от правителството бюджетни показатели при сегашното ниво на приходи, нашият симулационен анализ показва, че при отсъствие на външни шокове и в съчетание с една силна програма за структурна реформа, в средносрочен план е необходимо да се постигне малко намаление на разходите от порядъка на 1 процентен пункт от БВП. Ако правителството обаче предприеме по-нататъшно намаляване на данъчното бреме за фирмите, ще е необходимо и по-голямо намаляване на разходите, за да се постигнат заложените фискални цели. Следователно главното предизвикателство пред фискалната политика на страната е да работи за по-добро разпределение на разходите като постепенно понижава общото им равнище в средносрочен план в съответствие с фискалните цели и заложените приходи.

Този доклад има за цел да бъдат анализирани най-вече трудностите при усъвършенстване на разпределението на публичните разходи. Предизвикателството пред фискалната програма е усложнено от съществуващата нееластична структура на разходите в България, където социалните плащания възлизат на 33% от всички разходи. За да се подобри разпределението на публичните разходи, е необходимо да се създаде достатъчно гъвкава система на управление на разходите, която бързо и ефективно да се приспособява към макроикономическите шокове, а също и процес на фискално управление, който е насочен предимно към стратегическите аспекти с по-ясен акцент в средносрочен план и ориентиран към постигане на резултати. Наличието на паричен съвет в България прави още по-неотложно изпълнението на обсъжданите в този доклад реформи, за да бъдат постигнати набелязаните фискални цели.

Освен предизвикателствата, свързани с фиска и разходите, програмата за реформи в България включва широк кръг реформи за подобряване на инвестиционния климат, по-нататъшно усъвършенстване на публичната администрация и незавършената програма за приватизация. Всички те добиват още по-категорични измерения с оглед изискванията за членство в ЕС. Очевидно правителството трябва да действа на много фронтове, както прави това от 1997 г. насам. То трябва сериозно да помисли за стесняване на програмата си с цел разработване на реалистична "основна програма" с добре определени приоритети. Освен това е необходимо съдържанието и темпът на реформите да се обвържат със специфичните за страната обстоятелства. България се отличава с множество уникални особености и ограничения като демографската картина, включително етническия състав, закостенялата система на социална защита, наследството от миналото, системата за взаимодействие между различните нива на държавното управление, инвестиционния дефицит и пр. Тези характерни особености оказват влияние върху потребностите, приоритетите, обществената търпимост и резултатите.

Структура на разходите и тенденции

Поради строгата финансова дисциплина, наложена от паричния съвет, през последните години България поддържа малък бюджетен дефицит (в порядъка на 1% от БВП). Основният източник на финансиране на дефицита са постъпленията от приватизацията. През последните няколко години първичният излишък се поддържа на ниво от около 3%. Фискалното стабилизиране на България стана възможно предимно чрез увеличаване на приходите, а не чрез намаляване на разходите. Въпреки че през последните две години се наблюдава свиване както на приходи, така и на разходи, приходите остават на ниво доста над това отпреди кризата. През периода след кризата, в България беше извършено и съществено преструктуриране на разходите. Делът на лихвените плащания отбеляза огромен спад от 20% от БВП през 1996 г. на 4% през 2001 г., а нелихвените разходи се увеличиха значително.

Общото фискално състояние на България може да се определи като стабилно в сравнение с това на други страни от региона и с т.нар. "изравняващи се страни" от ЕС (Гърция, Ирландия, Португалия и Испания). Държавните приходи са доста над средното равнище за избрани страни от ЦИЕ, а разходите, въпреки неотдавнашното възстановяване, са в съответствие със средното ниво за ЦИЕ и малко над средното за "изравняващите се страни" от ЕС. При сравнението на публичните разходи по икономически елементи не се установяват съществени несъответствия с посочените страни, въпреки че класификацията по обобщени категории прикрива някои особености на разходите в страната. Например, докато числеността на държавните служители е малка в сравнение с "изравняващите се страни" от ЕС, заетостта в образованието и здравеопазването в България е сред най-високите в региона. Въпреки че в момента капиталовите разходи са съпоставими със средното ниво за ЦИЕ, остава скрито лошото състояние на обществената инфраструктура в резултат от дълго отлаганата поддръжка. На последно място, въпреки спада в обема на субсидиите, те все още са значителни и съсредоточени в инфраструктурата, което е за сметка на отложени разходи в други области.

Икономиите от намаляването на лихвените плащания с три-четвърти (спрямо БВП) за периода 1996-2001 г. са пренасочени към други сектори, главно социално осигуряване и подпомагане. Въпреки това функционалният състав на разходите в България в голяма степен съответства на структурата на държавните разходи в другите страни от ЦИЕ. Основното изключение като че ли са разходите за отбрана и сигурност, които, при дял 5% от БВП, в България са почти два пъти по-високи, отколкото във всички други страни от ЦИЕ.

В този доклад се повдигат редица въпроси и се дават препоръки за това къде разходите биха могли да се рационализират, а разпределението между секторите и вътре в тях да се подобри, като са взети предвид целите на държавната фискална политика, сравненията на разходите в България с тези в други държави и подробните секторни анализи, представени по-нататък. Докладът обаче не предписва оптимално по-ниско равнище на разходите, нито идеално разпределение между секторите.

Тези препоръки показват, че: а) разходите за някои икономически дейности, по-специално транспорт и съобщения (за железниците и субсидиите за електроенергията за битови нужди), отбрана и сигурност, както и за други общи държавни услуги изглеждат високи и подлежат на рационализация; б) при разходите за образование, здравеопазване и социална защита е необходимо да се преразгледат приоритетите вътре в секторите като например закриване на излишните заведения (училища и болници), намаляване на броя на персонала (учители и лекари) и рационализиране на програмите за социална защита като същевременно се увеличат разходите за подобряване на качеството (учебници и др.) и се подобри целевата насоченост на социалното подпомагане за бедните. Като цяло равнището на разходите в тези сектори изглежда почти приемливо. Изключение прави здравеопазването, където след рационализиране на болничната мрежа и анализ на нерегламентираните плащания може да се разкрие необходимост от по-високи публични разходи; в) в много сектори се очертава необходимост от по-големи капиталовложения, като инфраструктура, околна среда, образование и здравеопазване - някои от които са приоритетни за присъединяването към ЕС, а други трябва да включват участието на частния сектор. Въпреки че като цяло делът на публичните инвестиции в страната е в съответствие с този на другите кандидати за присъединяване в ЕС, ефектът от пренебрегването и отлагането на разходите за поддръжка в миналото може да наложи по-високо ниво на инвестиционните разходи. Следователно необходим е по-задълбочен поглед върху потребностите от публични инвестиции в цялата икономика, за да се определи дали е нужно тяхното увеличение или решението е в тяхното радикално преразпределяне. В заключение трябва да се има предвид, че целта на настоящия доклад не е разработването на програма за оптимално разпределяне на разходите, а само преглед на подбрани сектори. Следователно тези препоръки трябва да се приемат внимателно и като неокончателни, докато и други сектори се подложат на анализ, за да се получи по-пълна картина.

Структурни въпроси и приоритети

Образование. Въпреки че през последните пет години се наблюдава слабо увеличение на разходите за образование като процент от БВП и сега те почти отговарят на средното ниво за ЦИЕ, съществува сериозен проблем с неправилното разпределение на ресурсите в този сектор. От началото на прехода има значителен спад на броя на записаните ученици във всички нива на обучение, с изключение на висшето. Това в голяма степен се дължи на отрицателния прираст на населението в България, който се задълбочава от нетната емиграция. (На основата на броя на родените вече деца, се очаква намаление на броя на децата в училищна възраст поне до средата на настоящото десетилетие.) В резултат, съотношението ученици на един учител е много ниско и има излишък на учители и училища, особено в селата. Към това се добавя и проблемът с неравнопоставеността при предоставянето на образователни услуги, която се изразява в големи различия по отношение на образованието, включително качеството на образованието по области, общини и етнически групи, както и по степен на бедност. Налице е и силно централизиране на управлението на образователната система. Министерството на образованието и науката (МОН) отговаря за съдържанието на учебните планове, контрола върху качеството и политиката по кадровото осигуряване. Разходите се разпределят между държавата и 263-те общини на базата на сложна формула, която се одобрява всяка година и съдържа редица недостатъци.

Основното предизвикателство в образованието е в пренасочването на разходите за поддържане на излишен капацитет от учители и за неизползван училищен фонд – предимно в селата – към други дейности, допринасящи за повишаване на качеството, като се облекчи претовареността и обучението на смени в големите градове. Неотдавна правителството разработи план за оптимизация на училищната мрежа и пренасочване на учителите. Въпреки че това е добра първа стъпка, планът трябва да бъде разгледан внимателно, за да се прецени дали е достатъчно всеобхватен. Икономиите, реализирани от този план, трябва да се насочат за облекчаване на острия недостиг на средства за поддръжка и инвестиции, както и за осигуряване на материали и оборудване за учебния процес, особено в по-малките населени места.

Трябва спешно да се обърне внимание и на достъпа до образование. Необходимо е да се предприемат незабавни мерки за преодоляване на сериозния проблем с посещаемостта в училище и успеваемостта на ромските деца като отчасти се използва опита на целеви програми за ромите в други страни. Друг приоритет е промяната в подхода към децентрализация и финансиране на образователната система. В момента МОН упражнява прекомерен контрол върху ресурсите "на входа" (училища, учители и норми). Засилването на децентрализираното вземане на решения на общинско ниво за ресурсите на образователния процес ще осигури по-рационално разпределяне на отговорностите и отчетността. При настоящата формула се финансира ресурсът "на входа" (най-вече учителите), а при един ефективен механизъм трябва да се финансира продуктът "на изхода" - в случая обучението на учениците. Най-лесният начин за постигане на това е да се премине към прост модел на финансиране на база брой ученици с конкретна ставка за ученик при всяко образователно ниво. Рационализирането на учебните заведения и броя на учителите, като освободените ресурси бъдат пренасочени към повишаващи качеството продукти, ще бъде първа стъпка към подобряване на цялостното качество на основното и средното образование. Други приоритети в образованието са: а) установяване на сътрудничество между малките общини за постигане на по-ефективно разпределение на училищния фонд и преподавателския състав; б) рационализиране на висшите учебни заведения, свеждане до минимум на държавните разходи за висшето образование чрез повишаване на таксите като в същото време се подобри качеството; в) заместване на настоящата целева субсидия за капиталови разходи с механизъм, основан на добре документирани разчети по проекти - цел, валидна за всички сектори.

Здравеопазване. Здравните показатели на България са слаби в сравнение с тези на другите страни в преход. След началото на прехода повечето показатели или не са се променили съществено или са се влошили. Няколко са факторите, които са допринесли за относително лошия здравен статус на населението: а) скъпоструващият и прекомерен ресурс както от здравни заведения, така и от медицински специалисти – наследство от социалистическото минало; б) неефективното използване на този ресурс, което е видно от излишния капацитет на медицински персонал и от ниските нива на използване на материалната база, особено легловия фонд; в) лоша поддръжка на здравните заведения и оборудването; г) неадекватни нови инвестиции; д) прекомерно централизирана и негъвкава система на медицинско обслужване; е) ниско ниво на общите разходи за здравеопазване - в порядъка на 4% от БВП, което е едно от най-ниските нива за Централна и Източна Европа.

През 1999 г. правителството предприе широкомащабна реформа в здравеопазването. Централен елемент на новата система е Националната здравноосигурителна каса (НЗОК), която съчетава функции по рисково застраховане и закупуване на здравни услуги чрез договори с лекари, групови практики и болници. НЗОК се финансира от вноски за задължително здравно осигуряване, които не са обвързани с разходите. По-голямата част от вноските идват от целево облагане на трудовите възнаграждения, а останалата се плаща от държавата за бедните и неработещата част от населението. Болниците се финансират от НЗОК, държавата и общините. Общините финансират вноските на онези, които получават обезщетения за безработица. В резултат от проведените реформи вече е постигнато намаляване на броя на болниците и лекарите, въпреки че има какво още да се направи в това отношение. Налице са и някои признаци за това, че новата система може да се окаже труднодостъпна за някои групи от населението, например ромите и хората в отдалечени населени места. Накрая необходимо е да се промени и сегашния начин на неадекватно програмиране и финансиране на инвестициите в здравеопазването.

Като цяло моделът на новата система на здравеопазване в България е добър. Той се основава на модела на социалното осигуряване в Западна Европа, който през последните десет години е приет от много страни в ЦИЕ. Главният приоритет е системата да се внедри цялостно и внимателно, като се извличат поуки от постигнатото в процеса на изпълнението. Необходимо е да се въведат механизми за мониторинг на напредъка. Трябва да се наблюдават по-специално онези разходи за здравеопазване, които отиват за лекарите, за да се избегне допълнителното нарастване на тези разходи за сметка на крайно недостатъчната поддръжка и новите инвестиции, както това се е случвало в близкото минало.

Друг основен приоритет е решаването на проблемите, които произтичат от непълното използване на базата и са свързани със сериозното влошаване на качеството й и неадекватното обновяване на оборудването. Стабилизирането и поставянето на финансовото състояние на НЗОК на устойчива основа е третата необходима област на реформата в здравната политика. На последно място, както и при образованието, трябва да се реши проблемът с достъпа на хората в неравностойно положение – по-специално ромите, безработните и живеещите в отдалечени райони.

Социална защита. Програмите за социална защита включват: а) пенсии, б) програми за пазара на труда, в) социално подпомагане, г) краткосрочни обезщетения и семейни добавки. Съвкупните разходи по тези програми възлизат на 13,6% от БВП за 2001 г. Програмите за социална защита обхващат широк кръг от населението – повече от 80% от българите са получили поне един вид обезщетение през 2001 г. Като цяло от средата на 90-те години програмите за социална защита в по-голяма степен са насочени към бедните и играят основна роля за облекчаване на бедността. Делът на бедните намалява от 35,1% на 12,8% след получаване на обезщетения и помощи.

Пенсиите представляват най-голямата категория на разходи за социална защита с дял от 9,1% от БВП за 2001 г. През последното десетилетие общият брой на пенсионерите нараства поради застаряване на населението, докато броят на осигуряваните лица намалява в резултат от срива в заетостта. Доскоро програмата за пенсии включваше само един стълб (на базата на текущо финансиране), със средства от вноските в държавното общественото осигуряване, начислявани върху трудовите възнаграждения. Изправено пред продължителен финансов натиск, през 1999 г. правителството въвежда нова пенсионна система с три стълба: а) т.нар. първи или държавен стълб, представляващ рационализирана система на базата на текущо финансиране; б) т.нар. "универсален" стълб - задължително осигуряване в частни пенсионни фондове за всички родени след 1959 г., както и за някои определени професионални категории; и в) доброволно частно осигуряване.

Първият приоритет в реформата е да бъдат подобрени събираемостта и обхватът на държавния стълб и да се определят ясни правила за индексиране на пенсиите. Разширяването на обхвата на пенсионната система заслужава специално внимание, тъй като от самото начало на прехода някои икономически групи, като заетите в селското стопанство, са слабо покрити. Друг приоритет в краткосрочен план е да се наблюдава и ограничава нарастването на броя на пенсиите за инвалидност, тъй като по-строгите изисквания за пенсиониране доведоха до увеличаване на броя на молбите за пенсиониране поради инвалидност. Във връзка с частните пенсионни схеми е необходимо да се обърне по-сериозно внимание на тяхната законова, нормативна и надзорна рамка, по-специално уредбата на тяхното управление. Това изисква укрепване на капацитета на Държавната агенция за осигурителен надзор. В дългосрочен план е необходимо да се установи по-тясно интегриране между частните пенсионни схеми и другите финансови пазари в България и ЕС.

Програмите за пазара на труда заедно с фундаменталната реформа на трудовия пазар са ключов елемент в борбата с безработицата. От 1996 г. безработицата в страната непрекъснато расте като през 2001 г. достига ниво от 17,5% и е сред най-високите в региона. В България се изпълняват програми за пазара на труда, чиято цел е да се разшири реформата на трудовия пазар, така че той да установи динамична среда, благоприятна за растежа на заетостта, и да се помогне на загубилите работа си. Има два вида програми: а) изплащане на обезщетения при безработица или т.нар. "пасивни програми" и б) "активни програми за пазара на труда", които предвиждат мерки за насърчаване на заетостта, включително програми за общественополезен труд, обучение, субсидии за заетост и подкрепа за развитие на малки предприятия. **Фондът "Безработица"**, който от 1 януари 2002 г. наследи Фонд "Професионална квалификация и безработица", цели да подобри ефективността на помощите за безработни. Фондът се управлява от НОИ и цели да преодолее несъответствията между вноските в системата за задължително социално осигуряване и помощите, давани на безработни. Правото на обезщетения и техният размер са свързани с броя години, през които са правени вноски в системата като минимумът и максимумът на обезщетенията се определят всяка година със закон. Новият фонд "Безработица" покрива вноските за социално и здравно осигуряване на обезщетените.

Програмите за **социално подпомагане** включват няколко вида помощи, сред които най-важна е програмата за гарантирания минимален доход – парични помощи, правото на които се дава въз основа на проверка на материалното състояние. Те се изплащат на домакинства с доходи под определен праг и формират основната национална мрежа за социална защита. Системата за социална защита включва и **краткосрочни обезщетения**, които обхващат 12 категории плащания, включително при болест, майчинство, раждане, отглеждане на дете, трудови злополуки, деца с увреждания и др.

Изпълнението на фундаменталната реформа на пазара на труда е основен приоритет, за да се установи динамичен пазар на труда, който ще доведе до разширяване на възможностите за работа. Реформата в пазара на труда, програмите за трудовия пазар и политиката за социално подпомагане трябва взаимно да се допълват, за да нараснат стимулите за работа и увеличаването на заетостта. От ключово значение е да се следят внимателно: ефективността на фонда за осигуряване срещу безработица по отношение на очакваното нарастване на броя на регистрираните и вноските, периода на получаване на обезщетенията, делът на бенефициентите, които отново намират работа, и издръжката на фонда. Необходимо е също така да се следят отблизо активните програми за пазара на труда, за да се подобри тяхната ефективност и дългосрочен ефект за стимулиране на търсенето на работна ръка. В дългосрочен план трябва да се обмисли намаляването на данъчната тежест, свързана с политиката по заетостта, за да бъдат намалени разходите за работна ръка.

Постоянното предизвикателство пред системата за социална защита е да бъдат разглеждани възможностите за окрупняване и опростяване на програмите и предприемане на системен мониторинг на програмите, на разходите за осъществяването им и ползите от тях. Това се налага от съществуващите разнообразни програми за социална защита, които често се основават на сложни модели, както и от тяхното бреме върху държавата.

Държавните железници. Българските държавни железници (БДЖ) не функционират като предприятие на пазарни начала; то работи по-скоро като старо (отпреди прехода) държавно предприятие. Нетните приходи на БДЖ са отрицателни за целия период на прехода. Дефицитът достига 124 млн. лв. през 2001 г. или 21% от общите разходи, дори и като се вземе предвид субсидията за дейността, която предоставя държавният бюджет. БДЖ получава значителни средства от държавата за покриване на дефицита. През последните няколко години общият обем на субсидиите е средно 0,8% от БВП. Около половината от този размер е субсидия за дейността, а останалата част се използва за финансиране на инвестиции. Предоставяните субсидии не са довели до намаляване на сериозното влошаване на активите на железопътния транспорт в резултат на неадекватната поддръжка и обновяване.

Слабите финансови резултати на БДЖ се дължат на няколко фактора: голям брой нерентабилни услуги, възлагани от държавата; ниски пътнически тарифи; ниска производителност на труда и неподходяща рамка на стимули, която не благоприятства ефективното вземането на решения и отчетността.

За да се спре влошаването на състоянието на железопътния сектор, България трябва да предприеме редица действия. Първият приоритет е драстичното съкращаване на нерентабилните услуги, което да се осъществи на основата на внимателно разработен и обсъден план за рационализиране. Закриването на губещите дейности ще доведе до увеличаване на приходите. Допълнителните мерки за намаляване на разходите трябва да включват промяна в тарифите и - най-важното - съкращаване на работната ръка. От направените за този доклад прогнози се достигна до извода, че намаляването на числеността на персонала е най-важната мярка, която може да се предприеме за оздравяване на финансовото състояние на железниците. Въпреки че разделянето на БДЖ на две дружества - едното за експлоатацията, а другото за инфраструктурата, е стъпка напред, към това трябва да се добави ясна организация на фирменото управление, най-вече изолиране на новите предприятия от политическо влияние, особено по отношение на инвестиционните решения.

Енергетика. Енергийният сектор в България се характеризира с това, че държавата държи или контролира значителна част от ресурсите и в голяма степен субсидира енергопотреблението. Домакинствата са най-многобройната категория бенефициенти на държавни средства, тъй като в цените на електроенергията и топлоенергията за битови нужди има най-голям компонент на субсидия. Домакинствата с по-високи доходи, които са и по-големи потребители на енергия са пропорционално по-облагодетелствани от по-бедните домакинства, където енергопотреблението е много по-малко. Поради държавната собственост или контрол върху всички важни енергийни ресурси, на практика всички инвестиции са зависими от държавна подкрепа под формата на бюджетни средства или заеми с държавна гаранция. Повече от десетилетие секторът изпитва недостиг на инвестиции, поради ограничени налични публични средства. Нужни са значителни инвестиции за рехабилитацията на електроцентралите и системите за пренос и разпределение, за разработването на така необходимата система за газ ниско налягане, модернизирането на системата за централно отопление в няколко района на страната и рехабилитацията на някои въгледобивни мини.

Във връзка с това държавата трябва: а) да подобри административния капацитет на Държавната комисия за енергийно регулиране; б) да изпълни наскоро приетата програма за корекции в цените, за да се премахнат съществуващите изкривявания и през 2002–2004 г. цените да се изравнят с пълната си себестойност, като внимателно проследява механизмите, насочени към намаляване финансовата тежест върху домакинствата с ниски доходи и уязвимите групи от населението; в) да отложи скъпоструващите инвестиции в нови мощности за производство на електро- и топлоенергия до етап, на който ще се постигне по-добър напредък в реформите на нормативната уредба и докато инвеститорите (особено онези, които инвестират в мощности за износ) ще бъдат в състояние да поемат по-голям дял от пазарния риск в условията на подходяща регулация; г) да либерализира решенията за инвестиции, свързани с отрасъла за доставка на енергоносители и големите търговски потребители, на които да се даде възможност да договарят основната част от потребностите си от газ и електроенергия с частни доставчици, включително и чуждестранни.

Правителството е постигнало съществен напредък в реформите в енергийния сектор, които се разглеждат в този доклад. В средата на 2002 г. Министерският съвет одобри енергийна стратегия, която предвижда цените на електроенергията за битови нужди да достигнат пълната си себестойност за период от три години (2002–2004 г.). Държавната комисия за енергийно регулиране (ДКЕР) прие индикативен график за корекция на цените от 20, 15 и 10% съответно за всяка една от трите последователни години, започвайки от 2002 г. За да защити бедните от ефекта на ценовите корекции, правителството допълни ценовата реформа с два механизма: а) разширена програма за енергопотребление, която подпомага бедните до определени минимални нива на потребление; б) двустепенна ценова тарифа, при която цената за минимално енергопотребление остава непроменена, а при по-голяма консумация се заплаща по друга цена. Изпълнението на тези и други реформи в енергетиката заемат централно място в модернизирането на сектора.

Институционални въпроси и приоритети

Постигането на по-добро разпределение на разходите ще изисква на първо място по-добър процес на управление на разходите, който е едновременно стратегически ориентиран и насочен към постигане на резултати. За да осигури необходимата дисциплина в съответствие с изискванията на паричния съвет, правителството на България вече предприе поредица от реформи в управлението на публичните разходи. Дирекция "Бюджет и държавно съкровище" в Министерството на финансите модернизира функциите си, преструктурира организацията си и оптимизира персонала си; въвежда се информационна система за финансово управление; структурата на разпоредителите с бюджетни средства се рационализира и броят им се намалява. В началото на 2002 г. правителството въведе някои промени в процедурата по изготвяне на бюджета, чието прилагане ще започне с бюджета за 2003 г. Промените са насочени специално към подобряване на разпределението на бюджетните средства между отделните сектори. Правителството предприе и стъпки за въвеждане на програмен подход, по-специално към засилване на връзката бюджет-политика. Съгласно решението на Министерския съвет от януари 2002 г. разпоредителите с бюджетни средства трябва да разработят средносрочни бюджетни рамки (СБР) за сектора си на началния етап от изготвянето на бюджета за 2003 г. Правителството огласи намерението си да включи общата СБР в документацията, която внася в Народното събрание.

В резултат от тези реформи е установен ефективен контрол върху паричните потоци; постигнат е стриктен финансов контрол върху съвкупния обем на публичните разходи. Въпреки този значим напредък е необходимо да продължи и да се засили работата по провеждане на реформите, особено при: а) планирането на бюджета; б) изпълнението на бюджета, счетоводната отчетност и одита; както и в) финансовото управление на местно равнище. При управлението на публичните ресурси съществуват три възлови въпроса, свързани с институциите: а) как най-добре да се продължи и консолидира придвижването към програмно бюджетиране на база изпълнение и резултати; б) как да се подобрят подборът и бюджетирането на публичните инвестиции; и в) как да се укрепи финансовото управление на местно равнище в условията на подобрени отношения местно-централно управление. Гл. 5 посочва програмирането на инвестициите и управлението на разходите на местните власти като най-слабите звена в бюджетната система.

Акцентът на бъдещите реформи трябва да се постави върху три области. Първо, осъществяващите реформата трябва да разширят неотдавнашните инициативи за реформа в бюджетния процес, за да се премине към цялостен процес на бюджетиране в средносрочен план с по-добра стратегическа насоченост. Освен това процесът на изготвяне на бюджета трябва да бъде допълнен с някои действия, свързани конкретно с програмирането на инвестициите. Предложенията за капиталови разходи трябва да се формулират при твърди бюджетни ограничения и като неделима част от СБР, т.е. включени като приложение към документа за СБР. На общините трябва да се даде възможност да играят по-голяма роля при одобряването и изпълнението на инвестиционните разходи, в това число свободата да прехвърлят за следващата година неусвоени инвестиционни средства, вместо да се впускат в прекомерни текущи разходи както е при сегашната система.

Второ, системата на последващ контрол все още е слаба, а обратната информация от гражданското общество за качеството на услугите и целесъобразността на приоритетите на практика не съществува. Същевременно вътрешният финансов контрол, който е ключово изискване за членството в ЕС, трябва да се внедри за всички първостепенни разпоредители с бюджетни средства; в момента той съществува само на хартия като изключение правят само няколко министерства. Поради бюджетния натиск в резултат от неразплатени разходи в общинските бюджети и неясното разделение на правомощията между централно и местно управление, третият ключов приоритет за реформата е финансирането между различните нива на управление. Първата стъпка трябва да бъде изясняване на задълженията по отношение на разходите между различните нива, за да се избегне разпокъсването в управлението. Решаването на въпроса с отношенията между централно и местно ниво трябва да започне с ограничаване на различията между разпределението на приходите и възлагането на разходите. За да могат местните органи да увеличат приходите си, трябва да им се дадат по-големи правомощия по отношение на местните данъци и такси като резултат от всеобхватна реформа в системата на общинските приходи, която се очертава като необходима. Настоящата администрация е постигнала значителен напредък в това отношение – разработена е програма за фискална децентрализация в тясно сътрудничество и консултации с общините и другите заинтересовани лица. Наскоро Министерският съвет одобри тази програма за фискална децентрализация за 2002–2005 г., която цели провеждането на реформа, която ясно да разграничава задълженията по разходите и разпределението на приходите между различните нива на управление.

Въпроси и приоритети, обхващащи всички сектори

На практика всички институционални въпроси излизат извън рамките на отделните сектори. Други подобни въпроси са:

- **Държавната финансова подкрепа**, а именно намаляване на зависимостта от държавно финансиране или стабилизирането на това финансиране; опростяването на подкрепата чрез окрупняване на разнообразието от програми, по-специално тези за социална защита; и постигането на най-подходящата форма или съчетание от форми, като ценова подкрепа, подкрепа за доходите, косвена подкрепа и др.
- **Ролята на държавата**, в това число: а) ролята на различните нива на управление (централно, областно, общинско); б) отношенията между държавата и общините; и в) усилия за пренасочване на отговорности към частния сектор.
- **Ефективност на целевото насочване**: а) обхванати ли са целево подходящите групи; б) правилно ли са определени отделните домакинства или лица в целевите групи (бедните, уязвимите); в) помощите стигат ли до тези домакинства и лица, дали са от полза, има ли злоупотреби; г) подходяща ли е степента на подпомагане; д) има ли проблеми с обхващането на малцинствата, по-специално ромите.
- **Предоставяне на услуги**: а) качество на услугите; б) ефективност на осигуряването им; в) различия по отношение на достъпа и качеството в зависимост от областта или общината.

Значителният брой на въпросите, засягащи всички сектори, не означава, че централното управление ще играе пропорционално по-важна роля при тяхното решаване. Напротив, много от посочените въпроси и проблеми са в резултат от това, че политиката на централно ниво се разработва и прилага без оглед на специфичните местни условия и предпочитания, потребности и ограничения на отделните сектори. Това, което подсказват тези въпроси, по-скоро е, че общините трябва да получат по-голяма автономия и гъвкавост както при вземането на решения, така и при разпределянето на разходите.

Общи приоритети, засягащи всички сектори, са:

- **Приключване на започнатите реформи**. България е в процес на осъществяване на важни реформи в няколко области, като пенсиите, образованието, здравеопазването, железниците, енергетиката, приватизацията, банковия сектор. С оглед реализирането на пълните ползи от тези реформи и за осигуряването на заложения ефект върху финансовата стабилност и подобренията в качеството на услугите, реформите трябва да продължат, да се наблюдават постоянно, да се усъвършенстват според нуждите и да бъдат доведени докрай. Широката програма от вече започнати реформи подсказва, че правителството трябва да е много внимателно по отношение на инициативи за нови реформи; на този етап е по-добре да се работи за завършване на провеждащите се реформи, преди да се пристъпи към нови области, които биха отклонили вниманието на вземащите решения и капацитета на правителството за тяхното изпълнение.

- **Действия, насочени към засилване и доказване на ползите от реформите**. В много области трябва да се предприемат стъпки за наблюдение на ефекта от реформите, подобряване на целевото насочване на помощите и осведомяване на обществеността относно намеренията, свързани със съответните реформи.
- **Изпълнение на изискванията на ЕС**. Тези изисквания на практика засягат всички сектори на икономиката. Разчетите, направени от предишното правителство, показват потребност от разходи на централното управление в порядъка на 3-4% от БВП за изпълнение на изисквания за членство в ЕС през следващите няколко години. Тези разходи трябва да се посрещнат без увеличаване на съотношението разходи/БВП, което налага определяне на приоритетите сред разходните компоненти. Освен това има някои правни и нормативни изисквания, които трябва да се изпълнят, а това изисква преустройство и укрепване на държавната администрация в целия държавен сектор.

Приоритети за бъдещата работа

Предвид широката програма на правителството и факта, че това е първият ППРИ, налице са няколко области, свързани пряко или косвено с публичните разходи, върху които правителството, Банката и другите донори трябва да продължат да работят в тясно сътрудничество.

- **Изисквания във връзка с инвестициите**. Инвестициите са пренебрегвани на практика във всички сектори на икономиката, което има неблагоприятен ефект върху средата за развитие на частния сектор. Първият приоритет е да се запълнят празнотите в познаването на проблемите по сектори, свързани с поддръжката, рехабилитацията и инвестициите. Това трябва да се извърши чрез отчитане на реалното състоянието в момента (състояние на активите, изпълнение на текущите проекти и др.) от съответните ресорни министерства. Това също трябва да се обсъди и с частния сектор.
- **Фискална децентрализация и въпроси на взаимодействието между различните нива на управление**. Наскоро приетата от Министерския съвет програма за фискална децентрализация е стъпка напред в тази област. На тази основа в процеса на изпълнение на програмата е нужен един по-системен анализ на взаимодействието между различните нива на управление, за да продължи реформата със същата сила. Въпросите, свързани с рационализацията на училищата, учителите и болниците, управлението на разходите за социална защита, фискалния натиск в резултат от неизплатени общински разходи, изискват по-системен анализ на проблемите на централно и местно ниво, осъществяван в съответствие с текущата работа, за което оказват подкрепа ААМР, ЕС и други.
- **Оценка на капацитета и реформа на държавната администрация**. Ограниченията при капацитета на администрацията са характерни за всички сектори и са ключов елемент от предизвикателствата пред управлението. Едно допълнително проучване в контекста на програмните заеми за преструктуриране на Банката би спомогнало за набелязване на основните ограничения в области като планиране и управление на бюджета, които имат системен характер за всички министерства и нива на управление.

- **Пътища**. В този доклад вниманието е насочено само към проблемите на транспорта в железопътния сектор. Въпреки това има важни въпроси в сектора на шосейния транспорт, където активите са в лошо състояние и предприемачите изпитват необходимост от подобрения. Този сектор също е ключов приоритет по отношение на членството в ЕС.

- **Висше образование**. Въпросите, свързани със свръхкапацитет, равнопоставеност при достъпа до образование и рентабилност на разходите, които засягат най-вече основното и средното образование, се очертават и във висшето образование. България има голям брой университети за числеността на населението си; наблюдава се и известна инертност във финансирането на университетите, която нарушава принципа "парите следват студентите".

- **Разходи за отбрана и сигурност**. Разходите на България за отбрана са сред най-високите сред страните-кандидатки за ЕС, много от които са изправени пред същия бюджетен натиск, както и България във връзка с перспективата за членство в НАТО. Един обстоен преглед на тези разходи би бил полезен с оглед на цялостните усилия по осъществяването на фискалните реформи.

EXECUTIVE SUMMARY

The Strategic Setting

Until 1997, Bulgaria was one of the poorest performing economies of Central and Eastern Europe (CEE). The preceding decade was marked by massive external borrowing, stop-go stabilization policies and a slow pace of structural reforms. Fueled by a failure to establish market discipline, widespread rent-seeking and the prevalence of soft budget constraints among enterprises, banks and the Government budget, Bulgaria's problems culminated in a severe economic crisis in 1996–97, which saw cumulative GDP decline by about 14 percent. After a few months of chaos involving a hyperinflation episode, the collapse of the banking sector and a major foreign exchange crisis, Bulgaria adopted in July 1997 a Currency Board Arrangement (CBA). The CBA has been underpinned by a conservative fiscal policy and a significant acceleration of structural reforms. The wide-ranging structural program encompassed reforms of the social sectors, agriculture, energy, privatization, restructuring and financial discipline in the enterprise and banking sectors, and liberalization of prices and trade. Sound macroeconomic management and the acceleration of structural reforms have succeeded in restoring growth, abating inflation and improving public and investors' confidence.

Overall, Bulgaria has made substantial progress toward long-term macroeconomic stability—an important step along the way to its ultimate goals of improving living standards and accession to the EU. It has resumed economic growth and has laid the ground for faster growth. According to the Government's medium-term program, supported by the IMF, the World Bank and other donors, Bulgaria's real GDP is expected to grow by about 5 percent per annum over the next four years, and its GDP per capita to expand by close to 6 percent annually. Its internal accounts are projected to be roughly in balance, and Bulgaria's external indebtedness is projected to continue to decline. Fiscal management is one of the cornerstones of Bulgaria's medium-term program, and the Government has set ambitious, conservative targets for fiscal management to underpin macroeconomic stability and to establish an appropriate environment for private sector development.

The Government's economic program is feasible, and could even be exceeded in the longer term, provided that the policies and reforms that have served Bulgaria well are continued, strengthened and implemented with urgency. However, Bulgaria faces a number of challenges:

- **The poverty challenge.** Bulgaria's per capita income (US$1,560 in 2001) is low, amounting to only 31 percent of the EU average (based on purchasing power parity estimates). Despite the impressive improvement registered since 1997, poverty remains at twice the level of 1995. Besides, the improvement has not been evenly distributed, neither geographically nor by population group.
- **The unemployment challenge.** Bulgaria's unemployment rate of 17.5 percent in 2001 is among the highest in the region. Furthermore, 49.3 percent of the unemployed have been out of work for more than a year and are considered "long-term unemployed."
- **The demographic challenge.** Bulgaria has had a negative population growth averaging –0.7 percent a year during the 1990s. Population size has been eroded further by net out-migration in the last two decades.
- **The investment challenge.** Investment in Bulgaria has been neglected for a long time and has begun to recover only recently. Relative to GDP, it is significantly below the levels in other CEE countries, where it has been close to 30 percent.
- **The governance challenge.** According to independent studies, Bulgaria is among the countries where weak governance has been limiting investment and constraining the business environment. The Government has taken important steps to improve governance, but further efforts are needed, especially to address capacity weaknesses that permeate most levels of management and span most sectors.
- **The continuing challenge of macroeconomic stability.** While Bulgaria has made impressive progress in achieving macroeconomic stability, the country is almost certain to face large current account deficits in the years ahead. Attracting the capital inflows needed, while reducing the debt burden, will require significant inflows of foreign investment which will materialize only in a stable macroeconomic environment.

Fiscal and expenditures policies will play a central role in addressing the above challenges in the coming years. Under the Currency Board Arrangement, fiscal policy is the primary instrument for maintaining macroeconomic stability. A fiscal sustainability exercise conducted for this Report indicates that the Government's fiscal policy program, which is centered around reaching budget balance over the medium term is consistent with maintaining macroeconomic stability, reducing the debt-to-GDP ratio, and adjusting to a decline of privatization revenues as the privatization program is completed. Of course, this assumes that the Government continues to implement its structural reform program and there are no external shocks.

Given that the revenue burden is already high and the Government has announced its intention to reduce the level of taxation in the economy, expenditure policies must bear the brunt of the burden of achieving the Government's fiscal targets and compensating for any revenue loss emanating from tax reform. To achieve the Government's fiscal targets, at the current level of revenue performance, our simulations indicate that, in the absence of external shocks and in tandem with a strong program of structural reform, only a modest one percentage point reduction of expenditures relative to GDP needs to be achieved over the medium term. If, however, the Government moves to lower further the burden of taxation on the economy then a further reduction of expenditures will be required to meet its fiscal targets. Bulgaria's main fiscal challenges are, therefore, to work towards an improved allocation of expenditures, while gradually reducing the overall level of expenditures over the medium term in tandem with Bulgaria's fiscal targets and its revenue objectives.

This Report focuses primarily on analyzing the challenges of improving the allocation of public expenditures. This fiscal challenge is made more difficult by the existing rigid structure of Bulgaria's expenditures, with social outlays accounting for 33 percent of total spending. Meeting the challenge of improving the allocation of public expenditures requires creating an expenditure management system with enough flexibility to adjust quickly and efficiently to macroeconomic shocks, and a fiscal management process that is more strategic, has a clearer medium-term focus and is performance oriented. Bulgaria's Currency Board Arrangement makes implementing the reforms discussed in this Report to achieve these objectives even more pressing.

In addition to fiscal and expenditure challenges, Bulgaria's reform agenda includes broad-ranging reforms to enhance the investment climate, further improvements in public administration, and an unfinished privatization agenda, magnified by EU accession requirements. Clearly, the Government needs to act on multiple fronts, as it has since 1997. The Government needs to give serious consideration to narrowing the agenda to develop a realistic, properly prioritized "core agenda." Moreover, there is a need to place the content and pace of reforms in Bulgaria's own setting. Bulgaria has many unique features and constraints, such as its demographic characteristics, including ethnic composition, its entrenched social protection system, the legacy of its past, its system of inter-governmental relations, its investment deficit, and so on. These characteristics affect needs, priorities, tolerances, and results.

Expenditure Structure and Trends

Owing to the strict fiscal discipline imposed by the Currency Board, Bulgaria has maintained a low fiscal deficit (on the order of one percent of GDP) in recent years. The deficit has been financed mainly by privatization revenues. In the past several years, the primary surplus has been maintained at about 3 percent. Bulgaria's fiscal stabilization was made possible by revenue expansion rather than expenditure cuts. While both revenues and expenditures have contracted in the last two years, revenues remain considerably above their pre-crisis level. In the post-crisis period, Bulgaria also effected a major expenditure restructuring. Interest payments have dropped dramatically from 20 percent of GDP in 1996 to 4 percent in 2001—and non-interest expenditures have risen substantially.

Bulgaria's overall fiscal position appears strong, compared to other countries in the region and the so-called EU Cohesion countries (Greece, Ireland, Portugal, and Spain). Government revenues are far above the average for the sample of CEE considered, and despite their recent recovery, expenditures are in line with the CEE average and slightly above the average for the Cohesion countries. In terms of economic composition, comparisons of the structure of public expenditures in Bulgaria with these countries do not reveal major imbalances, although the classification by broad categories masks some peculiarities of Bulgaria's expenditures. For example, while the size of Bulgaria's civil service is small, compared to the Cohesion countries and the EU, employment in education and health in Bulgaria is among the highest in the region. While capital expenditures are now at par with the CEE average, this masks the poor condition of public infrastructure, because of the cumulative effect of delayed maintenance over time. Finally, while subsidies have declined, they are still considerable and concentrated in infrastructure and detract from spending in other areas.

The savings resulting from the drop of interest payments by three-fourth (relative to GDP) over 1996–2001 were allocated across sectors, the main beneficiaries being social security and welfare expenditures. Nevertheless, the functional composition of expenditure in Bulgaria is also broadly in line with the structure of government spending in other CEE countries. The main exception would seem to be defense and security expenditures which, at 5 percent of GDP, in Bulgaria are almost twice higher than in all other CEE countries.

Based on the Government's fiscal policy objectives, international comparisons of Bulgaria's expenditure levels, and the detailed sectoral analysis contained in the remainder of the Report, this Report does raise a number of issues and make recommendations with regard to where expenditures could be rationalized and where inter- and intrasectoral expenditure priorities could be improved, even though it does not prescribe an optimal lower level for expenditures nor an ideal intersectoral allocation of expenditures.

These recommendations indicate that: (i) expenditures levels on economic affairs, especially transport and communications (for the railway and subsidies for household electricity), defense and security, and general services appear high and are candidates for rationalization; (ii) education, health and social protection expenditures require a reallocation of intrasectoral priorities, such as eliminating excess facilities (schools and hospitals), lowering the number of personnel (teachers and doctors), and rationalizing social protection programs, and at the same time, an increase in expenditures on quality-enhancing inputs (textbooks, etc.) and a better targeting of existing social assistance resources to the poor. Overall expenditure levels in these sectors appear roughly appropriate, with the exception of health where after rationalization of hospitals and an analysis of private out-of-pocket expenditures may reveal the need for higher public outlays; and (iii) higher investments appear to be required in many sectors, such as infrastructure, environment, education and health—some of which are priorities for EU accession and some of which should involve the private sector. While the overall investment ratio is in line with other EU accession countries, the effect of past neglect of maintenance expenditures and delayed outlays in earlier years may require higher expenditures on investment. So a close look at public investment requirements throughout the economy is required to determine if higher public investment is needed or a significant reallocation of investment is the answer. In summary, one must be careful to note that this Report was not intended to derive an optimal expenditure program and it only examines selected sectors. Therefore, these recommendations should be treated as tentative and with caution, until other sectors are analyzed and a fuller picture is available.

Structural Issues and Priorities

Education.   While education expenditures as a percentage of GDP have risen slightly over the past five years and are now more or less equivalent to the average for CEEs, there is a serious problem of misallocation of resources in the education sector. Since the start of the transition, enrollments have declined significantly at all levels, except higher education. This is largely the result of Bulgaria's negative population growth rate, aggravated by net out-migration. (Based on the numbers already born, the school-age population is expected to decline at least through the middle of the current decade). As a result, student-teacher ratios are very low, and there is an excess number of schools and teachers, particularly in the rural areas. There is, in addition, an equity problem manifested in wide variations in education-related problems, including education quality, among regions, municipalities, and ethnic groups, and according to poverty status. Also, the management of the education system is highly centralized. The Ministry of Education and Sciences (MES) is responsible for education content, quality control and staffing policies. Costs are shared by the state and the 263 municipalities on the basis of a complex formula which is approved every year and has a number of shortcomings.

The main challenge in the education sector is to reallocate expenditures from surplus capacity in teaching staff and underused facilities largely in rural areas toward other quality-enhancing inputs, and relieving overcrowding and multiple shifting in the major urban areas. The Government has recently prepared a school and teacher redeployment plan. While this is a good first step, the plan needs to be closely examined to determine if it is far-reaching enough. The resources saved from this plan need to be allocated toward alleviating the acute underspending for maintenance and new investment, and the shortage of teaching equipment, particularly in the smaller communities.

Inequities in the access to education also need urgent attention. The plight of Roma children in terms of school participation and performance requires immediate remedial steps, drawing partly on the experience with Roma-targeted programs in other countries. Another priority is to change the approach to education decentralization and financing. Currently, the MES has too much control over inputs (schools, teachers and norms); more decentralization of input decisions to municipalities would better align responsibilities and accountabilities. The current financing formula finances inputs (mostly teachers); an efficient mechanism should finance outputs—in this case, the education of students. The simplest means of doing that is to move to a pure capitation model of financing, with specified per-student allocations for each level of education. Rationalizing facilities and teachers and redeploying the freed resources for quality-enhancing inputs will be a first step toward improving the overall quality of primary and secondary education. Other priorities in education are: (i) establishing collaboration among the small municipalities in order to achieve efficient deployment of educational facilities and staff; (ii) rationalizing higher education institutions, minimizing the cost of higher education to the Government by raising user fees and at the same time, improving its quality; and (iii) replacing the current earmarked subsidy for capital expenditures with a mechanism based on well-documented project evaluations—an objective that cuts across all sectors.

Health Care. Bulgaria's health indicators are poor, compared to those of other transition economies, and most indicators have changed little or have been deteriorating during the transition period. Several factors have contributed to this relatively poor health status: (i) costly, excess capacity of both facilities and health care specialists inherited from the socialist past; (ii) inefficient use of resources, as manifested through both excess capacity and low utilization rates of facilities, especially hospital beds; (iii) neglect of maintenance of facilities and equipment; (iv) inadequate new investments; (v) overcentralized, rigid system of medical care; and (vi) low level of overall health expenditure—on the order of four percent of GDP—one of the lowest levels in central and eastern Europe.

In 1999, the Government undertook a wide-ranging reform of the health sector. The central component of the new system is the National Health Insurance Fund (NHIF), which combines the roles of pooling risks and purchasing medical care through contracts with physicians, group practices, and hospitals. The NHIF is funded through mandatory contributions unrelated to costs, especially through the earmarked payroll tax and contributions from the state on behalf of the poor and the non-working population. Hospitals are financed by the NHIF, the state and municipalities. Municipalities finance the contributions of those receiving unemployment benefits. Under past and current reforms, a reduction in hospital capacity and the supply of doctors have already taken place, although there is considerable room for further reduction. There are also some signs that the new system may pose access problems for certain groups such as the Roma and those living in remote areas. Finally, the health sector needs to correct the current situation of inadequate investment programming and funding.

The design of Bulgaria's new health care system is generally appropriate; it builds on the social insurance model of Western Europe that has been adopted by many Central and Eastern European countries over the past ten years. The top priority is to implement the system fully and carefully, learning from experience as the implementation progresses. Mechanisms need to be put in place to monitor progress. There is a need to monitor, in particular, the proportion of health expenditures going to physicians to avoid further increases at the expense of starving maintenance and new investments, as in the recent past.

Another key priority is to address the concurrent problems of surplus capacity issues in health facilities, the serious deterioration in the quality of facilities, and the inadequate modernization of equipment. Stabilizing and placing the financial situation of the NHIF on a sustainable basis is a third area where policy reform is needed. Finally, as in education, there is a need to address access issues for the disadvantaged, especially the Roma, the unemployed, and people who live in rural communities.

Social Protection. Social protection programs consist of: (i) pensions, (ii) labor market programs, (iii) social assistance, and (iv) short-term and family benefits. Aggregate spending on these programs accounted for 13.6 percent of GDP in 2001. Social protection programs have wide coverage among the population, over 80 percent of Bulgarians received at least one type of benefit in 2001—however, only one-third of the population is of retirement age or poor. On the whole, social protection programs have become more pro-poor since the mid-1990s and are playing a major role in alleviating poverty. Among benefit recipients, the poverty headcount fell from 35.1 percent before benefits to a low of 12.8 percent after benefits.

Pensions constitute the largest social protection expenditure category, accounting for 9.1 percent of GDP in 2001. Over the last decade, the overall stock of pensioners rose as a result of the aging of the population, while the number of insured persons shrunk, mirroring the collapse of employment. Until recently, the pension program consisted of a single, pay-as-you-go pillar (labeled PAYG) financed through payroll taxes. In the face of continuing financial pressure, in 1999 the Government introduced a new pension system comprising three pillars: (i) the so-called first, or public, pillar tantamount to a rationalized PAYG; (ii) a so-called "universal" pillar—a mandatory, fully-funded private insurance for those born after 1959, and a similar "occupational" plan; and (iii) a supplementary voluntary private system.

The first priority for reform is to improve compliance with, and coverage of, the public pillar, and define a clear rule for indexing pensions. Expansion of the pension system's coverage merits special attention, as some economic groups (such as workers in the agriculture sector) have been poorly covered since the early transition days. Another priority in the short term is to monitor and restrain the rise in disability trends, as the stricter retirement provisions have generated a surge of disability claims. Regarding private pension plans, their legal, regulatory and supervisory framework, especially their governance structure, require growing attention. This should include strengthening the capacity of the State Insurance Supervision Agency and, in the longer term, establishing a closer integration of private pension plans with the rest of Bulgaria's financial markets and the EU.

Labor Market Programs together with fundamental labor market reform are critical elements in facing Bulgaria's unemployment challenge. At 17.5 percent in 2001, unemployment in Bulgaria has been rising steadily since 1996, and it is among the highest in the region. To complement labor market reform, which aims at creating a dynamic labor market conducive to employment growth, and to assist workers who lose their jobs, Bulgaria implements labor market programs. There are two kinds of labor market programs: (i) payment of unemployment benefits, or so-called "passive programs"; and (ii) "active labor market programs" (ALMPs), consisting of measures to promote employment, including public works programs, training, employment subsidies, and support for small business development. An *Unemployment Insurance Fund,* which succeeded the PTUF on January 1, 2002 aims to improve the effectiveness of unemployment benefits. The fund is managed by NSSI and is designed to close the gap between contributions to the compulsory social security system and the benefits provided to the unemployed. Eligibility and benefits are linked to the number of years of contributions to the system, and monthly minimum and maximum levels of benefits are determined annually by law. The new unemployment insurance fund is to cover the beneficiary's contributions to pension and health insurance.

Social Assistance programs encompass several kinds of benefits, the most important of which is the Guaranteed Minimum Income (GMI) Program, a means-tested cash benefit paid to low-income households below an income threshold, which constitutes the main national safety net. The social protection system also includes *short-term benefits* consisting of 12 categories of benefits, including sickness, maternity, birth, child care, work injuries, disabled children, etc.

A top priority is to implement fundamental labor market reform to establish a dynamic labor market conducive to expanding employment opportunities. Labor market reform, labor market programs, and social assistance policies should complement each other to promote work incentives and employment growth. At the same time it is critical to monitor closely the effectiveness of the unemployment insurance fund in terms of its expected increase in registry and contributions, profile of unemployment insurance beneficiaries, including duration of benefits, share of beneficiaries that return to employment, and costs of the fund. Similarly, there is a need to monitor the so-called ALMPs closely in order to improve their effectiveness and long-term impact in stimulating labor demand. Over the longer-term, consideration should be given to reduce the tax burden related to labor market policies in order to curtail labor costs.

Finally, given the plethora of social protection programs, the complexity of program design in many cases and their burden on the state, a constant challenge regarding the social protection system as a whole is to examine the opportunities for consolidation and simplification and engage in systematic monitoring of the programs, their costs and their effects.

The State Railway. The Bulgaria State Railway (BDZ) does not operate as a profit-oriented, commercial entity; it functions, rather, as an old (pre-transition) government enterprise. BDZ's net income has been negative since the economic transition. Its deficit reached 124 million Leva in 2001, or 21 percent of total costs, even after taking into account the operating subsidy provided by the central government. BDZ receives a significant contribution from the State to cover its deficit. The total state contribution has averaged 0.8 percent of GDP in recent years. About half of this amount represents an operating subsidy, and the rest a contribution to investment. The subsidies have not prevented the serious deterioration of railway assets due to their inadequate maintenance and renewal.

BDZ's poor financial performance is attributable to several factors: the large number of un-economic services mandated by the state; low passenger fares; low labor productivity; and an inappropriate incentive framework that is not conducive to efficient decision making and accountability.

To stem the deterioration of the railway sector, Bulgaria needs to undertake a number of actions. The first priority is a drastic reduction in uneconomic services, initiated on the basis of a carefully prepared and properly discussed rationalization plan. Terminating loss-making services should boost revenues. Further, cost-saving measures should include adjusting fares and, importantly, reducing the labor force. Projections undertaken for this Report concluded that reduction of labor is by far the most important measure that can be taken to redress the railway's financial situation. Although the breakup of BDZ into two entities—one for operations, the other for infrastructure—is a step forward, this should be complemented by clear corporate governance arrangements, especially to isolate the new entities from political interference, particularly where investment decisions are concerned.

Energy. Bulgaria's energy sector is largely government owned or controlled and energy consumption is heavily subsidized. Households constitute the largest category of beneficiaries as household electricity and district heating prices have the highest subsidy content. Higher income households, which consume larger amounts of energy benefit proportionately more than poorer households from these subsidies. With state ownership or control over all major energy assets, virtually all capital investment requires state support in the form of budget funds or state-guaranteed loans. As available public resources have been scarce, under-investment has afflicted the sector for more than a decade. Significant investments are needed to rehabilitate power generation plants, to modernize transmission and distribution systems, develop a much needed low-pressure gas system, to modernize the district heating system in several areas of the country, and to rehabilitate some coal mines.

In this connection the state needs to: (i) enhance the capacity of the State Energy Regulatory Commission; (ii) implement the recently adopted electricity price adjustment schedule to eliminate distortions, bringing prices to full cost recovery in 2002–04, and monitor closely the mechanisms aimed at easing the burden on low income and vulnerable groups; (iii) delay costly investment in new power and heat generation capacity until regulatory reforms are more advanced and investors (especially those investing in new capacity for export) can assume a larger share of the market risk under a suitable regulatory framework; (iv) liberalize investment decisions related to supplying industry and large commercial customers who should be allowed to contract the bulk of their needs of gas and electricity from private suppliers, including from abroad.

The Government has made important progress in the energy reforms discussed in this Report. In mid-2002, the Council of Ministers approved an energy strategy that envisages bringing household electricity prices to full cost recovery in a period of three years (from 2002–04). The State

Energy Regulatory Commission (SERC) adopted an indicative price adjustment of 20-15-10 percent in each of the three consecutive years starting in 2002. To protect the poor from the impact of the price adjustments, the Government supplemented this price reform with two mechanisms: (i) expanding the energy consumption program which supports a minimum energy consumption of households who are poor; and (ii) adopting a two-tier price system where the price for a minimum level of electricity consumption remains unchanged, and a second price is applied to higher levels of consumption. Implementation of these and other energy reforms remains central to the modernization of the energy sector.

Institutional Issues and Priorities

Achieving a better allocation of expenditures will require, first, an improved expenditure management process that is both strategic in focus and performance-oriented. To ensure the fiscal discipline necessary to support the Currency Board Arrangement, the Government of Bulgaria has already initiated a number of public expenditure management reforms. The Budget and State Treasury Department in the Ministry of Finance has realigned its functions, restructured its organization and strengthened its staff; a financial management information system is being introduced; and the structure of budget units is being rationalized and their number reduced. In early 2002, the Government introduced a number of changes in budget preparation procedures, which are to be implemented starting with the 2003 budget. The changes aim especially at improving intersectoral allocation. The Government has also taken steps to introduce a programmatic approach, particularly with a view to strengthening the budget-policy link. According to a Council of Ministers (COM) decision taken in January 2002, spending agencies are to prepare sectoral medium-term budget frameworks (MTBFs) at the initial stage of the 2003 budget preparation cycle. The Government has indicated its plan to include the global MTBF in the documents presented to Parliament.

As a result of these and related reforms, effective control over cash flows has been greatly improved; and aggregate public expenditures have been held under tight financial control. Despite this important progress, there is a need to continue and to broaden the reform effort, especially in: (i) budget formulation; (ii) budget execution, accounting and auditing; and (iii) financial management at the local government level. The key institutional issues in public expenditure management are three-fold: (i) how best to continue and consolidate the movement toward program budgeting, based on performance and outcomes; (ii) how to improve public investment selection and budgeting; and (iii) how to enhance financial management at the local government level in the context of improved local-central government relations. Chapter 5 has identified investment programming and local government expenditure management as the weakest links of the budget system.

The thrust of future reforms needs to focus on three areas. First, reformers need to broaden their recent budget formulation reform initiatives into a more robust and comprehensive budget preparation process that is medium-term in outlook and more strategically focused. Moreover, the budget preparation process should be supplemented by a number of actions specifically regarding investment programming. Capital expenditure proposals should be prepared under hard budget constraints and as an integral part of the MTBF, that is, included as an annex to the MTBF document. Municipalities should be allowed to play a greater role in approving and executing investment expenditures, including freedom to carry over investment expenditures, rather than over-indulging in current expenditures under the present system.

Second, systems of ex-post evaluation remain weak and feedback from civil society on service quality and appropriateness of priorities is virtually nonexistent. At the same time, internal audit, which is a key requirement for EU accession, needs to be made operational across all first-level budget agencies; currently, aside from a few ministries, it exists on paper only. Given the budgetary pressures arising from arrears in local government budgets and the unclear division of authority between the central and local governments, inter-governmental finance is the third key priority for reform. A first step is to clarify expenditure assignment between different levels of government in order to avoid fragmentation in management. Addressing the problem of central-local government relations needs to start with limiting the disparities between revenue allocations and expenditure assignments. To induce local governments to increase revenue collection, they should be granted increased authority over local taxes in the context of a comprehensive reform of the local revenue system, which seems to be needed. The current administration has made important progress by developing a fiscal decentralization program in close consultation and collaboration with municipalities and other stakeholders. The Council of Ministers recently approved this fiscal decentralization program for 2002–05 and aims at implementing a reform that clearly delineates intergovernmental expenditure assignments and revenue allocations.

Cross-cutting Issues and Priorities

Practically all institutional issues cut across sectors. Other cross-cutting issues include:

- **State financial support,** namely, reducing dependence on state financing or stabilizing such financing; simplifying the support by both consolidating the plethora of programs, especially for social protection; and the most appropriate form or combination of support, for example, among price support, income support, indirect support, and so on.

- **Role of the state,** including: (i) the role of the different levels of government (central, regional, municipal); (ii) the relations between the state and the municipalities; and (iii) efforts to devolve responsibilities to the private sector.

- **Effectiveness of targeting:** (i) are the right groups targeted; (ii) are the individual households or people within the targeted groups (the poor, the vulnerable) properly identified; (iii) do the subsidies reach those households and people, do they help, are there abuses; (iv) are the levels of the assistance appropriate; and (v) are there problems in reaching the minorities, especially the Roma.

- **Service delivery:** (i) service quality, (ii) efficiency of delivery; and (iii) the variability of access and quality by region or municipality.

The preponderance of cross-cutting issues does not imply that there is a proportionately large role for the central government to play in addressing them. On the contrary, many of the problems and issues highlighted arose because central government policies were designed and applied without sufficient attention to local conditions and preferences, and sector needs and constraints. What the issues point to, rather, is that municipalities should be given greater autonomy and flexibility in both decision making and expenditure allocation.

The overall cross-cutting priorities include:

- **Completion of reforms that have already been initiated.** Bulgaria is in the midst of implementing major reforms in a number of areas, for example, pensions, education, health care, railways, the energy sector, privatization, the banking sector. To realize the full benefits of these reforms and to ensure the intended impact on financial sustainability and improvements in the quality of services, these reforms need to be continued, continuously monitored, refined as needed, and completed. The large agenda of already initiated reforms implies that the Government needs to be very parsimonious in initiating new reforms; at this point, it seems advisable to work on completing ongoing reforms before opening new areas which would spread more thinly decisionmakers' attention and government implementation capacity.

- **Actions aimed at enhancing and demonstrating the benefits of reforms.** In many areas, steps need to be taken to monitor the impact of reforms, improve the targeting of benefits and inform the public of the intentions of the reform effort.

- **Meeting EU accession requirements.** These requirements cut across virtually all sectors of the economy. Estimates, which were prepared by the previous government, show the need for roughly 3–4 percent of GDP in central government expenditures for meeting EU accession requirements over the next few years. These expenditures would need to be accommodated without a rise in the expenditure to GDP ratio, implying the need for prioritization across the expenditure envelop. In addition, there are a number of legal and regulatory requirements that need to be met, and this will require reorganization and strengthening of public administration across the entire public sector.

Priorities for Further Work

Given the broad agenda that the Government has been following and the fact that this is the first PEIR, there are a number of areas related to public expenditures, directly or indirectly, where further work needs to be carried out by the Government, the Bank and other donors in close cooperation with each other.

- **Investment requirements.** Investment has been neglected in practically all sectors of the economy, and this is having an adverse effect on the climate for private sector development. The first priority is to close the knowledge gap concerning maintenance, rehabilitation and investment requirements, by sector. This should be done on the basis of the situation on the ground (state of assets, execution of ongoing projects, etc.), and undertaken by the line ministries. It should also be informed by a dialogue with the private sector.
- **Fiscal decentralization and intergovernmental fiscal issues.** The recently approved fiscal decentralization program by the Council of Ministers is a welcome step forward in this area. Building on this important achievement and as the program is implemented, a more systematic analysis of intergovernmental issues is needed to keep the reform momentum moving forward. Issues regarding the rationalization of schools, teachers and hospitals, the administration of social protection expenditures, and fiscal pressures arising from arrears in municipal finances, all call for a more systematic analysis of intergovernmental issues, in coordination with the ongoing work, supported by USAID, the EU and others.
- **Capacity assessment and public administration reform.** Capacity constraints permeate all sectors and is a key issue in the governance challenge. Further study in the context of the Bank's program of programmatic lending would help identify the key constraints in areas such as budget planning and management, which are systemic across ministries and levels of government.
- **Roads.** This Report has concentrated solely on transport issues in the railway sub-sector. Nevertheless, there are important issues in the roads subsector, where the stock is in bad shape and entrepreneurs perceive a need for improvements. The sub-sector is also a key priority for EU accession.
- **Higher education.** The issues of excess capacity, equity access and cost recovery, which affect primary and secondary education are also encountered in the higher education subsector. Bulgaria has a large number of universities for its population size, and there seem to be rigidities in university financing that violate the principle of money follows the student.
- **Defense and security expenditures.** Bulgaria's defense expenditures are the highest among EU accession candidates, many of which face the same spending pressures as Bulgaria as a result of their prospective NATO membership. A thorough review of these expenditures would be beneficial to the overall expenditure reform effort.

PART ONE:
THE MAIN REPORT

CHAPTER I

THE STRATEGIC SETTING

Performance and Prospects

Until 1997, Bulgaria was one of the poorest performing economies of Central and Eastern Europe (CEE). The preceding decade was marked by massive external borrowing, stop-and-go stabilization policies and a slow pace of structural reforms. Fueled by a failure to establish market discipline, widespread rent-seeking and the prevalence of soft budget constraints among enterprises, banks and the government budget, Bulgaria's problems culminated in a severe economic crisis in 1996–97, which resulted in a cumulative GDP decline of nearly 14 percent.

After a few months of chaos involving a hyperinflation episode, the collapse of the banking sector and a major foreign exchange crisis, Bulgaria adopted in July 1997 a Currency Board Arrangement (CBA). The CBA was considered the best cure to the soft budget constraints and commercial bank financing that kept loss-making enterprises afloat, and to the lack of fiscal discipline that led to hyperinflation.

The CBA has been underpinned by a conservative fiscal policy and a significant acceleration of structural reforms. The wide-ranging structural program encompassed reforms of the social sectors, agriculture, energy, privatization, restructuring and financial discipline in the enterprise and banking sectors, and liberalization of prices and trade. Sound macroeconomic management and the acceleration of structural reforms succeeded in restoring growth, abating inflation and improving public and investors' confidence.

Following the introduction of the CBA, interest rates dropped sharply, inflation declined dramatically, and the fiscal deficit was reduced to far more sustainable levels. Real output recovered and grew by an average of 4 percent per year after 1998 (Table 1.1). This improved performance took place in a difficult external environment marked by turmoil in international markets, unfavorable commodity price developments, the trade disruptions associated with the Kosovo crisis and, more recently, the global economic slowdown and the impact of the September 11 attack on the United States.

TABLE 1.1: SELECTED ECONOMIC INDICATORS

	1996	1997	1998	1999	2000	2001
Real GDP Growth (percent change)	−9.4	−5.6	4.0	2.3	5.4	4.0
GDP deflator (percent change)	120.8	948.3	23.7	3.7	6.7	6.5
CPI (End of Period, percent change)	310.8	549.2	1.7	7.0	11.4	4.8
Unemployment rate (registered)	11.0	14.0	12.4	13.8	18.1	17.5
Gross Domestic Investment (percent of GDP)	8.1	9.9	16.9	17.9	18.3	20.4
(of which public investment)	0.7	2.3	3.7	4.5	3.9	3.9
Primary Balance (percent of GDP)	9.2	7.1	5.3	2.8	3.0	2.9
Interest Payments (percent of GDP)	19.5	8.3	4.3	3.8	4.0	3.7
Overall Balance (percent of GDP)	−10.3	−1.2	1.0	−0.9	−1.0	−0.9
Interest Rates (BNB basic rate)	435.0	7.0	5.2	4.6	4.7	4.7
Current Account Balance (percent of GDP)	1.7	10.1	−0.5	−5.0	−5.6	−6.5
Merchandise Exports (US$ million)	4689	4809	4193	4006	4812	5099
Merchandise Imports (US$ million)	4567	4488	4574	5087	5988	6665
Foreign Direct Investment Inflows (US$ million)	109	505	537	819	1002	651
Gross Official Reserves (US$ millions)	793	2474	3057	3222	3460	3579
(in months of imports)	1.4	4.6	5.6	5.5	5.0	4.7
External Debt (in percent of GDP)	98.0	96.2	83.8	82.3	86.5	73.3
Exchange Rate (Leva per US$, e.o.p.)	0.487	1.777	1.675	1.947	2.102	2.219
(percent change, + means depreciation)	589.3	264.5	−5.7	16.2	8.0	5.6
Real Effective Exchange Rate (REER-CPI) (percent change, + means appreciation)	−38.8	77.4	5.2	0.5	3.3	3.3

Source: National Statistical Institute, Bulgarian National Bank, Ministry of Finance, IMF and World Bank.

The current account deficit widened from less than 1 percent of GDP in 1998 to nearly 6.5 percent in 2001, in response to external pressures. In 1999, a global financial crisis and low commodity prices lowered significantly the external demand for Bulgaria's exports, while the Kosovo conflict blocked transit routes to Western Europe, raising transport costs and causing losses in export markets. However, in 2000 and 2001, driven by higher demand from the Euro area, exports rebounded from their low level and registered a 10 percent volume growth. Inflows of foreign direct investment (FDI), which exceeded 8 percent of GDP in 2000, provided a comfortable cover for external financing requirements. In 2001, largely because of the lack of any significant privatization transaction, FDI inflows declined to about 5 percent of GDP, but they remained a primary source of BOP financing.

The government budget has been broadly in balance, registering a surplus of 1.0 percent of GDP in 1998 and a deficit of the same order of magnitude in the following three years. Inflation was contained at single digit levels in 1998–99. Because of pressures from international oil prices, the high US dollar and a summer drought, inflation grew to 11 percent in 2000 but fell back to 4.8 percent in 2001.

Two achievements since the crisis—other than those already cited-are noteworthy: (i) the reduction in poverty, and (ii) progress toward the divestiture of state-owned enterprises (SOEs). The 2001 poverty profile for Bulgaria shows a dramatic rebound of living standards since 1997, when poverty had escalated to 36 percent of the population. Using poverty lines updated from 1997, poverty fell by nearly two-thirds over the last four years to about 13 percent of the population, and the depth and severity of poverty have also improved (see Box 8.1 in Chapter 8).

Over the same period, close to 90 percent of the non-utility state-owned enterprises' assets have been divested; the bulk of these were privatized, and 13 percent were liquidated. More than half of the assets of all SOEs have been either sold or closed down. The Government has stated its commitment to complete the SOE privatization by the end of 2003.[2] Actually, with the new privatization law enacted recently, the Government is offering for sale all privatizable assets. Privatization in the financial sector, especially in the banking sector, has been almost completed, with more than 80 percent of bank assets now in private hands.[3]

A major exception to the positive recent trends has been the sharp rise in, and persistence of, unemployment. The unemployment rate, already high at 14 percent in 1997, grew steadily thereafter, exceeding 17 percent in 2000 and 2001. The reasons include the large number of people who lost their jobs due to enterprise restructuring, some productivity gains, skills and regional mismatches, labor market rigidities, and limited job creation due to the slow growth of new enterprises.

The Government's Economic Program.   Overall, Bulgaria has made substantial progress toward long-term macroeconomic stability—an important step along the way to its ultimate goal of accession to the EU. It has resumed economic growth and has laid the ground for faster growth. According to the Government's medium-term program, supported by the IMF and the World Bank, Bulgaria's real GDP is expected to grow by about 5 percent per annum over the next four years and its GDP per capita to expand by close to 6 percent annually.[4] Its internal accounts are projected to be roughly in balance, and Bulgaria's external indebtedness is projected to continue to decline. Fiscal management is one of the cornerstones of Bulgaria's medium-term program and the Government has set ambitious, conservative targets for fiscal management to underpin macroeconomic stability and to establish an appropriate environment for private sector development.

Challenges and Opportunities

The Government's economic program is feasible, and could even be exceeded in the longer term, provided that the policies and reforms that have served Bulgaria well are continued and strengthened. However, Bulgaria faces a number of challenges, in the form of constraints and pressures— as well as opportunities. Some of the constraints stem from the limitations of the physical resource base and are beyond Bulgaria's control. For example, Bulgaria does not have an economical indigenous source of energy; the only energy source it possesses is low-quality, polluting coal, or lignite. Yet it has the highest energy intensity among EU accession countries. Most of Bulgaria's challenges are, however, the product of past choices and performance. The main challenges include the following:

The Poverty Challenge.   Bulgaria's per capita income, estimated at US$ 1,560 in 2001, is low. It is only 31 percent of the EU average (at purchasing power parity), and less than half the average for Central Europe and the Baltics. Despite the impressive improvement registered since 1997, poverty remains at twice the level of 1995. Besides, the improvement has not been evenly distributed, neither geographically nor by population group. It has not benefited equitably the rural population or the Roma,[5] who (still) are 10 times as likely as the non-ethnic population to be poor.

---

[2] The Bulgaria Telecom, Bulgartabak Holding and a few energy distribution companies remain to be privatized, in addition to the sale of minority shares of the government in already privatized enterprises, plus a few small and medium-sized enterprises.

[3] Biochim Commercial Bank was privatized in July 2002. The remaining large entities are the State Savings Bank, and the largest insurance company, DZI, for all of which privatization strategies are being developed.

[4] Bulgaria has a negative population growth rate, as explained later.

[5] The Roma are the second largest ethnic minority of Bulgaria, after the Turks, and account for 4.6 percent of the total population. They are concentrated in cities and big towns, where they live in big families located predominantly in separate neighborhoods. They are disadvantaged in terms of education and employment, and rely on various forms of social assistance programs.

The Unemployment Challenge.   At 17.5 percent in 2001, unemployment in Bulgaria has been rising steadily since 1996, and it is still among the highest in the region. Furthermore, 49.3 percent of the unemployed have been out of work for more than a year, making them "the long-term unemployed." Unemployment persists partly because, as documented in Chapter 8, programs to reinsert workers into the active labor force have proven ineffective.

The Demographic Challenge.   Bulgaria has had a negative population growth, averaging −0.2 percent a year in the 1980s. The rate of population decline accelerated during the 1990s to an average of −0.7 a year. Of all the countries of Europe and Central Asia (ECA), only Latvia and Estonia experienced a faster shrinkage of population in the 1990s. The total fertility rate of Bulgaria, at 1.2, is just over half of the level required to maintain the population size constant over the long term. Population size has been eroded further by net out-migration, which was estimated at 8 percent of the population in 1989. Although this was a peak year for out-migration, population loss due to migration continued throughout the 1990s and is still continuing.

The Investment Challenge.   Investment in Bulgaria has been neglected for a long time and started to grow again only recently (see Table 1.2). Gross domestic investment as a share of GDP in Bulgaria has been slightly more than half of the levels in other CEE countries, where it has been close to 30 percent. In addition to catching up with long-deferred expenditures to rehabilitate its infrastructure and to cope with the EU's stringent requirements for accession, Bulgaria will need a sharp increase in new investments in the medium term. The need to expand investment is confirmed in every sectoral chapter of Part Two of this Report. It should be stressed that the degree of under-investment for the country as a whole is greater than suggested by the inter-country comparisons in Table 1.2 because of the cumulative effect of *persistent underinvestment* on the life and state of the physical assets.

The Governance Challenge.   Bulgaria is perceived as a country where corruption and weak governance are factors limiting investment and constraining the business climate. According to a recent report by the World Bank,[6] Bulgaria is characterized as a country with a high level of state capture—which is illicit, illegitimate and non-transparent forms of influence on state institutions—and a medium level of administrative corruption—which is a measure of the amount of illicit and non-transparent gains that accrue to public officials in the implementation of existing laws, rules and regulations. The existence and seriousness of corruption has also been documented in a number of studies, including the October 2001 EC Regular Report, which states that ". . . *Further steps are needed to ensure an efficient, transparent and accountable public administration. Corruption has continued to give serious cause for concern. Enforcing the legal framework effectively presents a challenge and greater focus is needed on prevention of corruption. . .*"[7] Similarly, other external independent reviews of corruption indicate that while the situation is improving, it is far from satisfactory. The problem is manifested through (i) the prevalence of corruption—both grand and petty (or administrative); and (ii) weak public confidence in the management of public resources. The problem is due to both the structure and the functioning of government—in particular, the concentration of power, despite progress toward decentralization, weak legal and regulatory framework, weak capacity to monitor corruption and enforce laws, a weak judiciary and weak overall accountability and transparency. The areas most affected have been customs, medical services, tax administration, higher education, and the courts.

---

[6] See, *Anticorruption in Transition: A Contribution to the Policy Debate,* The World Bank, Washington, D.C., 2000., pp. 14–16.

[7] See, *2001 Regular Report On Bulgaria's Progress Towards Accession,* Commission of European Communities, Brussels, 13.11.2001, SEC(2001) 1744, p. 96.

TABLE 1.2: GROSS DOMESTIC INVESTMENT						
(AS PERCENT OF GDP)						
	1996	1997	1998	1999	2000	2001[p]
Bulgaria	8.1	9.9	16.9	17.9	18.3	20.4
Czech Republic	35.0	32.8	30.2	27.9	34.9	30.4
Hungary	27.2	27.7	29.7	28.5	30.6	31.1
Poland	21.9	24.6	26.2	26.4	26.4	25.2
Romania	25.9	20.6	17.9	17.2	19.4	21.0
Slovak Republic	37.1	36.6	36.1	31.9	30.1	35.4
Average (excl. Bulgaria)	**29.4**	**28.5**	**28.0**	**26.4**	**28.3**	**28.6**

Source: National authorities, WB staff estimates and projections, except EIU for Hungary for 2000.

In recent years, the Government has taken a number of steps to improve governance, in recognition of the problem. The anti-corruption measures taken by the Government include the adoption, in 1998, of a National Strategy for Combating Corruption, and of a series of measures designed to strengthen control within the Tax Administration, Customs, the Ministry of the Interior, and the National Security Service. There is both anecdotal and documented evidence (through surveys) of progress: the 2001 Regular Report of the European Commission notes that there has been progress in many areas, especially in the area of public administration, as do some external, independent surveys. Furthermore, a recent extensive survey of governance and corruption in South East Europe concluded that Bulgaria presented "a mixed picture," placing above average in some areas, and below average, in others.[8]

Despite the apparent improvement regarding governance-cum-corruption, which needs further confirmation, both require continued attention in the current context due to (i) the EU pre-accession requirements; (ii) their role in shaping the business climate; (iii) their relevance to stimulating the private sector and attracting foreign investors, in particular; and (iv) their impact on: access to services, service delivery, the overall effectiveness of public expenditures, and especially the functioning of the system of targeting as intended.

The framework for addressing administrative corruption has improved with recent public administration reforms, but capacity weaknesses at all levels of government—central and municipal, managerial and technical—remain formidable. As highlighted throughout this Report (see Chapters 4 and Part II), capacity deficiencies of one kind or another span most sectors, including health, social protection and even railways. These constraints cover activities as varied as expenditure budgeting, especially within a Medium-Term Budget Framework (MTBF) at the sector and national levels, poverty monitoring, social assistance targeting, and debt management. While the needs are real, it is easy to exaggerate existing capacity deficiencies for several reasons: it is easy to confuse the capacity problem with those associated with governance, or decision-making, i.e., to separate the problems of demand and those of supply; it is also easy to mistake the lack of motivation and incentives for lack of skills; and finally, the problem of capacity may be exacerbated by the

---

[8] The survey was undertaken by seven countries which formed an alliance for voluntary, mutual, "peer review" style monitoring of governance. While South East Europe is not necessarily the best comparator to draw positive conclusions from, this disadvantage is partly offset by the sophistication of the survey. The indicators used ranged from measures of revenue predictability and civil liberties to the size and wage level of the central government employment and the waiting time for telephone lines. On the positive side, the survey found Bulgaria to be relatively decentralized, its revenue predictability to be relatively good, and to be among the better countries with respect to civil liberties. On the negative side, Bulgaria had a high "state capture" index, implying a need to open the economy to competition; its budgetary volatility was the highest in the region, as was the waiting time for a telephone line. (World Bank, Europe and Central Asia Region, *Measuring Governance in South East Europe,* draft, April 2002.)

breadth and ambitiousness of the reform agenda. Nevertheless, capacity needs are accentuated by at least three factors: (i) the complexity of the second-generation structural reforms, compared with the first-generation ones; (ii) EU pre-accession requirements, which call for strengthened capacity in a number of areas and treat capacity enhancement as a requirement in itself; and (iii) the close link between capacity and governance.

The Continuing Challenge of Macroeconomic Stability. Bulgaria has made progress in the past few years in achieving and maintaining macroeconomic stability. But, the Government's macroeconomic projections imply a large current account deficit for the medium term, as the imports required to support needed investment outlays and manufacturing exports will continue to surpass Bulgaria's improving export capacity. As a result, large capital inflows will be needed to finance the current account deficit and to sustain an adequate level of reserves to maintain confidence in the Currency Board Arrangement. Continued implementation of tight fiscal policy and strict incomes policy are central to maintaining macroeconomic stability under the Currency Board Arrangement. In addition, attracting adequate capital inflows, while at the same time, reducing Bulgaria's debt burden, requires significant inflows of foreign investment, which, in turn, requires an investment climate that is conducive to such inflows and a continuation of the privatization program. Furthermore, the large external imbalances under the base scenario imply that Bulgaria is vulnerable to external shocks, such as a continuation of the slowdown in EU economic activity or adverse oil price trends.

Opportunities. Despite the depth and breadth of these challenges, Bulgaria also has significant opportunities in the next decade. The last few years of solid growth has established a good base. Sustaining the growth momentum offers the possibility of further reductions in poverty and meaningful reductions in unemployment. Moreover, Bulgaria stands on the threshold of joining the European Union, which would likely accelerate economic growth and convergence of incomes towards Western European levels. The desirability of faster growth can hardly be over-emphasized. At the 5.5 percent growth of GDP projected for 2005, and at the current population trend, it would still take about a decade for Bulgaria's per capita income of US$ 1,560 (Atlas methodology, 2001) to reach the current level of the Czech Republic, Poland and Hungary.

While Bulgaria's physical resource base is fixed, and demographic realities can change only slowly, most of the challenges faced are the result of past and current policies. They include the policies responsible for: the slow start of transition; the neglect of maintenance, rehabilitation and new investments; the misallocation of resources, responsible for, inter alia, costly surplus capacity in some areas; institutional and capacity bottlenecks; and deficiencies in governance. There is thus a growth potential that can be released which can contribute to faster growth—and the promise of growth—beyond the medium term.

Policy Priorities: The Fiscal Challenge

Bulgaria faces a daunting agenda in the next decade, if it is to meet these challenges and seize the opportunities offered by higher growth and integration into the European Union. By any criterion, the first priority is to complete the ongoing reforms, especially those bearing on the transition to a market economy, the decentralization of decision making, the privatization of government assets, and the improvement of the business climate. This should be based on close monitoring of results—the cost-benefit of individual actions—and pursued with flexibility to adjust policies, as needed.

Bulgaria's policy framework is centered on the Currency Board Arrangement and supported by tight fiscal policy, strict incomes policy, and a broad agenda of structural reforms. Macroeconomic performance has been robust: for the third consecutive year, the fiscal deficit has been under 1 percent of GDP, the primary surplus has been about 3 percent of GDP, the Fiscal Reserve Account has remained at least 90 percent of next year's gross public debt service requirements, inflation has remained at single digit levels, and international reserves have remained at about 5 months of imports. However, the external current account deficit is large—reaching 6.5 percent of GDP in 2001. In the medium term, the external account deficit is expected to remain at about 6 percent of GDP—the deficit is expected to be financed largely by private capital flows, particularly by foreign direct investment flows. Provided the Government maintains fiscal discipline, a strict incomes policy, and accelerates structural reforms, the CBA provides a stable nominal anchor and facilitates the political economy of reform but the Government needs to monitor the situation closely especially in light of the high current account deficit and unemployment rate. To provide some cushion against external shocks the Government has identified contingency measures—totalling about ¾ percent of GDP—in the event that, in the short run, the external current account deficit worsens or international reserves decline significantly below set targets.[9]

Fiscal and expenditure policies, which are the main focus of this Report, will play a central role in addressing Bulgaria's major challenges in the coming years. Under the CBA, fiscal policy is the primary instrument for maintaining macroeconomic stability. Moreover, expenditure policies will be critical in protecting those members of society who are bypassed by the growth process. Financing the infrastructure and investment needs for an acceleration of economic growth and to meet EU accession requirements will also require additional expenditures. These expenditure priorities, in combination with the demands on fiscal policy from a macro-economic perspective, will require careful management, difficult tradeoffs, and a medium term strategic perspective.

An Analysis of Fiscal Sustainability. At the outset, it is essential to assess what constitutes an appropriate government fiscal stance, that is, a fiscal policy stance that is sustainable in the medium term. For the purposes of this Report, we have estimated the 'sustainable level' for the primary balance over the medium term.[10] Our fiscal sustainability calculation is based on a declining level of debt, consistent with the Government's objective to meet the Maastricht Treaty targets over a five year period. For medium-term planning targets, it seems prudent to assume a rate of inflation of 3.5 percent, a growth rate of 4 percent and an interest rate on future borrowings in Euros of 8–9 percent. Our assumption regarding seignorage revenue is 1 percent per year. The estimated sustainable level for the primary surplus is roughly 2.5–3 percent of GDP.

The sensitivity of this estimate to changes in assumptions about real growth and interest rates, keeping the other assumptions unchanged, is shown in Table 1.3. The table shows that fiscal sustainability is very sensitive to changes in growth and interest rates. An additional percentage point of growth would enable the government to run a smaller primary surplus of about 0.8 percent of GDP. An additional 200 basis points on the interest rate raises the required surplus by 1.3 percent of GDP. As stated earlier, Bulgaria is currently in the fortunate position of servicing its debt at low interest rates, but if it were to suffer a sustained rise in interest rates, it would soon need to run a larger primary surplus to maintain an equivalent reduction in debt. The other implication is that, if Bulgaria is unable to sustain a high level of growth, a higher primary surplus would be necessary to achieve its debt reduction objectives.

Evaluation of Government's Medium-Term Fiscal Framework. To support their medium-term economic program, the Government has committed to a sound fiscal policy stance. This fiscal policy stance is designed to support the CBA and to reduce the debt-to-GDP ratio to below 60 percent of GDP. The key component of the Government's fiscal commitment is to reduce the

---

[9] Contingency measures include: (i) continuing the 90 percent rule for some categories of discretionary expenditure through the end of 2002; (ii) limiting the share of the interest savings that is to be used for arrears clearance by imposing additional reform measures; (iii) fully saving the accrued interest revenue and remainder of the interest saving; (iv) not spending part of the structural reform contingency resources; and (v) postponing a number of investment projects.

[10] For details see "*Fiscal Sustainability in Bulgaria*" by A. Craig Burnside, The World Bank, mimeo, May 2002.

TABLE 1.3: SIZE OF NECESSARY PRIMARY SURPLUS FOR FISCAL SUSTAINABILITY

(PERCENT OF GDP)

REAL GROWTH RATE (PERCENT)	INTEREST RATE (%)				
	5	7	9	11	13
3	1.1	2.4	3.7	4.9	6.2
4	0.4	1.6	2.9	4.1	5.4
5	−0.4	0.8	2.1	3.3	4.6

Assumptions: Inflation rate = 0.035, and the size of the monetary base, $m = 0.14$.

Note: Fiscal sustainability is defined as a declining level of public debt, falling from 72 percent of GDP in 2001 to roughly 60 percent in 2005.

fiscal deficit from roughly 1 percent of GDP in 2001 to near balance over the medium term. Given the expected course of interest payments during this period, this implies a primary surplus of 2.5–3.0 percent of GDP. The Government's strategy is consistent with the sustainability exercise above, implying the Government's fiscal program is likely to assure sustainability over the medium term, in the absence of external shocks and if the Government continues to make progress on structural reforms.

An Appropriate Fiscal Strategy.   There is limited scope for achieving the Government's fiscal priorities through additional revenue measures. In fact, the Government recognizes the need to lower the tax burden, as the level of taxes is quite high. Taxes have already been raised to a near maximum; as illustrated in the next chapter, the reduction in the government deficit since 1997 was achieved primarily by increasing revenues rather than cutting expenditures. To boost growth and ease the fiscal burden, the Government, which took office in July 2001, has introduced a series of personal income and company tax reductions and is considering alleviating the excessive burden of payroll taxation in order to boost employment and reduce tax evasion. A further easing of the overall tax burden, especially payroll taxes, is highly desirable. But, given the macroeconomic risks that Bulgaria faces and its considerable debt burden, the prudent approach would be to defer reductions in the tax burden, until expenditures are restructured and fiscal policy is placed on a more sustainable footing. The fiscal strategy also faces the challenge to adjust for the decline in privatization revenues as the privatization program is completed.

Meeting the Government's fiscal objectives will, therefore, have to rely on rationalizing expenditures and improving their effectiveness. This is consistent with the Government's overall objectives of improving the functioning of the public sector and of the economy as a whole to improve the standards of living of all Bulgarians. It is also consistent with the fact that the public sector commands a very large share of the economy's resources—above 40 percent—which likely limits Bulgaria's potential output growth. To achieve the Government's fiscal targets, at the current level of revenue performance, our simulations indicate that, in the absence of external shocks and in tandem with a strong program of structural reform, only a modest one percentage point reduction of expenditures relative to GDP needs to be achieved over the medium term. If, however, the Government moves to lower the burden of taxation on the economy, which is high, then a further reduction of expenditures will be required to meet its fiscal targets. Rationalizing expenditures, within a consistent fiscal framework, would likely be in line with the Government's announced policy of allowing the private sector to take the lead in the expansion of investment, output, and employment while the state focuses on the efficient delivery of public goods, including an efficient and effective social safety net.

Thus, expenditure priorities and processes, which are the main topic of this Report, are critical to achieving Bulgaria's stability, growth and poverty reduction objectives in the medium term. As discussed throughout this Report, the existing rigid structure of expenditures is a key issue that needs to be confronted. Bulgaria's public expenditures are dominated by social protection expenditures, which account for 33 percent of total spending. This is due to a combination of demographic trends (resulting in an aging population), economic developments (responsible for the very high rate of unemployment), and the need to pull a large share of the population out of poverty. Social protection expenditures are, indeed, staggering: they account for 13.6 percent of GDP; pensions alone are equivalent to 9.1 percent of GDP. Maintenance and investment expenditures (excluding defense and security) are low (23 percent of total spending), but need to be raised urgently. The wage bill is not high (14 percent of total spending), and interest payments absorb another 9 percent of total expenditures. Defense and security spending is also high. Clearly, there is little room left for mechanical expenditure cuts without hurting the quality of public services and the already low living standards of a large segment of the population.

The priorities for action concerning public expenditure management are discussed in Chapter 4, after reviewing the current situation (Chapter 2) and public expenditure issues by sector (Chapter 3).

Summary

This brief discussion of recent economic developments, development challenges, and fiscal priorities has four main conclusions:

- The fiscal sustainability exercise undertaken for this Report indicates that the Government's macroeconomic and fiscal program is both sound and appropriate. The targets set for fiscal policy should help ensure macroeconomic stability, including adjusting to a decline in privatization revenues, and achieve a reduction in the debt-to-GDP ratio, which will help in lowering external vulnerability and interest costs, easing future pressures on the budget.
- There are, however, risks. The largest risk would seem to be in the balance of payments, where an external shock, such as a slowdown in EU economic growth or an increase in oil prices, or a slowdown in FDI could pose threats to macroeconomic stability through either downward pressures on reserves or a need for higher external borrowing. Since Bulgaria has a CBA, a tightened fiscal stance would be required to regain macroeconomic stability.
- Given that the current course of fiscal policy is basically appropriate, Bulgaria's main fiscal challenge is to work towards an improved allocation of expenditures, while reducing the level of expenditures over the medium term in tandem with fiscal targets and revenue objectives. Overcoming existing expenditure rigidity and allocating public expenditures to support growth, EU accession, and to protect the most vulnerable members of society are the key issues for policy makers. Given Bulgaria's developmental constraints, these will require tough choices and difficult tradeoffs.
- Improving the allocation of expenditures and creating an expenditure management system with enough flexibility to adjust quickly and efficiently to macroeconomic shocks implies the need for an improved fiscal management process that is more strategic, has a better medium-term focus and is performance-oriented. Better monitoring of the benefits from public spending, feedback from civil society on priorities for expenditures and the quality of public services, and internal and external auditing of specific government programs and projects will all help to ensure better expenditure outcomes.

In addition to the fiscal and expenditure challenges which are the subject of this Report, Bulgaria's reform agenda also includes broad ranging reforms in the investment climate, including further improvements in public administration, the legal and judiciary system and an unfinished privatization agenda. Needs in these areas are also further enlarged by EU accession requirements. Clearly, the Government needs to act on multiple fronts, as it has since 1997. The Government also needs to give serious consideration to narrowing the agenda to develop a realistic, properly-prioritized "core agenda". This will permit aiming higher and getting there faster. Moreover, there is a need to place the content and pace of reforms in Bulgaria's own setting. Bulgaria has many unique features and constraints (in combination, if not individually), such as its demographic characteristics, including ethnic composition, its entrenched social protection system, the legacy of its past, its system of inter-governmental relations, its investment deficit, etc. These characteristics affect needs, priorities, tolerances, and results. Finally, a close partnership between the Government, the people and external partners, based on consensus, information, and clarity of communication needs to be forged.

CHAPTER 2

PUBLIC EXPENDITURE STRUCTURE AND TRENDS

Recent Fiscal Developments

Owing to the strict discipline imposed by the Currency Board, Bulgaria has maintained a very low fiscal deficit. Importantly, the fiscal deficit has been financed mainly by privatization revenues. Since 1997, external financing has been negative, except for in 1999, while domestic financing has been so far limited. The primary surplus has declined substantially, from more than 9 percent of GDP in 1996 to about 3 percent in 1999–2001 (see Table 2.1).

Bulgaria's fiscal stabilization was made possible by revenue expansion rather than expenditure cuts. Total revenues soared from about 33 percent of GDP in 1996 to over 41 percent in 2001. Total expenditures marked a sharp decline in 1997 only to increase to about their 1996 level (43 percent) by 2000 and reached 41 percent of GDP in 2001. While both revenues and expenditures declined in 2001, revenues remain considerably above their 1996 level.

The Economic Composition of Expenditures

Behind the initial fall in expenditure and its subsequent rebound during the review period, a major expenditure restructuring was taking place (see Figure 2.1 and Table 2.1). Since the 1996–97 crisis, interest payments have dropped sharply from 20 percent of GDP in 1996 to 3.7 percent in 2001[11] (see Table 2.2). Yet, total expenditures have fallen by only 2.4 percentage points of GDP since 1996. Thus, while there has been a sharp drop in the fiscal deficit, there has also been a significant rise in primary (i.e., non-interest) expenditures. This has included large increases in benefits and capital expenditures. Social benefits increased by 5.7 percentage points of GDP since 1996 to reach 15 percent of GDP in 2001—of this increase, about 1.3 percentage points of GDP is

---

[11] Bulgaria restructured its debt to the Paris Club in 1992 and to the London Club in 1994, easing its external debt burden by a third. Domestic debt, however, had been on the rise since 1993, as it was the main source of deficit financing.

TABLE 2.1: SUMMARY OF GENERAL GOVERNMENT OPERATIONS, 1996–2002

(PERCENT OF GDP)

	1996	1997	1998	1999	2000	2001	2002[p]
Total revenue and grants	32.9	37.5	39.8	40.7	41.4	40.0	40.5
Total expenditure and net lending	43.2	38.6	38.8	41.7	42.4	40.8	41.3
Primary balance	9.2	7.1	5.3	2.8	3.0	2.9	2.4
Overall fiscal balance	−10.3	−1.2	1.0	−0.9	−1.0	−0.9	−0.8
Financing	10.3	1.2	−1.0	0.9	1.0	0.9	0.8
External	−2.8	0.3	−0.6	1.2	−1.5	−0.3	−0.3
Domestic	13.2	−2.3	−2.0	−2.5	1.2	0.6	−0.8
Privatization revenue	0.0	3.1	1.6	2.2	1.3	0.6	2.0

Note: Consolidated general government expenditure since 1997. Includes social contributions paid by the Government on behalf of government employees.

[p] 2002 figures are preliminary projections.

Source: Ministry of Finance.

related to the introduction of health insurance in 2001. From their very low levels during the crisis in 1996–97, capital expenditures (including state reserves) grew to 4.8 percent of GDP in 1999 and steadied at about 4.2 percent of GDP in 2000 and 2001. Wages and salaries also grew from 3–4 percent of GDP in 1996/1997 to 5.4 percent of GDP in 1999, and declined to about 4.4 percent of GDP in 2001, as a result of the ongoing public sector reform (including downsizing). Other goods and services (which include operation and maintenance expenditure and scholarships) also rebounded after the 1996 crisis, gaining close to 3 percentage points of GDP in 2000 but spending has declined since. Along with the restructuring of the public enterprise sector, subsidies fell from 2.2 percent of GDP in 1997 to 1.1 percent in 2000. Subsidies in 2001 rebounded due to the inclusion of the subsidy provided to the health sector of about 1.4 percent of GDP.

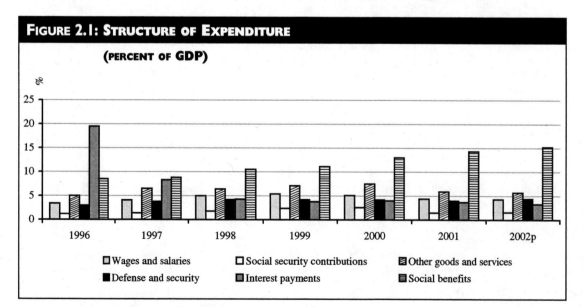

FIGURE 2.1: STRUCTURE OF EXPENDITURE

(PERCENT OF GDP)

Legend:
- Wages and salaries
- Social security contributions
- Other goods and services
- Defense and security
- Interest payments
- Social benefits

[p] Data for 2002 are preliminary projections.
Source: Ministry of Finance.

TABLE 2.2: ECONOMIC COMPOSITION OF GENERAL GOVERNMENT OPERATIONS, 1996–2002[1]

(PERCENT OF GDP)

	1996	1997	1998	1999	2000	2001	2002[P]
Total revenues and grants	**32.9**	**37.5**	**39.8**	**40.7**	**41.4**	**40.0**	**40.5**
o.w. Grants	0.0	0.6	0.6	0.9	0.8	1.2	1.6
Current revenue	30.5	36.3	38.8	39.8	40.6	38.7	38.9
Tax revenue	26.8	28.9	31.6	31.4	32.5	31.0	31.6
Total expenditure and net lending	**43.2**	**38.6**	**38.8**	**41.7**	**42.4**	**40.8**	**41.3**
Current expenditure	41.8	35.2	34.3	35.7	37.6	36.4	37.2
Goods and services	9.6	12.0	13.2	14.9	15.2	11.8	11.5
Wages and salaries	3.4	4.1	5.0	5.4	5.1	4.4	4.3
Social security contributions	1.2	1.4	1.8	2.4	2.6	1.5	1.6
Other goods and services	5.0	6.5	6.4	7.1	7.5	5.9	5.7
Defense and security	3.0	3.8	4.2	4.2	4.2	4.0	4.4
Interest payments	19.5	8.3	4.3	3.8	4.0	3.7	3.3
Subsidies[2]	0.8	2.2	2.0	1.6	1.1	2.4	2.4
Social benefits	8.5	8.8	10.5	11.1	13.0	14.3	15.2
Other[3]	0.3	0.2	0.2	0.1	0.1	0.2	0.1
Capital expenditure	0.7	2.7	4.1	4.8	4.2	4.2	3.4
Net lending	0.0	0.8	0.3	1.1	0.4	0.3	
Other n.e.i.[4]	0.7						
Contingency	0.0	0.0	0.0	0.1	0.1	0.0	0.7
Overall deficit/surplus	−10.3	−1.2	1.0	−0.9	−1.0	−0.9	−0.8
Primary deficit/surplus	9.2	7.1	5.3	2.8	3.0	2.9	2.4
Current deficit/surplus	−11.4	1.1	4.5	4.1	2.9	2.3	1.7

[1] Consolidated general government expenditure since 1997. Includes social contributions paid by the Government on behalf of government employees. Intergovernmental transfers for 1999 and 2001 which are not consolidated are shown as non-tax revenues. Data for 2002 are preliminary projections.

[2] Includes subsidies provided for health care since 2001, accounting for about 1.4 percent of GDP.

[3] Includes membership remittance and payments to banks under the Deposit Guarantee Law.

[4] Includes extrabudgetary accounts in 1996.

Source: Ministry of Finance.

Bulgaria's fiscal position appears strong compared to other countries in the region and the so-called Cohesion countries.[12] Government revenues are far above the average for the sample of CEEs considered, second only to Hungary. Moreover, the recovery in expenditures has brought overall expenditures in line with the average of the CEEs and slightly above the average of the EU Cohesion countries (see Table 2.3). In terms of economic composition, the comparison does not reveal major imbalances in the structure of public expenditures in Bulgaria. While Bulgaria's economic composition of expenditures compares favorably with other CEE economies and the Cohesion countries, three issues deserve further discussion (and these are discussed in the remainder of this section):

- **Wages and salaries.** Bulgaria's wages and salaries exclude defense and security wages and salaries which are included in other goods and services. Taking these into account, Bulgaria's

---

[12] Greece, Ireland, Portugal, and Spain.

TABLE 2.3: CONSOLIDATED GENERAL GOVERNMENT REVENUES AND EXPENDITURES, 2000

(PERCENT OF GDP)

	AVERAGE FOR THE CEE COUNTRIES	BULGARIA	CZECH REPUBLIC	HUNGARY	POLAND	ROMANIA	SLOVAK REP.	AVERAGE FOR COHESION COUNTRIES
Total revenue and grants	38.3	41.3	39.8	43.9	39.4	31.5	36.8	41.1
Total expenditure	42.0	42.0	44.3	46.2	42.7	35.1	41.8	40.7
Current expenditure	37.0	37.4	38.4	39.1	39.6	32.0	36.0	35.5
Goods and services	12.4	17.2	8.7	14.5	16.2	12.6	10.1	16.6
Wages and salaries	6.0	5.1	3.6	7.4	8.2	5.5	5.2	11.2
Other G&S	6.4	12.2	5.1	7.1	7.9	7.1	4.9	5.4
Subsidies and other current transfers	21.1	15.9	28.6	18.6	20.7	14.6	23.0	13.3
Interest	3.5	4.3	1.1	6.1	2.7	4.9	2.9	4.0
Capital expenditure	5.0	4.6	5.9	7.1	3.1	3.1	5.8	5.2

Note: The average for the CEE countries excludes Bulgaria. Compensation of employees for the cohesion countries, i.e., wages and salaries including social security contributions. Military and police staff wages are included in other goods and services for Bulgaria.

Source: Government Finance Statistics, IMF, and General Government Data, European Commission.

wages and salaries exceed the CEE average, and there are issues regarding the composition of civil service employees that is not shown clearly in the aggregate numbers;

- **Capital expenditures.** While spending on public investment has recovered and is now on par with the CEE average, this masks the poor condition of public infrastructure and the considerable investment backlog needed to support growth and EU accession; and,
- **Subsidies.** While subsidies have declined, there are still considerable subsidies in the infrastructure sector. The elimination of these subsidies would permit higher spending in other areas.

Wages and Salaries. With a wage bill of about 5 percent of GDP in 2000, Bulgaria's aggregate spending on wages and salaries is not high by regional or international standards. It is, rather, the structure of employment that is a matter of concern (see Figure 2.2). CEE countries (with the exception of the Czech Republic) tend to have a high share of health and education employment. In contrast with Cohesion countries, they also tend to have a low level of local government employment—a clear legacy of the socialist past.

Analysis of civilian government employment over the last five years also indicates that the size of Bulgaria's civil service is small compared to the Cohesion countries and the EU as a whole (see Table 2.4). Government employment in Bulgaria is 6.4 percent of the population, lower than in Hungary and the Czech Republic, and only slightly higher than the CEE average (5.9 percent). However, employment in education and health in Bulgaria is among the highest in the region and twice as high as in the Cohesion countries. Issues related to rationalizing employment particularly in education and also in health are discussed in detail in Chapters 6 and 7. Similarly, the size of defense and security employment are large in comparison to other CEEs and the Cohesion countries. For example, military employment as percent of population in Bulgaria was almost twice higher than the average for the EU in 1996–2000. (However, if the army is reduced to 45,000,

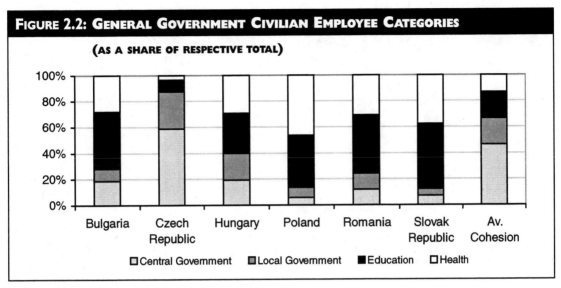

FIGURE 2.2: GENERAL GOVERNMENT CIVILIAN EMPLOYEE CATEGORIES

(AS A SHARE OF RESPECTIVE TOTAL)

Source: Ministry of Finance World Bank, OECD and EU.

the percentage will be about 0.6 compared with 1.5 for the EU.) The Government is also planning to address employment issues in these sectors.

Employment trends in health, education, central government and local government during the review period indicate that progress on rationalizing the civil service has been uneven (see Figure 2.3). Total government employment in 2000 was 19 percent below the 1997 level. Two-thirds of the employment reduction was related to the recent restructuring of the health sector, discussed in Chapter 7, where public sector employment shrank by 40 percent. In the education sector, the decline in employment was more modest—11 percent between 1997 and 2000. However, there is considerable scope for further rationalization of the education sector, given the large decline in the school-age population. To optimize the use of public resources, the Government is preparing a redeployment plan for the teaching staff, which will take effect in 2002/2003.

TABLE 2.4: GOVERNMENT EMPLOYMENT AS PERCENT OF POPULATION, AVERAGE 1996–2000

	TOTAL	CENTRAL GOVERNMENT	LOCAL GOVERNMENT	EDUCATION	HEALTH
Bulgaria	6.4	1.2	0.6	2.8	1.8
Czech Republic	8.1	4.8	2.3	0.7	0.3
Poland	5.2	0.3	0.4	2.1	2.4
Romania	4.2	0.5	0.5	1.9	1.3
Hungary	7.6	1.5	1.6	2.3	2.2
Slovenia	3.8	1.4	0.2	1.3	0.9
Slovak Republic	6.4	0.5	0.3	3.2	2.4
Average CEE, excl. Bulgaria	5.9	1.5	0.9	1.9	1.6
Average Cohesion countries	6.9	3.2	1.4	1.4	0.9
Average EU	8.9	2.6	3.2	1.8	1.4

Source: World Bank Administrative and Civil Service Reform thematic group, OECD public sector employment data and EU accession country governments.

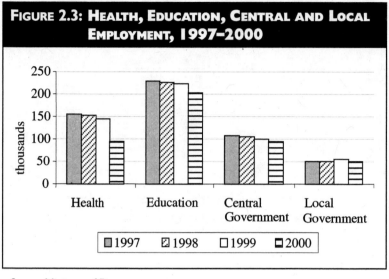

FIGURE 2.3: HEALTH, EDUCATION, CENTRAL AND LOCAL EMPLOYMENT, 1997–2000

Legend: ■ 1997   ▨ 1998   □ 1999   ▤ 2000

Source: Ministry of Finance.

Capital Expenditures. Government capital expenditures in Bulgaria, which collapsed to below 1 percent of GDP in 1996, have recovered to over 4 percent of GDP since 1998. In 2000, capital expenditures were at the average level for the CEE countries. Environmental and infrastructure investment along with general public services have absorbed the lion's share of capital expenditure in Bulgaria over the past five years (see Figure 2.4). The composition and efficiency of public investment are, however, as important as its level, and Bulgaria policy makers need to pay attention to these three key aspects of public investment.[13]

In line with the investment requirements of EU accession, spending on public investment may need to rise to the levels prevailing in other, more advanced EU accession countries, such as Hungary or the Czech Republic. As discussed in Box 2.1, the perceptions of the quality of Bulgaria's

---

[13] For further discussion of public investment issues, see *Managing Fiscal Risk in Bulgaria,* The World Bank, Policy Research Working Paper No. 2282, and *Bulgaria: The Dual Challenge of Transition and Accession,* op. cit.

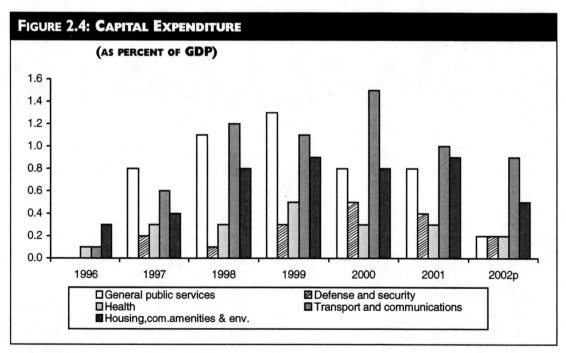

FIGURE 2.4: CAPITAL EXPENDITURE

(AS PERCENT OF GDP)

Legend: □ General public services   ▨ Defense and security   □ Health   ■ Transport and communications   ■ Housing, com. amenities & env.

Source: MOF.

BOX 2.1: THE QUALITY OF PUBLIC INFRASTRUCTURE: WHAT DO FIRMS SAY?

In a survey of enterprise owners and senior managers in Bulgaria and other transition economies, respondents were asked about their perception of the quality of infrastructure in their country. The responses for Bulgaria are startling and informative (see the Figure below). The Figure below compares Bulgaria's performance to four CEE transition countries, which will be in the first wave of EU accession. The results strongly support the conclusions of this Report that **inadequate public infrastructure is a key impediment to the investment climate and investment in infrastructure is a key priority for public expenditure.**

The main conclusions relevant for this Report are:

- 78 percent of Bulgarian entrepreneurs surveyed perceived **the road network** in Bulgaria to bad or very bad, and less than 5 percent of the respondents felt that the road network was good or very good; this can be compared to the next worst country, Poland, where only 49 percent of the respondents felt the roads were bad or very bad.
- 15 percent of the respondents felt that the **telephone service** was bad or very bad; this is almost three times worse than the next worst country in the sample—Slovak Republic.
- 19 percent of respondents feel the **electricity service** is bad or very bad; again this is more than double the next worst country.
- 18 percent of the respondents also feel **the water services** are bad or very bad; this is more than three times the next worst country—Hungary.

The implications of these entrepreneurs perceptions of the adequacy of public infrastructure for business are obvious for foreign investment inflows, as well as domestic investment.

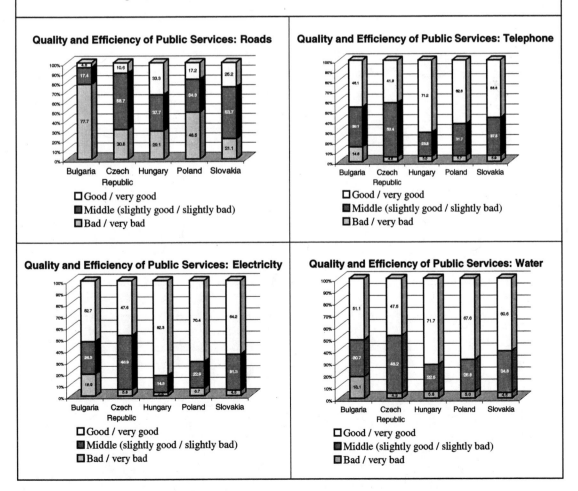

infrastructure by private entrepreneurs is negative and this is likely to be one important factor in the low overall level of investment in the economy. Moreover, comparative data on the availability of infrastructure services, such as waiting time for a telephone line (see Figure 2.5), indicate a need to improve availability and to enhance the involvement of the private sector. Given the high demand for public investment stemming from the backlog of infrastructure maintenance and past environmental damage, Bulgaria needs to ensure enough public investment in infrastructure and the environment, as well as allowing private sector involvement in areas where it is appropriate and the regulatory environment is adequate.

Subsidies.[14]   Reflecting slow restructuring and serious inefficiencies, the infrastructure sectors absorb the majority of the fiscal subsidies from the budget. In 2001, the energy sector absorbed 19 percent of total subsidies (17 percent for the District Heating companies and 2 percent for the mining sector), and the transport sector (mainly railways) another 29 percent (Figure 2.6). While the share of subsidies provided to the energy sector has contracted severely since 1997, there is considerable cross-subsidization in the energy sector. Subsidies to the transport sector have continued to grow. Further analysis of the railway and energy sectors in Chapter 9 and 10 respectively, will shed light on the evolution of subsidies in recent years. The agriculture sector, which is not discussed in this report, has been a recipient of larger amounts of subsidies. While in 1998 there were practically no subsidies for agriculture, by 2001 these reached 22 percent of total subsidies—more than double the amount provided in 2000—and the budgeted subsidies for 2002 may be even higher.

---

[14] Excluding subsidies provided for health care.

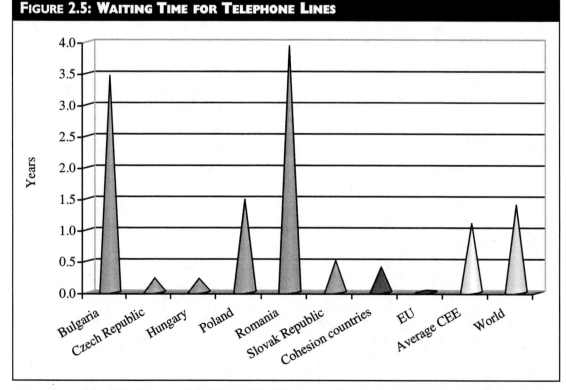

FIGURE 2.5: WAITING TIME FOR TELEPHONE LINES

Source: International Telecommunication Union's World Telecommunication Development Report 2000, and World Development Indicators, 2001, World Bank.

FIGURE 2.6: STRUCTURE OF SUBSIDIES, 2001

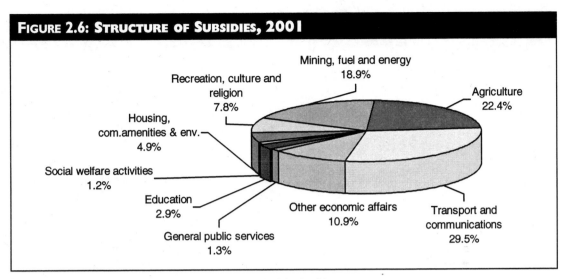

Source: Ministry of Finance. Excludes subsidies provided for health care.

The Functional Composition of Expenditures

Overview

The main development that marked the post crisis period was the drop of interest expenditure from an unsustainable 20 percent of GDP in 1996 to about 4 percent in 2001. The resulting savings were substantial and they permitted a rapid expansion of other expenditures which were reallocated across the various sectors. Social security and welfare expenditures rose by 5 percentage points of GDP, split about equally between pensions and social assistance and compensation (see Table 2.5). Gains were also made by the executive and legislative branch of government (1.6 percentage points), the police and security (1.1 percentage points), and transport and communications (1.3 percentage points). Both health and education outlays rose immediately after the crisis in 1997 and have remained relatively stable since then.

As noted earlier, Bulgaria's overall expenditure level is broadly in line with other CEE countries. The functional composition of expenditure in Bulgaria is also broadly in line with the structure of government spending in other CEE countries (see Table 2.6). From the comparative perspective, the main issue would appear to be defense and security expenditures, which average a total of 5.5 percent of GDP in Bulgaria, compared to only 3.5 percent of GDP in the comparator countries. The share of defense spending is almost twice higher than in all other CEE countries. Issues in defense and security are discussed briefly below, but they deserve closer scrutiny by the Government in the period ahead. Like the other CEE countries, social sector expenditures dominate all spending, accounting for more than half of total expenditures. While on a comparative basis, education and health appear slightly under-funded, inefficiencies and poorly designed programs in the other CEE countries may bias their average upwards. Nevertheless, there are many important issues in these sectors in Bulgaria that are examined in detail in Chapters 6 and 7. Issues regarding social protection expenditures—the largest level of outlays in the budget—are discussed in Chapter 8.

Defense and Security. Expenditures on defense and security are largely shaped by Bulgaria's international and regional integration agenda. Nevertheless, Bulgaria's spending on defense and security is the highest of all EU accession countries, even those which are restructuring their armed services and security apparatus to make them compatible with NATO and EU requirements. Defense spending at 3 percent of GDP is about twice the level of other EU accession

TABLE 2.5: CONSOLIDATED GOVERNMENT EXPENDITURE BY FUNCTION, 1996–2002[1]

(PERCENT OF GDP)

	1996	1997	1998	1999	2000	2001	2002[p]
Total	43.2	38.6	38.8	41.7	42.4	40.8	41.3
General public services	1.3	2.4	3.0	4.0	3.5	3.2	2.6
Executive and legislative organs	1.0	1.6	2.0	2.2	2.3	2.6	2.1
General services[2]	0.0	0.4	0.6	0.4	0.8	0.3	0.1
Science	0.2	0.4	0.4	0.4	0.4	0.3	0.4
Education	3.2	3.9	3.9	4.2	4.2	4.0	4.1
Health	3.1	3.6	3.6	3.9	3.7	4.0	4.3
Defense and security	3.4	4.3	4.7	5.1	5.3	4.9	5.1
Defense	2.2	2.6	2.6	2.8	2.8	2.5	2.5
Police and security	0.9	1.4	1.7	1.8	1.9	1.9	2.0
Judiciary[3]	0.3	0.2	0.3	0.3	0.4	0.4	0.4
Prison adm. and maint.	0.0	0.1	0.1	0.2	0.1	0.2	0.2
Social security and welfare	9.0	9.5	11.3	12.3	14.1	13.6	14.3
Pensions	6.9	6.2	8.0	8.2	9.5	9.1	9.4
Social assist. and compensations	1.6	2.6	2.5	2.9	4.0	3.7	4.3
Social welfare activities	0.4	0.7	0.7	1.2	0.7	0.8	0.6
Housing, comm. amenities and env.	1.2	0.9	1.6	1.7	1.7	1.8	1.1
Recreation, culture and religion	0.5	0.6	0.8	1.0	0.8	0.7	0.8
Economic affairs[4]	1.5	5.1	5.6	5.7	4.8	4.8	5.1
Mining, fuel and energy	0.2	1.3	1.3	0.7	0.4	0.3	0.2
Agriculture	0.2	1.0	0.9	0.7	0.8	0.9	0.9
Transport and communications	0.7	1.8	2.7	2.4	2.8	2.0	1.7
Manufacturing and construction	0.1	0.0	0.1	0.0	0.0	0.0	0.0
Other economic affairs	0.2	1.0	0.6	1.8	0.8	1.6	2.3
Other expenditure	20.2	8.3	4.3	3.9	4.2	3.7	4.0
Interest - total	19.5	8.3	4.3	3.8	4.0	3.7	3.3
Contingency	0.0	0.0	0.0	0.1	0.1	0.0	0.7
Other n.e.i.	0.7			0.0		−0.1	

[1] Consolidated general government expenditure since 1997. Includes social security contributions.

[2] Includes the activities of the National Statistical Institute, registries, etc.

[3] Judiciary and prison administration are aggregated in 1996.

[4] Includes activities of ministries and agencies other than administrative and executive activities (land commissions, testing and measuring, waste storage, etc.).

[p] Data for 2002 are preliminary projections.

Source: Ministry of Finance.

countries; security outlays at 2.5 percent of GDP are nearly one-third higher than those countries; and, employment in these sectors is also relatively high. Regarding the latter, for instance, personnel costs in 2001 represented close to 60 percent of the overall defense budget. Personnel costs do include one-time severance payments to the military staff, but these payments are small, only about 0.13 percent of GDP in 2002. While a detailed examination of issues in defense and security are outside the scope of this Report, the Government should examine closely expenditure levels

TABLE 2.6: CONSOLIDATED GOVERNMENT EXPENDITURE BY FUNCTION, 2000

(PERCENT OF GDP)

	AVERAGE FOR THE SELECTED CEE COUNTRIES	BULGARIA	CZECH REPUBLIC	HUNGARY	POLAND	ROMANIA	SLOVAK REP.
Total expenditure	42.3	42.0	44.3	47.3	42.7	35.5	41.8
General public services	2.9	3.5	2.5	4.6	2.5	1.5	3.4
Defense	1.6	3.0	1.9	1.1	1.4	1.7	1.9
Public order and safety	1.9	2.5	2.1	1.6	1.8	2.0	1.6
Education	4.4	4.1	4.2	4.8	5.9	3.1	3.9
Health	5.2	3.7	6.7	4.2	4.2	3.7	7.1
Social security and welfare	13.7	14.8	14.8	14.5	18.7	10.0	10.7
Housing & comm. amenities	2.3	1.7	3.2	1.6	3.0	1.9	1.9
Recreation, culture	0.9	0.8	1.1	1.2	0.8	0.6	0.9
Economic affairs	5.4	4.7	6.0	5.1	2.9	5.0	8.1
Fuel and energy	0.1	0.4	0.2	0.0	0.2	n.a	0.0
Agriculture	1.3	0.7	1.0	1.4	0.8	1.2	2.0
Non-fuel mining and mineral	0.4	0.0	0.1	0.2	0.3	0.8	0.6
Transport and communications	2.3	3.0	3.2	2.3	1.4	2.7	1.9
Other economic	1.4	0.6	1.5	1.5	0.2	0.3	3.5
Interest payments	3.5	4.3	1.1	6.1	2.7	4.9	2.9

Note: The average for the CEE countries excludes Bulgaria. Total expenditure and net lending for Hungary and Romania.

Source: Government Finance Statistics, IMF.

in defense and security with a view to eliminating waste, reducing inefficiencies and modernizing security forces.

In the defense sector, delayed reforms in the past kept Bulgaria out of NATO's first round enlargement. The Government feels that Bulgaria's economic and political stability, its central location in the Balkans, and its role as a de facto ally of NATO during the Kosovo crisis have all improved Bulgaria's membership prospects, and it has recognized the need to revamp its outdated Soviet-style army into a small efficient force compatible with NATO standards, to realize its membership objectives. NATO membership will entail a sharp restructuring of Bulgaria's defense expenditures to increase outlays for upgrading military equipment and to reduce wage expenditures through a contraction of personnel. These plans are outlined in the Ministry of Defense's (MOD) restructuring plan for the Bulgarian army—"Plan 2004"—which involves complete or partial closures of garrisons, the relocation of units, and the retrenchment of personnel. The Government currently plans to reduce military personnel to 45,000 by 2004, which would lower wage costs to about one-third of total military spending. A large number of servicemen to be released are between 40 and 55 years old, partly well educated, highly qualified but with little labor market experience. Hence, the plan includes a reinsertion and civil adaptation program. The resource envelop is estimated at US$10.3 million, of which US$1.75 million will be provided by the MOD, with the rest to be mobilized from bilateral donors and others.

Bulgaria has also initiated the overhaul of its police system to meet key security-related EU accession requirements. With support from the EU, Bulgaria is implementing a Border Police program involving the institutional strengthening of the Bulgarian Border Police, the creation of a modern border police training center, aimed at introducing effective border control systems, the strengthening of criminal information systems, and improvement of management techniques. The program spans the control of external and maritime borders as well as the development of a national anti-drug strategy. Most of the funding needs will be covered by the EU. According to the Ministry of Interior budget projections, overall expenditures for security are expected to grow by 0.8 percent of GDP between 2001 and 2004, which includes a reduction of wage costs to below 50 percent. This increase in expenditures needs to be examined carefully in light of Bulgaria's already large spending in this area.

Directions for Reform

Given the need to reduce the tax burden, the government needs to improve substantially intersectoral allocations. This could be done in the context of the medium-term expenditure framework (MTEF) which is now being prepared in close consultations with the line ministries. The options for moving away from activities that could well be provided by the private sector are more or less limited although a thorough analyses may show areas where certain gains may be achieved. The existing spending policies need to be revisited to identify sectors which could produce the same outcomes with less resources, and sectors that need more resources to achieve better coverage, quality of service, or improve equity and standards of living. Comparing functional expenditure levels with other countries could also give an idea of the resources needed for the provision of certain services.

How to make the difficult trade-offs between the various sectors? There is no one single prescription for the optimal size of each sector. The review of the sectoral allocation trends so far shows that further adjustments are needed to improve the efficiency of use of public resources and reduce the burden on the budget. It is very important to reassess which activities could be shifted to the private sector. For example, private sector could enlarge its participation in the higher sector education (see Chapter 6) and free up resources for improvements in quality and coverage of primary and secondary public education. The huge investment needs in the energy sector could be partly borne by the private sector. Efficiency gains may also come from downsizing activities which have not been a focus of this Report but do not necessarily need public intervention.

Another priority is to review activities that are increasingly demanding public resources due to worsening demographics or the need to cope with the consequences of structural reforms. However, given the resource constraint, there is not much room for increased financing of these sectors. So the main challenge would be to improve the intrasectoral allocations by optimization of existing structures in the health and education sectors, better targeting of social assistance programs, and termination of non-economic services in the railways to reduce the needed state support. A third priority is to downsize resources that absorb a larger portion of public resources compared to other EU accession countries. Finally, defense and security spending in Bulgaria appears to be high.

Summary

This chapter has undertaken a detailed examination of expenditure trends and composition. From this analysis, the primary issues raised are the following:

- In the post-crisis period, Bulgaria has effected a major expenditure restructuring. Interest expenditures have declined dramatically and non-interest expenditures have risen substantially. Overall expenditure levels are now roughly on par with other CEE countries and, ceteris paribus, only a modest reduction in expenditures relative to GDP over the medium term is needed to be consistent with the Government's medium-term fiscal program, including importantly, lowering the debt burden.

- The implication of these trends for expenditure is that Bulgaria faces an important allocative challenge—aligning spending with Bulgaria's emerging development priorities: achieving rapid income growth to close the income gap with other EU accession countries; reducing poverty and protecting those people whom the growth of the past few years has left behind, especially the unemployed; and, joining the European Union.

- The analysis revealed several issues that merit further attention, some of which are discussed in detail in this Report and others, which require additional analysis. The key issues include:

  ➤ the structure of public employment, especially in the health and education sectors, where changing demographics and population shifts have led to overstaffing and other inefficiencies;

  ➤ remaining subsidies in the energy sector and transport, especially the railways;

  ➤ a large level and rapid expansion of spending on social protection, and the fiscal sustainability of existing programs and the targeting of social benefits;

  ➤ the adequacy of infrastructure for promoting economic growth; and

  ➤ the overall level of resources devoted to defense and security, which, by regional standards appear to be high.

The remainder of this Report looks in depth at some of these issues. In close consultation with the Government on its immediate priorities, this Report examines sectoral issues in education, health, social protection, the railways and the energy sector (Chapter 3) and institutional expenditure management challenges (Chapter 4). A detailed analysis of each of the sectors is contained in Part Two (Chapters 6-10). Chapter 5 concludes by suggesting areas for future analysis.

EXPENDITURE REFORM PRIORITIES IN KEY SECTORS

Introduction

The first two chapters of this Report confirmed the appropriateness of the Government's macro-fiscal program and documented the need for a reallocation of expenditures to support the mutually re-enforcing goals of improving the living standards of all Bulgarians, especially the poor, and joining the European Union. These chapters also showed the necessity of completing ongoing reforms in certain sectors (education, health, and pensions) to consolidate efficiency gains and to achieve expected fiscal savings, as well as analyzing other sectors for potential improvements and savings. Realizing the potential for efficiency gains from a reallocation of expenditures will depend on a two-pronged approach:

(a) Significant reforms of major spending programs to reduce or contain their spending while maintaining or improving program impact. This is the topic of this Chapter.

(b) Continued improvements in the institutions, capacities and processes for managing public spending. Chapter 4 will focus on the priorities in this area.

This Chapter discusses issues and priorities in a number of important sectors, mostly where the Government has ongoing reform programs. It stops short of suggesting the make-up of an optimal public expenditure program with precise expenditure levels or shares. The objective is, rather, to point out the desirable policy directions and to facilitate decision-making. While there are some important measures identified in this Chapter (and the detailed discussions in Part Two of this Report) that can be taken in the short term, the most important reforms to rationalize expenditures in a sustainable way will require a thorough, comprehensive review of the overall expenditure program, not as a one-shot exercise, but as a continuous process of identifying, refining and implementing reforms of the main expenditure programs. This will involve choices over time of what the public sector should do, how much it should do, and how it can do it most effectively. Most of these choices are politically sensitive, so an important part of the effort needs to be aimed at developing a political consensus for the need for and the broad outlines of these reforms.

This chapter presents the major public expenditure issues and recommendations in five key sectors: Education (Section B), Health (Section C), Social Protection (Section D), Railway Transport (Section E), and Energy (Section F). Each section is in two parts, the first summarizing the current situation and issues in each area, and the second identifies key priorities and recommendations for reform. Each of these sectors are examined in a separate Chapter in Part Two of this Report. These individual sector Chapters provide the detailed analysis behind the identification of issues and specific recommendations.

It should be emphasized that the sectors covered in this Chapter and the background papers in Part Two of this Report were selected in close coordination with the Government. Some important expenditure areas not here (for example Environment, Roads, Defense and Security) should also be subjected to a similar rigorous review. The most important areas for future work are outlined in Chapter 5, along with a number of cross-cutting issues and overall priorities.

Education[15]

Current Situation

Bulgaria's education system consists of optional pre-school education, an eight-year primary cycle, a secondary cycle, which was recently extended from three years to four years, and various higher education programs. Attendance at school is compulsory from ages 7 to 16, coinciding with the end of the first year of secondary schooling. Most education is public; private primary and secondary education is quite limited accounting for less than 1 percent of enrollments. Most education is also free; parents of children in public pre-school pay an annual fee of about 300 leva, which covers less than a third of the cost. There are no fees for attendance in public primary and secondary schools. Cost recovery in higher education was introduced in 1991, though on a highly discriminatory basis; students with entry scores above a certain threshold attend free of charge, while others are required to pay a relatively high tuition.

Education expenditures as a percentage of GDP have risen slightly over the past five years to a level (about 4 percent of GDP) that is more or less equivalent to the average for CEEs. Despite the level of expenditures, there is strong evidence of a serious problem of misallocated resources in the education sector.

Since the start of the transition, while school enrollments have declined significantly due mostly to demographics, *enrollment ratios have improved*, as enrollments have declined less than the number of school age children. Enrollments have declined significantly at all levels except higher education (see Table 3.1). This is largely a result of Bulgaria's negative population growth rate in the last two decades—the only country in Europe and Central Asia with such a trend—which has been aggravated by net out-migration. This trend is expected to continue, with important implications for the education sector. Despite the decline in absolute enrollment, net enrollment "ratios" have increased for every age group, because of the still sharper contraction of population

---

[15] For a more detailed discussion, see Chapter 6 of Part Two.

TABLE 3.1: ENROLLMENTS BY LEVEL, 1990/91 AND 2001/2

	PRE-SCHOOL	PRIMARY	SECONDARY	HIGHER
1990/91	303,779	975,095	391,832	188,479
2001/02	199,206	708,092	334,813	228,394
percent change	−34.4	−27.4	−14.6	21.2

Source: National Statistical Institute. See Chapter 6, Table 6.1.

in each age cohort and the country as a whole (see Table 3.2).

Declining enrollments have led to very low student/teacher ratios, especially in primary and secondary schools (see Table 3.3) and there is an excess number of schools and teachers particularly in rural areas. Moreover, based on the numbers already born, the school-age population is expected to decline at least through the middle of the current decade.[16] This will likely lead to further drops in student/teacher ratios unless school and teacher rationalization is further pursued.

Improving enrollment ratios mask, however, an apparent growing problem with *school attendance*. Data derived from household surveys show school attendance lower than enrollment ratios and indicate several issues:[17] (i) secondary school attendance rates are much below official enrollments; (ii) rural school attendance rates are much lower than urban rates and attendance for rural students dropped alarmingly in the last four years; (iii) school attendance rates for the poor are much lower than the non-poor and again, there is a significant drop at the secondary school level for the poor; and (iv) Roma attendance rates are lower than other ethnic groups at all levels of education, but attendance has improved slightly since the mid-1990s.

Despite the increase in enrollment ratios during the past five years, there is evidence of *an emerging equity problem*. This conclusion is strengthened by the data on attendance. There are wide variations in trends and enrollment and attendance data point to problems across regions, municipalities and ethnic groups, and according, in particular, to poverty status (see Table 3.4). At the secondary level, for example, the nationwide net enrollment ratio for the poor, 34 percent, is less than half the ratio for the non-poor (84 percent). Moreover, data on attendance show differences of between 94 percent (non-poor) and 70 percent (poor) at the primary level and more strikingly, 52 percent (non-poor) and 13 percent (poor) at the secondary level. These trends are largely attributable to the low school attendance in rural areas and

TABLE 3.2: NET ENROLLMENT RATIOS BY LEVEL, 1994/95 AND 2001/02

(IN PERCENT)

	1994/95	2001/02
Pre-school education	59.7	70.6
Primary education (grades 1–4)	92.8	96.4
Junior high education (grades 5–8)	79.0	84.2
Secondary education (grades 9–12)	61.4	68.3
Higher education	22.1	n.a.

Note: Figures for 2001/02 are calculated on the basis of the preliminary 2001 census data and take into account the out-migration flows.

Source: National Statistical Institute. See Chapter 6, Table 6.2.

TABLE 3.3: AVERAGE STUDENT/TEACHER RATIOS BY LEVEL OF EDUCATION

	STUDENT/TEACHER RATIO		
	PRIMARY	SECONDARY	HIGHER
Bulgaria	13.5	10.7	10.6
Canada	21.0	22.1	14.6
New Zealand	24.7	21.0	15.5
United Kingdom	22.0	16.7	17.7
United States	16.5	15.9	14.6
Spain	16.0	12.1	17.2
Germany	21.6	15.5	12.5
OECD Average	17.1	15.2	14.6

Source: OECD, *Education at a Glance, 2001*. Data for Bulgaria from the Bulgarian National Statistical Institute. Primary education in Bulgaria covers grades 1–8.

---

[16] The primary school age group in 2005 is projected to be at least 27 percent smaller than in 1998, with similar declines in prospect for the other age groups.

[17] See Chapter 6, Table 6.3.

TABLE 3.4: NET ENROLLMENT RATIOS BY EDUCATION LEVEL AND POVERTY STATUS, 1997 AND 2001

(IN PERCENT)	1997	2001
Primary		
Poor	84.1	74.2
Non-Poor	97.5	97.6
Secondary		
Poor	59.6	34.0
Non-Poor	77.1	83.9

Source: Bulgarian Integrated Household Survey (BIHS), 1997 and 2001.

importantly, among Roma children.[18] The few Roma children that do attend primary school are often stigmatized by being assigned to schools for the handicapped, because of language difficulties or other environmental handicaps rather than innate limitations.

While there are only limited data, the information that is available indicates that there is also a *deterioration in the quality* of education in Bulgaria. The most inclusive source of internationally comparable data for the CEEs, which includes Bulgaria, is the TIMSS international science and math assessment.[19] Bulgaria participated in the 1995 and 1999 surveys. According to the results, Bulgarian student's mean math and science scores declined between the two surveys and the mean scores in both subjects fell below the international average in 1999 (see Table 3.5). Currently, the Ministry of Education and Sciences (MES) uses measures of input-based measures of quality, such as class size and teaching hours; there is a need to move towards output based measures, which monitor directly what students are learning and use these results to target corrective actions.

The financing of education is being increasingly decentralized, but the management of the education system remains highly centralized. The Ministry of Education and Sciences is responsible for educational content, quality control, and staffing policies, including the appointment and firing of school principals. The Ministry must also approve all requests by municipalities for school

---

[18] The problems are related to the Roma's language, low income and social traditions.

[19] The survey was carried out for a nationally representative sample of eighth-grade students in 24 countries in 1995 and 39 countries in 1999.

TABLE 3.5: TIMSS 8TH GRADE STUDENT ASSESSMENT RESULTS FOR SCIENCE AND MATH, 1995 AND 1999

	MATHEMATICS		SCIENCE	
	1995 MEAN SCORE	1999 MEAN SCORE	1995 MEAN SCORE	1999 MEAN SCORE
Czech Republic	546	520	555	539
Slovak Republic	534	534	532	535
Slovenia	531	530	541	533
Hungary	527	532	537	552
Bulgaria	527	511	545	518
International Average	**519**	**521**	**518**	**521**
Latvia	488	505	476	503
Romania	474	472	471	472
Lithuania	472	482	464	488

Source: TIMSS 1999: International Mathematics Report, International Association for the Evaluation of International Achievement, December, 2000, and TIMSS 1999: International Science Report, International Association for the Evaluation of International Achievement, December, 2000.

closure or school creation, including the licensing of schools. Costs are shared by the state and the 263 municipalities. Municipalities' contributions are made up of: (a) revenues collected at the local level, and (b) subsidies from the state. The subsidies are calculated according to a complex formula which is approved every year. In addition to its complexity and changeability, the formula suffers from being based almost exclusively on personnel costs, to the exclusion of the costs of books and other teaching inputs. It does not compensate sufficiently for differences in municipalities' ability to raise revenues. It legitimizes an inefficient system of too many schools with too many teachers and other staff. Efficiency suffers also because, while municipalities are, in principle, free to spend the subsidy as they please, in reality, they have little flexibility in the matter since virtually the entire amount goes to pay salaries and benefits, over which they have little control. The system produces fluctuations in financing and wide variations in education quality, depending on the financial resources of the municipalities. It also can have very negative implications for poorer communities, as they cannot supplement state financing and hence, education quality suffers.

Reforms are also needed in *higher education*. Currently, there is also strong evidence of excess capacity at the university level. Bulgaria has 37 public universities, which is far in excess of EU countries of comparable population size. Moreover, as shown in Table 3.3, student-teacher ratios at the university level are also low. Finally, there is anecdotal evidence that students in some faculties, such as engineering, which were popular during the socialist period, have declined to minimal levels, as student demand has shifted to other disciplines deemed more useful in market economies. Also, cost recovery levels are well below the 30 percent specified in the new Law.

Finally, due to the limited funds available to municipalities to finance current expenditures, which now constitute roughly 93 percent of their overall budgets, the last decade has seen *a contraction of capital expenditures in the education sector*—for both maintenance and new investment—to practically insignificant levels.[20] The results are visible throughout the education system in the form of deferred maintenance of school facilities.

Recommendations

The main challenge in the education sector is to reallocate expenditures from surplus capacity in teaching staff and under-used facilities largely in rural areas towards other quality enhancing inputs and relieving overcrowding and multiple shifting in the major urban areas. This will require school closures or consolidation, and staff reductions as a first step. The Government has recently prepared a school and teacher redeployment plan. While this is a good first step, the plan needs to be closely examined to determine if it is far reaching enough. The resources saved from this plan, as a first priority need to be allocated to alleviating the acute under-spending for maintenance and new investment, and the shortage of teaching-related supplies, particularly in the smaller communities. Significant expenditures are needed to re-equip schools, to modernize the curriculum and teaching equipment, to maintain and rehabilitate school infrastructure, and to rationalize the school network.

Second, inequities in the access to education also need urgent attention. Improvements in education quality that result from more non-teaching inputs should help to reverse declines in attendance in rural areas, as will economic growth, since this will raise the returns to education overall. The plight of Roma children in terms of school participation and performance, however, requires continued close attention and remedial steps, drawing partly on the experience with Roma-targeted programs in other countries. As education has a central role in securing improvements in welfare and economic status, improving access and quality for Roma children is crucial to improving their income status over the long term.[21] One approach is expanding pre-school education for Roma, as these programs can provide essential preparations for the classroom environment, such as

---

[20] Barely 3 percent of total education expenditures in primary and secondary education, and 8.6 percent in the case of higher education.

[21] See, Dena Ringold, *Roma and the Transition in Central and Eastern Europe: Trends and Challenges*, The World Bank, 2000, pp. 40–41.

overcoming language and cultural differences. Another suggestion that has worked in other countries is the use of Roma teaching assistants to help in classrooms with Roma children. These teaching assistants can also provide a link with the Roma communities. Schools also need to foster links with Roma parents and get them involved at all levels; there is a clear connection between parental involvement in schools and attendance and performance.

A key constraint to improving basic education is the control retained by the MES overall inputs (schools, teachers, principals and norms for class size and teaching hours). The experiences of the past decade have shown that these input controls are not effective instruments for quality assurance. The decentralization formula should be changed to better align responsibilities and accountabilities. Another priority is to change the approach to education financing. The current formula finances inputs (mostly teachers); an efficient mechanism should finance outputs—in this case, the education of students. The simplest means of doing this is to move to a pure capitation model of financing, with specified per-student allocations for each level of education (see Chapter 6). Also, the current earmarked subsidy for capital expenditures needs to be replaced with a mechanism based on well-documented project evaluations—an objective that cuts across all sectors.

Rationalizing facilities and teachers and redeploying the freed resources for quality enhancing inputs will be a first step towards improving the overall quality of primary and secondary education. Serious attention also needs to be given to measuring educational quality and addressing identified deficiencies. Under the current system, the main instruments for quality control in the sector are the centrally mandated norms on class size and teaching hours. These are not in all cases necessary, effective or efficient to guarantee quality. A more direct and efficient approach is to monitor what students are actually learning—through a system of student assessment—and to take corrective action, where needed.

While to date, the rationalization of schools and teachers has focused almost exclusively on primary and secondary education, higher education should not be spared from close scrutiny, further rationalization and other reforms. There is an excess number of public universities and some rationalization is needed. One method to achieve this outcome is to limit funding to those institutions, that meet agreed standards of quality and efficiency (in terms of resource use and student completion). Institutions which do not meet these standards could continue, but only as private institutions. Student fees in higher education also need to be increased, both to mobilize resources and to reduce excessive consumption of services. An appropriate goal is to achieve an overall cost recovery ratio of 30 percent, as specified in the Law. The means-tested scholarship program and the loan scheme that are being developed can be used to deal with access problems for qualified low-income students. Finally, the capitation formula should be based upon the students completing a given higher education program, rather than the number of students enrolled, to help eliminate the problem of grade repetition.

Health[22]

Current Situation and Issues

Bulgaria's health indicators are poor, compared to those of other transition economies; most indicators have changed little or have been deteriorating during the transition period. For example, life expectancy at birth has been more or less steady at about 71 years, while the trend in most other transition countries has been upward. The incidence of new cases of tuberculosis in Bulgaria has risen steadily during the nineties, and the incidence of hepatitis stubbornly remains four to five times the level in Central European transition economies. Especially worrisome has been the sustained drop in immunization coverage in Bulgaria (see Table 3.6).[23]

---

[22] For a more detailed discussion, see Chapter 7 of Part Two.

[23] The incidence of HIV/AIDS is very low at 314 reported cases, which, however, is no reason for complacency.

Several factors have contributed to this relatively poor health status: (i) costly, excess capacity of both facilities and health care specialists inherited from the socialist past; (ii) inefficient use of resources, as manifested through both excess capacity and low utilization rates of facilities, especially hospital beds; (iii) neglect of maintenance of facilities and equipment; (iv) inadequate new investments; (v) over-centralized, rigid system of medical care; and (vi) low level of overall health expenditure. Bulgaria's total public expenditures in the health sector in the last five years have been in the order of 4 percent of GDP[24]—one of the lowest levels in Central and Eastern Europe during the transition and well below the average for Western European countries (around 8 percent). More than 90 percent of these outlays represented current expenditures and less than 10 percent (5 percent in 2001) capital expenditures.

TABLE 3.6: POLIO IMMUNIZATION RATE		
(IN PERCENT OF CHILDREN UNDER TWO IMMUNIZED)		
COUNTRY	1989	2000
Bulgaria	99.7	94.4
Czech Republic	99.0	97.4
Hungary	98.5	99.8
Poland	—	94.8
Romania	89.4	96.3
Slovak Republic	98.8	—

Source: Trans MONEE. See Chapter 7, Table 7.1.

In 1999, the Government undertook a wide-ranging reform of the health sector centered on the introduction of an insurance-based system. The new system is described in Chapter 7. Its key features are as follows. The central component of the new system is the National Health Insurance Fund (NHIF), which combines the roles of pooling risks and purchasing medical care through contracts with physicians, group practices and hospitals. The system is essentially a publicly-administered insurance fund, implemented through private providers of care. It affords consumer choice, and it contrasts with the old system under which most health care was delivered through polyclinics and hospitals. It introduces the concept of General Practitioner (GP) as the first point of entry into the system. All physicians are permitted to provide care privately and to charge a negotiated fee.

The NHIF is funded through mandatory contributions unrelated to costs, through an earmarked payroll tax, and contributions from the state on behalf of the poor and the non-working population. Hospitals are financed by the NHIF, the state and municipalities. Municipalities also finance the contributions of those receiving unemployment benefits. For the working population, currently, the contribution rate is 6 percent of wages up to a ceiling of 850 leva per month. Since the rate is the same for all those within this broad income range, the scheme is somewhat regressive. The self-employed are required to contribute 6 percent of their declared income. Physicians are paid on a capitation basis, i.e., a fixed amount per patient (which varies by the patient's age), with a premium for patients with chronic diseases—not according to the treatment administered.

The new system, which is still evolving, continues the reforms toward a leaner and more efficient health system initiated in the early 1990s. Under these reforms, a significant reduction in hospital capacity and the supply of doctors has already taken place. While experience with the new system is too short to draw firm lessons from it, a few emerging issues are already evident.

Despite reductions in capacity, *surplus capacity* still remains an issue in the sector. This is especially the case with hospitals. Hospital occupancy rates are still low. According to officials in the health sector, there are possibly as many as 12,000 surplus hospital beds (out of a total of

---

[24] Not allowing for an undetermined amount of unreported (under-the-table) private spending which is known to take place.

62,000). Also, in many cases, the bed reductions that have been effected were achieved by reducing the number of beds per room. While this may have led to small quality improvements, the overall impact on costs is small, as staffing costs, heating and other utility costs change very little. Moreover, the usage of hospital beds is highly inefficient, as the average length of stay in the hospital is still twice the level of Western Europe and one a half times the Czech Republic. The introduction of day surgery and more efficient management practices are, therefore, likely to exacerbate excess capacity issues.

There is an issue regarding the management and coordination of hospitals. Even though the proportion of hospital costs to be provided by the NIHF is expected to rise to 50 percent, funding and oversight of hospitals will remain the responsibility of the NIHF, the Ministry of Health (MOH) and municipalities, all of which will be responsible for funding some portion of hospital costs. The Ministry of Health is preparing an accreditation program to identify the providers of high quality care, but the current governance structure is not conducive to achieving the needed rationalization in hospital facilities.

Capacity issues also arise in the structure of health sector employees. Bulgaria still has more medical doctors than most Central and Eastern European countries. In spite of the surplus of doctors, the introduction of the new system has led to a five-fold increase in the incomes of physicians. Consistent with this pattern, Bulgaria has had a much lower ratio of nurses to physicians than other countries in the region, except for Hungary. Anecdotal evidence from interviews with officials suggests that, particularly in the primary care sub-sector, the supply of nurses remains low.

The *financial sustainability* of the NIHF is also an issue. In the near term, the fund is accumulating a surplus. Surplus reserves are currently being held with the Bulgarian National Bank, earning a return which is below the interest costs of government debt. These reserves are also not being used to improve quality in the sector. System funding is being re-centralized under the NIHF. The share of municipal funding has declined from about 50 percent in 1997–2000 to 24 percent in 2001. This and the expansion of the role of the NHIF in hospital financing are the main reasons that the Fund is projected to run a deficit by 2003. With the emerging deficit, the financial sustainability of the fund will require additional revenue mobilization if projected deficits continue into the future. In this case, the Government must decide whether to raise contribution rates above the current 6 percent or reduce the costs to be covered by the Fund.

There are also some signs that the new system may pose *access problems* for certain groups. This is identified as a problem for the Roma and the population in remote areas. The greater autonomy provided to physicians has led to withdrawals from Roma neighborhoods and rural areas. The Roma and other minority groups may also face an additional constraint—under the GP system, clients must register and GPs have some discretion in who they register. Examining the possibilities for improving the incentives for physicians to service these groups or organizing some type of special service is another challenge facing policy makers. The new insurance system has also resulted in access problems for pensioners, the poor and the unemployed. For these individuals, who do not have a NHIF contribution history, the municipalities are supposed to make contributions on their behalf. Yet, given the poor state of their finances, some municipalities do not make the required contributions, and the GPs and health facilities deny these individuals access to health care.

Finally, the health sector also needs to improve the current situation of *inadequate investment programming and funding*. The hospital sector appears to be in need of significant refurbishment and replacement of key diagnostic and therapeutic equipment. It is possible that some of the savings from hospital closures could be used to finance the required investment in the sector. However, these savings are far from certain, especially as regards timing; yet, the quality of health facilities continues to decline. In addition, the governance problem discussed above, which results in unclear authority over hospitals among the NIHF, the MOH and the municipalities, is complicating investment planning in the sector.

Recommendations

The design of Bulgaria's new health care system is generally appropriate; it builds on the social insurance model of Western Europe that has been adopted by many Central and Eastern European countries over the past 10 years.[25] The top priority is to implement the system fully and carefully, learning from experience as the implementation progresses. Mechanisms need to be put in place to monitor progress and public perceptions of reform. There is a need to monitor, in particular, the proportion of health expenditures going to physicians in order to avoid that further increases on them do not take place at the expense of starving maintenance and new investments, as in the recent past. It is relevant to note that the over-supply of physicians inherited from the centrally planned era implies that physicians' income were not unattractive even before the new system was introduced. The recent survey by the National Institute of Public Health on public mechanisms is another positive step in evaluating the progress of reform and determining what changes, if any, are needed. Not only should this instrument be repeated in the health sector, similar surveys need to be undertaken in other sectors as well.

The first key priority is to address the concurrent problems of surplus capacity issues in health facilities, the serious deterioration in the quality of facilities, and the inadequate modernization of equipment. From the point of view of relieving the financial burden on the state and municipalities, the top priority is to proceed with a further round of reduction in the over-supply of hospital beds and doctors. Neither decision is easy; both should be made as transparently as possible and in close consultation with representatives of civil society, including NGOs and professional associations, and with approaches which result in meaningful and sustainable change (for example, closing entire wards of hospitals, instead of reducing the number of beds per room).

Addressing the deterioration in quality and modernization issues requires augmenting the funds allocated to investment in the sector. While the share of investment in total health expenditure in Bulgaria (7 percent) is higher than the average for mature economies (3–4 percent), it should be higher than that level (8–10 percent), given the neglect of physical assets during the transition. To guide the choice of investments, Bulgaria needs to undertake a careful inventory of medical equipment and structures, possibly on the basis of a random survey of establishments, as opposed to carrying out an exhaustive census, and to supplement it with indicators of demand. Consideration should be given to establishing a sustainable capital improvement fund with the accumulated surpluses of the NHIF.

Stabilizing and placing on a sustainable basis the financial situation of the NHIF is the third area for policy reform. NHIF's financing requirements will increase as it assumes greater responsibilities. Our analysis shows that the NHIF will begin to run a deficit as early as 2003. Thus, the financial sustainability of the fund will require additional revenue mobilization if projected deficits continue into the future. In this case, the Government must decide whether to raise contribution rates above the current 6 percent or increase its contribution on behalf of non-working individuals. Improving compliance through the introduction of the Unified Revenue Agency will also help the system's finances.

At the institutional level, there is a need to delineate more clearly the functions of the NHIF, the Ministries of Health and Finance, and the municipalities. Each of these institutions will continue to play important roles, although their scope and scale will change as the NHIF assumes greater responsibility for hospital financing. The Ministry of Health needs to take the lead role in rationalizing hospital capacity, based on the accreditation program that it is now preparing. The Ministry of Finance will need to act in a coordinating capacity, to ensure that changing responsibilities are matched by corresponding changes in resource flows. There is a pressing need to develop the parameters of a "steady state" health financing system, including the long-term division of

---

[25] The extent to which the system relies on the provision of services by the private sector has varied among countries. Bulgaria has adopted a middle of the road approach, choosing to treat medical care providers as regulated private agents, while publicly operating the insurance function.

responsibilities and revenue sources between the MOH and the NHIF. Over the medium term, it seems appropriate that the NHIF would provide the bulk of financing to hospitals, with only a minimal role for municipalities and the Central Government, except in the case of university hospitals.

Finally, as in education, there is a need to address access issues for the disadvantaged, especially the Roma, the unemployed and people who live in rural communities. Adequate resources need to be provided to municipalities to ensure that contributions are paid for those who lack a contribution history. Regarding the shortage of medical care givers in Roma communities, this is currently being addressed by training Roma nurses and doctors. It is preferable to provide financial incentives to nurses and doctors, regardless of their ethnic backgrounds, to serve in minority communities. Moreover, the Government needs to make a special effort to reach the Roma community.[26] A first step is to initiate a monitoring effort to ascertain needs; this should be concentrated on communicative diseases, such as tuberculosis, hepatitis and HIV/AIDS. One approach that has proven effective in other countries is the use of Roma mediators to work in Roma communities to engage in health promotion activities, in particular women's reproductive health.

Social Protection[27]

Current Situation

With the exception of guaranteed employment, Bulgaria's pre-transition social protection system of cradle-to-grave benefits and services remained largely intact during the 1990s. Moreover, the system has been expanded to include new "western" types of assistance, primarily unemployment insurance and benefits, and a variety of social assistance or welfare benefits aimed at helping individuals and households cope with transition-related shocks. During the crisis in 1996–97, due to escalating fiscal pressures, total social protection expenditures, which peaked at 15 percent of GDP in 1993, fell to 9.5 percent by 1997 (see Figure 3.1). Despite large, unsustainable public expendi-

---

[26] This is drawn from *Roma and the Transition in Central and Eastern Europe: Trends and Challenges, op. cit.*

[27] For a more detailed discussion, see Chapter 8 of Part Two.

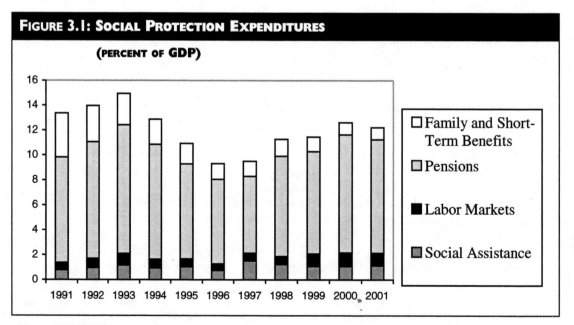

FIGURE 3.1: SOCIAL PROTECTION EXPENDITURES

(PERCENT OF GDP)

Source: MOLSP, MOF.

tures on social protection, individual benefits had become so compressed that they could no longer assist those that most needed them. The combination of benefits proliferation, rising number of beneficiaries due to adverse demographic trends (aging population) and generous early retirement provisions, and increasing unemployment severely undermined the sustainability and the adequacy of the system. This led the Government to initiate a series of reforms of the pension and social assistance programs, aimed at improving targeting and achieving fiscal sustainability. While the level of spending on social protection is now close to that of the early 1990s, its composition has changed and the targeting improved.

Social protection programs consist of: (i) pensions; (ii) labor market programs; (iii) social assistance; and (iv) short-term and family benefits. Aggregate spending on these programs accounted for 13.6 percent of GDP in 2001; the majority of expenditures (9.1 percent of GDP) goes to pensions. Social protection programs have wide coverage among the population; over 80 percent of Bulgarians received at least one type of benefit in 2001—however, only one-third of the population is of retirement age or poor. On the whole, social protection programs have become more pro-poor since the mid-1990s and have played a major role in alleviating poverty. The poverty headcount fell from 30 percent before benefits to a low of 12 percent after benefits (see Table 3.7). Social protection programs also succeeded in reducing the depth and severity of poverty.

Pensions

Issues.   Pensions constitute the largest social protection expenditure category, accounting for 9.1 percent of GDP in 2001. The program comprises a variety of contributory and non-contributory benefits: old age, survivor, disability, veteran, merit and social pensions, etc. Over the last decade, the pension system came under severe pressure. The overall stock of pensioners rose as a result of the aging of the population, while the number of insured persons shrank, mirroring the collapse of employment. To cope with the financial problem created by this situation, successive governments reduced the benefits while raising the payroll taxes, eventually reaching limits on both sides.

Until recently, the pension program consisted of a single, pay-as-you-go pillar (labeled PAYG), financed through payroll taxes. In the face of continuing financial pressure, in 1999, the Government introduced a new pension system comprising three pillars: (i) the first, or public, pillar tantamount to a rationalized PAYG; it incorporated, inter alia, an increase in the retirement age from 55/60 to 60/63 for female/male over a 10/6 year period; (ii) a mandatory second "universal" pillar—a mandatory, fully-funded private insurance for those born after January 1, 1960, and an "occupational" plan for those working under hazardous labor conditions, financed by employers' contributions; and (iii) a voluntary private system.

As with health reforms, the new pension reform, which is described more fully in Chapter 8, constitutes a major leap forward in building a more secure and stable pension system. Although the basic legal and institutional foundations of the new system are operational, there are a number of issues that could adversely affect the successful implementation of the system. First, while our simulations show that the system will reach a sustainable financial position by the next decade, this can only be realized with an improvement in compliance. Recently, compliance has been weak, as evidenced by declining revenues (see Table 3.8). Second,

TABLE 3.7: POVERTY LEVELS WITH AND WITHOUT SOCIAL PROTECTION BENEFITS 1995, 1997, 2001			
	1995	1997	2001
Population	100	100	100
Poverty Headcount (%)			
Without	20.5	47.7	29.9
With	5.5	36.0	11.7

Source: BIHS, 1995, 1997, 2001. See Chapter 8, Table 8.3.

TABLE 3.8: FINANCIAL PERFORMANCE OF THE PUBLIC PILLAR 1991-2001

(PERCENT OF GDP)

	1991	1993	1995	1997	1998	1999	2000	2001
Revenues	9.1	10.7	8.4	7.7	9.4	9.3	8.7	8.1
Expenditures	9.8	11.6	8.4	7.0	9.3	9.5	9.8	9.7
Balance	−0.7	−1.0	−0.1	0.7	0.1	−0.2	−1.1	−1.6

Source: National Social Security Institute (NSSI) and World Bank estimates. See Chapter 8, Table 8.4.

the new system does not define a transparent rule for indexing benefits, which leaves the system open to policy discretion and engenders uncertainty among beneficiaries. Third, regarding the "universal" pillar, the contribution rate is not set in legislation (this is also true for the public pillar), which engenders uncertainty among beneficiaries; transfers into private funds are not yet fully reconciled nor have they been automatic; and the legal and supervisory framework needs to be strengthened. Finally, there needs to be stricter provisions regarding disability claims, which have recently surged.

Recommendations. The first priority is to improve compliance with, coverage of, the public pillar, and define a clear rule for indexing pensions. Improving compliance can be achieved by the rapid implementation of the Unified Revenue Agency, which will unify collection of social security contributions and taxes. Until the new Agency becomes operational, the joint audits between the NSSI and the General Tax Directorate should be continued and broadened. Expansion of the pension system's coverage merits special attention, as some economic groups (such as workers in the agriculture sector) have been poorly covered since the early transition days.

The new legislative framework set forth clear criteria for determining benefits but failed to define a transparent rule for indexing benefits, retaining a fair amount of policy discretion in this area. Discretion can help control short-term volatility in the system, but it can equally foster inappropriate management of pension expenditures. Beneficiaries would also prefer a more predictable pension indexation provision in order to enjoy a smoother income and consumption pattern rather than confronting *ad hoc* changes. At a minimum, the indexation rule should aim to preserve the real value of benefits. The gradual improvement in the dependency ratio, which results from the retirement age increase, suggests that benefits could be indexed to inflation plus a modest percentage of real wage growth (25 percent) transferring to pensioners some of the substantial wage recovery gains expected over coming years. Full indexation to real wage growth would likely have adverse consequences on the financial position of the public pillar, and as a consequence, hinder efforts to increase the contribution rate to the second pillar.

For both the public and universal plans, it is difficult for contributors to assess their potential future retirement income, as the contribution rate to both pillars is not set in separate legislation and can be changed annually within the budget cycle. From a retirement planning perspective, it would be preferable to establish a set contribution rate for both the public pillar and the universal pillar in legislation and remove it from the vagaries of the budget process. In the years ahead, consideration should be given to harmonizing the retirement age of men and women; this would affect all pillars.

Another priority in the short term is to monitor and restrain the rise in disability trends, as the stricter retirement provisions have generated a surge of disability claims. It is recommended that the NSSI carefully examine disability regulations and administrative procedures, if recent trends continue.

The legal, regulatory and supervisory framework for the private pension funds and private plans require growing attention. This should include: in the short term, strengthening the institutional capacity of the State Insurance Supervision Agency (SISA) to foster the sound development of private pension plans; in the medium term, strengthening the legal framework of private pension plans, especially their governance structure; and in the long term, establishing a closer integration of private pension funds with the rest of Bulgaria's financial markets and the EU.

To summarize, the main reforms for pensions are:

In the short term:

- Enhance compliance and coverage of the public pillar, control the rise in disability payments and define a clear rule for indexing pensions.
- Ensure a prompt and transparent transfer of contributions to private pension plans and proper management of contributions that have not yet been reconciled.
- Strengthen the institutional capacity of SISA and upgrade regulations to foster the sound development of private pension plans.
- Define a transparent plan for the universal pillar to eliminate current uncertainties on its future.

In the medium term:

- Strengthen the legal framework of private pension plans, especially the governance structure of private plans, and the authority and independence of the supervisory agency, and make the investment regime more flexible.

In the long-term:

- Seek closer integration of private pension funds with the rest of Bulgaria's financial markets and the EU.
- Harmonize the retirement age of men and women.

Labor Market Problems

Issues.   Improving effectiveness of labor market programs and implementing fundamental market reform are critical elements to address Bulgaria's unemployment challenge. At 17.5 percent of the labor force in 2001, unemployment in Bulgaria has been rising steadily since 1996, and it is among the highest rates in the region. The labor is also characterized by low flows out of unemployment into jobs and a high share of discouraged workers—those workers who have stopped looking for a job and drop out of the labor force all together. In 2001, long-term unemployment is 49.3 percent—a disturbing development, as the long-term unemployed face the greatest obstacles in re-entering the labor market. Thus, to complement fundamental labor market reform and assist workers who lose their jobs, Bulgaria implements labor market programs. There are two kinds of programs: (i) payment of unemployment benefits, or so-called "passive programs"; and (ii) "active labor market programs" (ALMPs), consisting of measures to promote employment, including public works programs, training, employment subsidies, and support for small business development. Expenditures on all programs together correspond to 1 percent of GDP, with three-fourths of it (or 0.7 percent of GDP) accounted by unemployment benefits.

Up to 2001, all unemployment programs have been financed through an extrabudgetary fund, the Professional Training and Unemployment Fund (PTUF), in turn financed by payroll taxes.[28] Because of the increase in unemployment, since 1997, the PTUF has run a deficit which had to be covered by the state budget. In 2001, state transfers to the Fund amounted to 33 percent

---

[28] The contribution rate is currently 4 percent of gross wages, with 1.0 percent paid by the employees and 3 percent by the employer in 2002.

of PTUF receipts. The targeting of unemployment benefits has been more problematic than that of other social assistance cash-transfer programs. In 2001, roughly two-thirds of the benefits went to the non-poor. The *employment promotion* programs, or ALMPs, are non-contributory, i.e., financed entirely by the state. A recent study of the experience with ALMPs concluded that while the results were positive, the programs' overall impact was limited. These programs peaked during the economic crisis of 1996–97 but have been scaled back since given their low effectiveness.

Recent Reforms.   The amendments to the Mandatory Social Insurance Code, which became effective on January 1, 2002, introduced important reforms on eligibility criteria and benefits to the unemployed. The amendments incorporated an unemployment insurance fund which succeeds the PTUF. The unemployment insurance fund is designed to cover insured risk of unemployment and it is managed by NSSI. Workers are now eligible for unemployment benefits if they are registered with the NSSI, if they have been contributing to compulsory social insurance for at least 9 months during the last 15 months before termination of the social insurance contributions, and if they are willing to accept a job or training, if offered. Benefits are no longer linked to the minimum monthly wage but instead to a minimum and maximum levels determined annually in the Law of the Budget of the State Social Insurance. In 2002, the minimum level was set to 70 leva and the maximum to 130 leva. In addition, duration of benefits are linked to the number of years contributing to the compulsory social insurance system. Moreover, the unemployment insurance fund is to cover the beneficiary's contributions to pension and health insurance.

Recommendations.   A top priority is to implement fundamental labor market reform to establish a dynamic labor market conducive to expanding employment opportunities. Labor market reform, labor market programs, and social assistance policies should complement each other to promote work incentives and employment growth. At the same time, it is critical to monitor very closely the effectiveness of the unemployment insurance fund and its fiscal costs. Similarly, there is a need to monitor the so-called Active Labor Market Programs closely in order to improve their effectiveness and long-term impact in stimulating labor demand. Over the longer-term, consideration should be given to reduce the tax burden related to labor market policies in order to curtail labor costs.
To summarize, the main reforms for labor market programs are:

- Enhance consistency among labor market programs, social assistance and fundamental labor market reform—all components should complement each other to promote work incentives and employment growth.
- Monitor closely the effectiveness and fiscal costs of the new unemployment insurance fund.
- Continue the on-going monitoring of ALMPs to ensure the effectiveness and long-term impact of programs to ensure these assist vulnerable groups.
- Over the longer-term, reforms should aim at reducing the tax burden related to labor market policies to decrease labor costs.

Social Assistance

Issues.   Social assistance programs account for about 14 percent of total social protection expenditures under the social protection system and represent 1.1 percent of GDP. They encompass several kinds of benefits: (i) the Guaranteed Minimum Income (GMI) Program, a means-tested cash benefit paid to low-income families below an income threshold, which constitutes the main national safety net; (ii) the energy benefits program, a cash supplement to the GMI which is paid during the winter heating season; and (iii) other benefits designed to meet the needs of specific groups, such as children and the disabled. All of these programs are non-contributory,[29] their financing

---

[29] The energy benefits program is financed by the state only.

being provided by the state and the municipalities, in equal shares in 2001. Three-quarters of the financing is covered by the state budget, starting in 2002. Many municipalities have difficulty in mobilizing the resources necessary to contribute their share. Benefits are often paid irregularly, late or in kind. The Ministry of Finance earmarks funding for this purpose in its budget, but the amount required is constantly underestimated (see Figure 3.2). And the formula for allocating transfers is too complicated and changes annually, making planning at all levels of government difficult. An entirely new approach for allocating subsidies to municipalities is envisioned under the fiscal decentralization program approved by the Council of Ministers (COM) in mid-2002.

Chapter 8 presents and discusses the effectiveness of the various social assistance programs, based on their: (i) coverage–the percentage of beneficiary households that are poor; (ii) targeting–the percentage of the resources distributed that go to the poor; and (iii) adequacy–the ratio of resources received by the poor to the pre-benefit consumption (available resources) of the poor. While the effectiveness of the programs has generally improved, there is further room for improvement, particularly with regard to targeting (see Table 3.9). Some benefits are perhaps too high and others too low to have an impact on poverty. Some are not targeted at all and may, in fact, be regressive. A common problem is that the identification of poor households is weak.

Recommendations. Attention needs to be given, first, to strengthening the Guaranteed Minimum Income (GMI) program, which is the nation's main safety net benefit. While the move under the 2002 budget to shift 75 percent of the funding of the GMI program to the Central Government was a positive step, it is important to fully centralizing its funding (as is currently the case for the energy benefit). The Government has indicated its intention to move in this direction and implement this approach possibly starting in 2003 (see Box 4.1). This would avoid the chronic underfunding of municipalities' contributions and reverse the current situation where the burden of fiscal sustainability issues at the municipal level is borne by the most economically vulnerable members of society. The provision of in-kind benefits rather than cash, which may be largely a function of cash constraints at the municipal level, should be discontinued.

The targeting of the various sub-programs can and should be enhanced by improving, inter alia, the identification of poor households and the information system needed for proper means testing. Improved targeting is needed especially with regard to energy benefits and child allowances. This would be greatly facilitated by the establishment of a national poverty line and

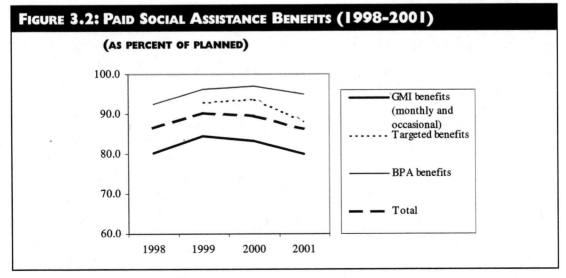

FIGURE 3.2: PAID SOCIAL ASSISTANCE BENEFITS (1998–2001)

(AS PERCENT OF PLANNED)

Legend:
- GMI benefits (monthly and occasional)
- Targeted benefits
- BPA benefits
- Total

Source: MOLSP.

TABLE 3.9: BENEFIT INCIDENCE BY (EX ANTE) CONSUMPTION QUINTILE[1]

CONS. QUINT	EXTENDED GMI (INCLUDING IN-KIND)			GMI (CASH BENEFITS ONLY)			ENERGY BENEFIT
	1995	1997	2001	1995	1997	2001	2001
1	47.3	18.4	68.3	54.7	20.3	60.5	52.9
2	16.9	18.5	12.4	9.9	7.4	17.6	21.7
3	2.7	11.6	8.2	0.2	17.4	12.4	11.9
4	19.4	26.5	8.5	0.0	38.9	9.3	10.0
5	13.8	25.0	2.5	35.2	16.1	0.3	3.4

[1] Table shows the incidence of the benefit, estimated in the absence of the benefit.
Source: BIHS 1995, 1997, 2001.

then, the alignment of social assistance payments with this line. Another priority concerning targeting is to eliminate payment of regressive medical and transportation benefits.

To summarize, the main reforms for social assistance programs are:

- Strengthen the GMI program by fully centralizing funding for the program (the Government has indicated its intention to implement this approach possibly starting within the framework of the 2003 budget).
- Improve targeting of social assistance by: (i) training social workers to identify poor households; (ii) improving information systems to facilitate means-testing and reduce payment of duplicative benefits; and (iii) expanding communication activities to inform beneficiaries about eligibility criteria and application procedures.
- Improve targeting of the energy benefit to benefit poor households.
- Target expenditures on child allowances to the poor. Evaluate program design options for expanding coverage to children currently not covered by the benefit.
- Eliminate provision of GMI benefits in-kind.
- Eliminate payment of the regressive medical and transportation benefits.

Short-Term and Family Benefits

Issues.   The Social Protection System also includes short-term benefits consisting of some 12 categories of benefits, including sickness, maternity, birth, child care, work injuries, disabled children, etc. Financing comes from different sources, depending on the benefit: payroll taxes, contributions by the self-employed, state contributions on behalf of civil servants, and the employers. Total spending on short-term benefits declined from 3.5 percent of GDP in 1991 to 1.6 percent in 2001, largely because of the declining expenditures on child allowances, driven by the demographic decline. While most of the benefits involved play an important role, some may be too generous, as explained in Chapter 8.

Recommendations.   A new Law was enacted on April 1, 2002, to improve the adequacy of child benefits and target them better to poor households. However, it is important to note that the income threshold in the Law (150 leva) is too high and the increase in benefit level (to 15 leva) too low to have more than a modest impact on poor children, especially those in one child households. There is also a need to expand coverage of child benefits to the uninsured self-employed, because 23 percent of poor children are not covered by this benefit. Other priorities include monitoring sick leave claims, which have increased since 2000. Some countries exempt the first few days of sickness from sick pay to prevent abuse. Adjusting benefits that appear too generous or are burdens on employers, such as child care, is another measure that should be considered. This can be achieved in some cases by changing the program design rather than the benefit level.

To summarize, the main reforms for short-term and family benefits are:

- Monitor sick leave payments and incentives.
- Reduce period of child care leave benefits to one year.
- Eliminate the job reentry guarantee for mothers on child care leave.
- Shift responsibility for paying social insurance contributions for individuals on child care leave from employers to the NSSI.

Overall Recommendations

Given the plethora of programs, the complexity of program design in many cases and their burden on the state, a constant challenge regarding the social protection system as a whole is to examine the opportunities for consolidation and simplification and engage in systematic monitoring of the programs, their costs and their effects. Among sub-programs, those deserving the highest priority are pensions, which account for the lion's share of social protection expenditures and benefit the largest segment of the population, and labor market programs, which should complement fundamental labor market reform, given the high rate of unemployment and the still higher rate of long-term unemployment.

The State Railway[30]

Current Situation and Issues

At the outset, it is important to note that the analysis in this PEIR is focused on railway transport. There are serious issues affecting other modes of transport, but they are generally not as pressing as those affecting the railway. The other main land transport mode, road transport, has changed dramatically in the last decade; road transport enterprises have been privatized and with deregulation, have been restructured. As a result, road transport is today competitive and efficient: for freight, road transport had gained 55 percent share and complements rail transport; for passengers, road transport competes aggressively with the railways. On the other hand, rail transport had not fully restructured, is not efficient and still is a major drain on the budget. It should be noted, however, that Bulgaria's main road network does require attention, as maintenance is poor and it is a negative factor influencing the investment climate. As noted in Chapter 5, further analytical work on the road network is a key priority for the future.

The Bulgaria State Railway (BDZ) does not operate as a profit-oriented, commercial entity; it functions, rather, as an old (pre-transition) government enterprise. BDZ's net income has been negative since the economic transition. Its deficit reached 124 million leva in 2001, or 21 percent of total costs, even after taking into account the operating subsidy provided by the central government. BDZ receives a significant contribution from the State to cover its deficit. The total state contribution has averaged 0.8 percent of GDP in recent years.[31] About half of the this amount represents an operating subsidy, and the rest a contribution to investment. The subsidies have not prevented the serious deterioration of the railway assets due to their inadequate maintenance and renewal.

---

[30] For a more detailed discussion, see Chapter 9 of Part Two.

[31] This is a conservative estimate. Not counted in this figure are other forms of state support such as arrears to state-owned companies (such as utilities), interest payments on loans to BDZ from the European Investment Bank, and provision of sovereign guarantees for World Bank and EBRD loans.

BDZ's poor financial performance is attributable to several factors (see Table 3.10). BDZ operates *a large number of uneconomic services*, mandated by the State and constituting public service obligations (PSOs). To a large extent, this is a legacy of the past, as economic efficiency was not a prime objective during the socialist era. The railway was given a dominant role in land transport then, with road transport receiving scant attention. As the economy evolved, demand for railway services declined, to the benefit of road transport, which developed rapidly. This is evidenced by the low intensity of use of the railway network, as shown in the statistics on the number of traffic units per km of line in Table 3.10.

Another reason for BDZ's poor performance is *low passenger fares*. Revenues from passenger services cover, on average, only 27 percent of costs because of the low level of standard fares. In addition, a large number of passengers benefit from substantial discounts. These fares and discounts are generally justified on the basis of the need to serve the poor or low-income people. However, while incomes are indeed low in Bulgaria, there is no evidence that rail users are poorer than the average non-motorized population. The benefits of cheap railway transport are, therefore, not necessarily well targeted.

Low labor productivity is a third major problem of the railway. Although BDZ has considerably reduced its labor force throughout the 1990s, it still has 36,600 employees, making it one of the largest employers in the country. BDZ's labor productivity is less than half that of Western Europe and lower than in most Eastern European countries. BDZ's wage bill accounts for about 40 percent of its total cost.

BDZ suffers from *an inappropriate incentive framework* that is not conducive to efficient decision making and accountability. Most strategic decisions about the railway services provided, passenger fares, senior staff appointments, labor reductions, and capital investments are taken directly or indirectly by the State. Moreover, BDZ is entirely dependent on the State for its investments, which are financed from state budget or through foreign loans (guaranteed by the State) and grants. This results in a weak and flawed investment planning process. BDZ's management is not in a position to define, by itself, a commercial strategy and to select the investments that would best serve that strategy. BDZ does not have a multi-year business plan; nor does the State have a multi-year investment program for the sector. It is doubtful that this setting leads to optimal investment selection.

BDZ and the State have taken a number of important steps to improve the railway's financial situation. Labor has been cut by 37 percent since 1995; operating costs have been reduced; passenger and freight rates have been raised; most of BDZ's ancillary (non-core) businesses have been divested; some of the enterprise's surplus assets have been sold; and under a new Railway Law enacted in November 2000, BDZ has been split into two separate enterprises: one in charge of infrastructure, the other of railway operation. While these actions have helped unit revenues to rise significantly, many of the decisions have been too limited in scope to turn BDZ around. BDZ's financial situation remains fragile and its future uncertain.

TABLE 3.10: COMPARATIVE RAILWAY STATISTICS, 2000

	BULGARIA	POLAND	ROMANIA	WESTERN EUROPE
Use of railway network, million traffic units/km	2.5	4.2	3.3	3.5
Labor productivity, traffic units per employee	223,000	431,000	284,000	600,000
Average revenue per t/km, US$	0.019	0.023	0.022	n.a.
Average revenue per passenger/km, [US$]	0.008	0.018	0.010	n.a.

Source: BDZ, Polish and Romanian Railways, World Bank Railways Database.

Projections with a 10-year horizon were prepared for this Report to assess the likely conse-quences of the present situation for BDZ's finances.[32] The results show that in the absence of further reforms, BDZ's annual losses would increase rapidly to a level of 170–180 million leva—more than twice the estimated 2002 level. BDZ's net cash generation would remain negative even after factoring in an operating subsidy of 60 million leva, as in recent years, to cover public service obligations. The State would have to provide an additional "contribution to solvency" of more than 100 million leva to ensure that BDZ continues to operate. The State's total support to the railway sector would exceed 200 million leva, or 0.7 percent of GDP. If loans and grants from the European Union were taken into account, the total State support would come to 413 million leva, or 1.3 percent of GDP. The inevitable conclusion is that if present policies are allowed to continue, the railway sector risks becoming an unsustainable burden on the State.

Recommendations

To stem the deterioration of the railway sector, Bulgaria needs to undertake a number of actions. The analysis undertaken for this Report shows that unless deep structural reforms are taken, the railways will be a growing source of fiscal drain on the budget. The first priority is a drastic reduc-tion of uneconomic services, especially on branch lines and low-volume freight trains. Some of the regular inter-city lines should also be reconsidered, as the distances are too short, the stops too frequent and the passengers too few to ever compete successfully with buses. The reduction in uneconomic services should be initiated on the basis of a carefully prepared and properly discussed "rationalization plan" which carefully considers alternatives and costs. Terminating loss-making services should boost unit revenues.

Further cost saving measures should include removing fare discounts, increasing freight rates and importantly, reducing the labor force. Fare discounts—for which there is no strong justifica-tion on equity grounds—should be reduced, although this should be attempted gradually. There is also some scope for raising freight rates, which are somewhat lower in Bulgaria than in neigh-boring countries. The top priority on the cost side is, however, a further reduction in the labor force, so as to increase productivity. As shown in the financial projections prepared for this Report, a labor force reduction would make the single most important contribution to improving the financial position of BDZ. In some cases, this will require changes in technology and complemen-tary investments to achieve it.

Although the break-up of BDZ, the Bulgarian state railway, into two entities—one for opera-tions, the other for infrastructure—is a step forward. This should be complemented by clear cor-porate governance arrangements, especially to isolate the new entities from political interference, particularly where investment decisions are concerned. Investment decisions should be based on strict economic criteria. The importance of formulating sound investment policies is accentuated by the poor shape of the railway infrastructure. Infrastructure renewal needs are estimated at 200 million leva per year. Given the constraint on resources, despite the availability of European funds, it is essential to optimize the selection of investments.

To shed light on the intensity of the efforts required, financial projections for 2002–20 were prepared under three alternative reform scenarios with increasing strength, labeled Mild, Medium and Strong Reform Scenarios. Strength varied according to the assumptions concerning labor retrenchment, fares and tariffs, and termination of service, specified in Chapter 9. The projections led to three important findings: (i) only the Strong Reform Scenario results in a turnaround in the financial situation of the railway in terms of the requirement for government contribution to

---

[32] The assumptions, which are detailed in Chapter 9, include a decline in passenger traffic until 2006, with a lev-eling off thereafter; little change in freight traffic over the next five years and moderate growth after that; stable overall revenues; unchanged labor force and wages; some increase in the cost of materials, to stem the accumulation of deferred maintenance; substantial clearing up and/or cancellation of arrears to suppliers and Government; and a modest amount of new infrastructure investments and equipment replacement.

solvency and investment; (ii) reduction of labor is by far the most important measure that can be taken to redress the railway's financial situation; and (iii) nevertheless, a "comprehensive package" of reforms is necessary to address the many issues. Chapter 9 presents such a package, distinguishing between measures that need to be taken immediately, within 18 months and within 36 months. The focus is on the sequence rather than the timing of the actions.

Energy[33]

Current Situation and Issues

Bulgaria's energy sector is largely government owned or controlled and energy consumption is heavily subsidized. Since household electricity and district heating prices have the highest subsidy content, households are the main beneficiaries of these subsidies. Household energy consumption is cross-subsidized by non-household consumers. With state ownership or control over all major energy assets, virtually all capital investment in the sector requires state support in the form of budget funds or state-guaranteed loans. This is largely responsible for the under-investment which has afflicted the sector for more than a decade.

Bulgaria has the *highest energy intensity* among EU accession candidates due to lagging sector reforms. Yet, except for pollution-producing lignite coal, Bulgaria does not have economical energy resources. The bulk of Bulgaria's electricity (about 80 percent) is generated from nuclear fuel and indigenous, low-quality lignite, which pose environmental and safety hazards. A low-pressure natural gas distribution system is virtually absent. Yet, the country has an electricity surplus, which it exports, especially to neighboring Turkey. Moreover, under the right policies, the sector offers scope for internal demand management and energy efficiency, improving Bulgaria's competitiveness, and increasing government revenues through privatization.

State subsidies to the energy sector take many forms. The most important are explicit, or direct, subsidies, mostly of two kinds: (i) district heating (DH) subsidies, provided to DH companies to cover operating costs not covered by tariffs; and (ii) the "Winter Energy Benefits Program," discussed in Chapters 8 and 10 under which low-income families receive an energy-linked cash supplement during five winter months. Explicit subsidies (excluding capital investment) have contracted by more than two-thirds since 1998, from 1.8 percent of GDP to 0.4 percent. Within this group, subsidies to suppliers have been steadily declining, while those for vulnerable consumers have been rising. The State also provides energy suppliers and consumers with so-called "quasi-fiscal subsidies." They arise from, or compensate for: (i) the operating losses of the state-owned district heating companies which are not covered by tariffs or explicit subsidies; and (ii) non-payment (or delayed payment) for energy consumption by state-dependent entities such as schools, hospitals, government buildings, etc. The below-cost pricing of electricity for household consumers constitutes another major form of subsidy which, however, has limited impact on the state budget, as it is cross-subsidized by all other consumer categories.

Investments in the energy sector have been supported by the State through the process of assuming *contingent liabilities*. The National Electricity Company (NEK) and DH companies have received state-guaranteed loans and/or (in the case of NEK) guarantee of performance under power-purchase contracts signed with plants. The existing legal and regulatory framework does not allow private investors or consumers of electricity to assume any significant market risk, thus expressly leaving a significant portion of investment risk with the Government.

Bulgaria has taken important steps over the last three years to reduce the operating subsidies to DH and coal entities, adjust tariffs, increase the transparency of sector operations, and amend the legal framework to facilitate the commercialization of the energy sector. While subsidies, both direct and quasi-fiscal, have been reduced, this has been accompanied by: (i) an increase in household

---

[33] For a more detailed discussion, see Chapter 10 of Part Two.

demand for costly electricity; (ii) excessive government attention on building new plants to meet future electricity demand, instead of developing policies to promote a more efficient and rational use of energy; and (iii) government reluctance to liberalize investment decisions and to allow consumers (particularly large industries) and investors to take on a greater share of investment and supply risks, as well as rewards. Furthermore, the failure to modernize the DH facilities and to enforce payment for DH services (due to the legal barriers and technical difficulty of disconnecting individual consumers) has delayed the further commercialization and privatization of this subsector.

Recommendations

Actions are needed to bring the energy sector and legislation in line with EU directives. Management and strengthening public administration are vital to the overall process. This will allow the process to be internalized and ongoing to meet different, changing and emerging priorities.

The first and most pressing priority in the energy sector—to separate policy-making, economic regulation and ownership functions—has been achieved to a considerable degree with the recent amendments to the Energy and Energy Efficiency Act. Now the challenge is to consolidate all regulatory functions in the State Energy Regulatory Commission and improve its stature and competence, which would contribute to a better balancing of consumer and supplier long-term interests.

In mid-2002, the State Energy Regulatory Commission (SERC) adopted a schedule of electricity price adjustments aimed at bringing electricity prices to full cost recovery levels in the next three years (2002–04). Complementing this price adjustment schedule, the Government adopted two mechanisms to protect the poor by: (i) expanding the winter energy subsidy program which supplements the winter income of low-income families; and (ii) by adopting a two-tier price system whereby a subsidized tariff will be maintained for a life-line level of consumption until 2005, and a higher tariff is applied to consumption above this level. The next pressing issue is to implement these electricity price adjustments to reach full-cost recovery by end-2004, eliminate these costly distortions; and monitor the targeting of the mechanisms aimed at easing the burden on low income and vulnerable households. In addition, in areas not served by district heating, the development of low-pressure natural gas services should be a priority in order to facilitate consumer choice for more efficient and clean space heating. However, it is critical to delay costly investment in new power and heat generation capacity until regulatory reforms are more advanced and investors (especially those investing in new capacity for export) can assume a larger share of the market risk under a suitable regulatory framework.

Closer attention needs to be given also to investments in the energy sector—their volume, mix, selection, planning and programming, and financing. Significant investments are needed to rehabilitate power generation plants, to modernize transmission and distribution systems, to develop a much needed low-pressure gas system, to modernize and rehabilitate the district heating system in several areas of the country, and to rehabilitate some of the coal mines. (Cost estimate of these requirements are provided in Chapter 10.) In this connection, the State needs to:

- Strengthen its analytical and planning capacity to ensure that vital investments, whether publicly or privately financed, are undertaken to support clear and well-justified public objectives.
- Accelerate cost-effective rehabilitation of existing assets, ideally through privatization, even if this requires substantial state support in the interim.
- Defer investment in new power and heat generation capacity until regulatory reforms are more advanced and investors (especially those investing in new capacity for export) can assume a larger share of the market risk under a suitable regulatory framework.
- Liberalize investment decisions related to supplying industry and large commercial customers; these should be allowed to contract the bulk of their needs of gas and electricity from private suppliers, including from abroad.

CHAPTER 4

INSTITUTIONAL CHALLENGES IN PUBLIC EXPENDITURE MANAGEMENT

The previous chapter discusses sectoral and expenditure reform priorities in a number of key sectors. Nevertheless, undertaking a thorough review of expenditure policy in Bulgaria would require a similar detailed analysis across the entire budget, subjecting all sector programs and policies to a vigorous, detailed and systematic review. This, of course, is beyond the realm of this Report. This chapter, therefore, focuses on institutional and expenditure management priorities in budget processes, which would enhance the Government's own ability to undertake a detailed review of expenditure policies and programs.

In all countries, reallocating and rationalizing expenditures requires a political and technocratic process that determines strategic priorities for the Government. Therefore, a crucial element of public sector reform is a reform of budgetary management processes. This reform should ensure that institutional arrangements and processes are put in place to allow policy makers to make strategic choices based on an informed analysis of public expenditure issues, to transform these choices into actions, to ensure that budget expenditures are monitored and audited, and to make budgetary choices and outcomes transparent to all elements of society. As a result of the macroeconomic and financial crisis of 1996–97, Bulgaria began the process of budgetary management reform and has now made significant progress in ensuring aggregate fiscal discipline and in budget execution and financial controls.

This chapter examines issues with regard to public expenditure management. After a brief introduction (Section A), Section B discusses the current budget preparation process and reforms to improve the process of budget formulation. Section C looks at budget execution, accounting and auditing—areas where Bulgaria has made significant strides as part of the imposition of fiscal discipline in the post-crisis period—yet areas also where progress is still required, especially to meet EU requirements. Finally, Section D describes issues of local government finance. Reforms in all of these areas are critical to meeting the allocative challenge laid in the first three chapters of this report.

Introduction

With the adoption of the Currency Board Arrangement in 1997, the Government of Bulgaria committed itself to strict fiscal discipline and initiated a number of public expenditure management reforms:

- The Budget and State Treasury Department in the Ministry of Finance has realigned its functions, restructured its organization and strengthened its staff.
- The structure of budget units is being rationalized and their number reduced.
- A Treasury Single Account at the Central Bank has been set up and is gradually being extended to include all budget units and funds.
- A revised chart of accounts, which is broadly consistent with the standards of the EU and the revised Government Finance Statistics (GFS) Manual of the IMF, has been approved and is being implemented. A financial management information system is being introduced.
- Bulgaria has also strengthened the legal and administrative framework for financial control: (i) the role and responsibilities of the Public Internal Financial Control Agency have been clearly defined under a new law approved in 2000; and (ii) a substantial reform in the procurement legislation was initiated, by law, in 1999.

As a result of these and related reforms, Bulgaria has established appropriate institutional and implementation arrangements to ensure aggregate fiscal discipline; effective control over cash flows has been ensured; and aggregate public expenditures have been held under tight financial control. As a result of these improvements, in January 2000, Bulgaria became the first EU accession candidate accredited to manage Special Accession Program for Agriculture and Rural Development (SAPARD) funds under the same guidelines as EU member states. Despite this important progress, there is a need to continue and to broaden the reform effort into the areas of better prioritizing budgetary allocations according to strategic priorities and improving the efficiency and effectiveness of expenditures. There are three areas—discussed below—where the reform effort should be concentrated: (i) budget formulation; (ii) budget execution, accounting and auditing; and (iii) financial management at the local government level.

Budget Formulation

Current Situation and Issues

Until recently, the budget formulation process in Bulgaria started with the preparation of macroeconomic projections and the setting of fiscal targets in June, and was concluded with the review and approval of the sectoral requests by the MOF in October and the submission of the draft budget to the National Assembly shortly thereafter. The process has proven effective in ensuring aggregate fiscal discipline under the oversight of the MOF, which was properly empowered to supervise the process. Yet the process has had a number of weaknesses as regards allocative efficiency, in particular: (i) spending agencies did not normally take into account financial constraints when preparing their budget requests and failed to prioritize their programs; (ii) the budgeting process did not allow the Government to make the appropriate trade-offs among investments and between current and capital expenditures. The practice has been to place an overall ceiling on investment expenditures, and making the intersectoral allocations of capital and current expenditures independently of each other; (iii) the investment programming processes have been fragmented, with several central agencies being involved; (iv) little information has been available—or used—on the performance of existing programs, with the result that the budget has concentrated almost exclusively on financial compliance rather than achievement of objectives, or outcomes; and (v) spending agencies have been hindered by a lack of standards or methodology for project appraisal, as well as a weak capacity in this area.

Recently (early 2002) the Government introduced a number of changes in the budget preparation procedures to make the process more strategic and to involve the line ministries more and earlier in the budget formulation process. The changes aim especially at improving intersectoral allocation. These changes are being introduced starting with the 2003 budget. They include: preparation of a "budget policy paper" defining intersectoral priorities and estimating the fiscal impact of policy changes; issuing improved guidelines earlier in the year; adoption of a revised preparation calendar; setting detailed expenditure ceilings; requesting multi-year expenditure estimates; and prioritizing of programs by spending agencies. Together, the changes represent the first steps toward performance-based budgeting. The procedures will need to be revised after at least a year's experience with implementation.

To further improve the budget preparation process and to achieve the desired results from the recent reform of budget preparation, the Government needs to consider further reforms in five areas:

(a) Making the underlying macroeconomic framework more robust;
(b) Developing a programmatic approach;
(c) Enhancing the multi-year approach to budgeting;
(d) Incorporating investment planning more fully in the process; and,
(e) Improving the budget documentation.

Several changes are needed in the preparation of the macroeconomic framework to facilitate making the budget process more robust. While CBA has been effective in imposing fiscal discipline, it leaves limited room for accommodating potential fiscal risks. Bulgaria's ability to absorb fiscal risk is limited. To show the medium-term implications of fiscal risks for the overall fiscal position, the baseline medium-term projections prepared for the budget could be supplemented with various scenarios taking into account specific risks and possible variations of economic parameters, such as interest rates or the exchange rate. They should include debt scenarios and discuss the potential future impact of contingent liabilities. Guarantees and implicit promises of contingent government support should be subject to the same scrutiny as budgetary programs. In particular, the non-guaranteed debt of public enterprises and guarantees or other initiatives of local government that present fiscal risks need to be monitored. To ensure that policy makers adequately reflect fiscal risks in their fiscal plans, they must become accountable for their analysis and assumptions. In order to increase the legitimacy of the macroeconomic framework, it is advisable to make it widely available. External reviews of the macroeconomic framework need to be institutionalized. The National Audit Office (NAO) and budget reports should comment on, and evaluate ex post, government risk analyses and risk management. The Government should encourage competing analyses from the academic community and the private sector.

The Government has also taken steps to introduce a programmatic approach, particularly with a view to strengthening the budget-policy link. The Ministry of Defense has been developing and following such a program on a pilot basis since 1999. The experience is encouraging, and a similar budgeting program will be initiated in the environment sector in 2003. According to a Council of Ministers decision in January 2002, spending agencies are to prepare sectoral MTBFs at the initial stage of the 2003 budget preparation cycle. The global MTBF will be included in the documents presented to Parliament. While there may be some data constraints to proceeding with these plans, they seem to be exceeded by capacity constraints that need to be overcome.

The medium-term perspective of the budget can be developed by extending the medium-term framework to include sectoral and sub-national disaggregations. Completing the macroeconomic exercise with the preparation of a rolling Medium-Term Budget Framework (MTBF) that includes multi-year expenditure estimates by line ministry and/or by program will reinforce the budget-policy link. A start has been made with Decision No. 96 of January 2002, spending agencies will prepare sectoral MTBFs at the initial stage of the budget preparation cycle. These MTBFs will provide information on sectoral policies to the Council of Ministers to help in establishing intersectoral resource allocations. In 2003, further improvements could consist of strengthening the strategic and initial phase of budget preparation through setting up sectoral multi-year ceilings that are consistent with the fiscal projections of the macroeconomic framework to frame both the budget and MTBF preparation. They could then be reviewed by the Council of Ministers, together with the budget policy paper. The line ministries and sub-national governments that prepare program-budgets would do that within these medium-term expenditure ceilings. The MTBF should also be included in the budgetary documents presented to Parliament.

One area where the budget formulation process has especially been weak is investment planning. Pressure to limit the budget deficit in earlier years resulted in under-investment, mis-investment or excessive postponement of capital spending. Inefficiencies in investment evaluation and programming have contributed to this; in fact, investment programming has emerged as one of the weakest aspects of budget formulation. Currently, in Bulgaria, project appraisal is often understood as an engineering analysis, and capacity for microeconomic analysis—to question project proposals and to assess their social and economic benefits—is usually weak. Staff in the Ministry of Finance are inundated with a voluminous amount of technical documents of limited usefulness, with little capacity to synthesize, evaluate or prioritize. Similarly, investment planning and programming is also weak in a number of specific sectors, especially transport and energy, as demonstrated in the sector summaries that follow.

Budgetary information presented to Parliament should include all the elements needed to assess government fiscal policy and its future impact. The current budgetary documentation includes a statement of budget policy, supplemented with a number of annexes, but information on the ministry objectives and the expected results is lacking. Ideally, the budgetary documents should include:

- policy statements;
- medium-term fiscal projections;
- narrative statements and indicators on the main programs;
- medium-term expenditure estimates over the MTBF period;
- a statement on contingent liabilities and an estimate of payments likely to be required under those guarantees during the budget year and the MTBF period; and
- a statement on tax changes.

The budgetary documents are made public by posting them on the web-site of the Ministry of Finance. However, further progress in the quality of published documents is desirable in order to make them more instructive and accessible to ordinary citizens through, for example, disseminating a "budget brief."

Recommendations

The thrust of future reforms of the budget preparation process should be designed to develop a *more robust and comprehensive budget preparation process that is medium-term in outlook, more strategically focused, and performance oriented*. While a good start has been made with the changes in the budget preparation process for 2003, further efforts are needed. The four principal areas for reform are:

To consolidate overall fiscal control and improve transparency:

- develop analyses of contingent liabilities and fiscal risks; and
- reinforce the status of the macroeconomic framework, through notably making macro-economic projections public and encouraging external reviews of the macroeconomic framework.

To improve resource allocation:

- design streamlined budget preparation processes, including an associated calendar and procedures. The modernized procedures would include: (i) preparation of a three-year rolling Medium-Term Budget Framework (MTBF); (ii) preparation and cabinet review of a policy paper and initial ceilings to frame the budget and MTBF preparation; (iii) strengthened coordination between annual budget preparation and investment programming; and (iv) improved format and content of budget submissions prepared by line ministries;

- prepare a plan for implementing MTBF activities and the modernized budget preparation processes; organize appropriate seminars and training on implementation;
- develop capacities in project appraisal by establishing guidelines for project screening and evaluation and organizing training, seminars, etc.; and
- prepare an MTBF investment annex, under "hard budget constraint."

To develop a "performance concern":

- extend progressively the program-budgeting exercises to all major line ministries.

To contribute to public scrutiny and confidence:

- improve the budgetary documentation and its dissemination so as to make the budget accessible to the wide public.

Budget Execution, Accounting and Auditing

Current Situation

The Government has introduced important reforms in budget execution. It has implemented a Treasury Single Account (TSA) at the Central Bank. The first-level spending units, the extra-budgetary funds and the second-level spending units make their payments through the TSA, by submitting payment orders to the Central Bank. The MOF has established a system that allows all other budget units to submit their payment orders through zero-balance accounts in commercial banks. Such arrangements present the advantage of keeping cash under control and allow efficient cash management, while maintaining a certain degree of decentralization in budget management. Bankservice, which is responsible for inter-bank settlements, has developed a simple scheme for the monitoring and control of the payment orders from the budget units. Its information system allows the first-level units to monitor the flow of payment orders and to stop orders that would go beyond the payment limits they have distributed to their subordinate units.

The Government is, moreover, implementing an integrated Financial Management Information System (FMIS). All budget units will have electronic links with the MOF and access the FMIS through these links. The first implementation phase of the FMIS is completed; it covers the first-level spending agencies. The second implementation phase was expected to start in 2002. The FMIS currently includes accounting, budget control and cash management modules. Assets management and cost accounting modules will be developed during the second implementation phase, as well as electronic links with the banks.

For the purpose of managing EU assistance, a National Fund has been established. The National Fund is a central treasury entity within the MOF. EU funds are transferred to the National Fund accounts through the respective servicing bank, where there exists a separate account for each financial memorandum and a separate sub-account for each project. However, these accounts are not yet fully integrated into the budget. Moreover, so far, foreign exchange deposit accounts are kept outside the TSA. To improve transparency, facilitate decision making and fiscal control, such accounts should be integrated into the TSA, although under special management procedures in order to take into account their specificity.

The MOF has established agreements with the commercial banks regarding processing payments, but the banking arrangements for collecting revenues should also be reviewed with a view to establishing strict requirements for processing times within the banks.

In 1998, a substantial reform of the procurement legislation was initiated, and a new Public Procurement Law was enacted in June 1999. The role and responsibilities of the Public Internal Financial Control Agency have been clearly defined in the Public Internal Financial Control Act passed in 2000. An audit law was presented to Parliament in 2001. However, setting up the legal framework and organization arrangements is only the first step in improving financial control, which needs time and continuous efforts. Also, the legal framework has to be complemented with secondary or tertiary legislation.

A new chart of accounts on a cash and accrual basis is being implemented on a partial accrual basis. This chart of accounts is broadly consistent with EU standards ESA95 and the 2002 Government Finance Statistics manual.

During budget implementation, cash releases are tightly controlled. Monthly cash plans are established; in addition, the MOF issues cash limits for the budget units on a weekly basis. Currently, the MOF releases budget funds on the basis of only 90 percent of budget appropriations. During the fourth quarter, the Cabinet can review progress in budget implementation and decide whether and how to release the balance. This measure is aimed at keeping budget execution under control. However, it weakens the function of the budget as central instrument for resource allocation. It can even have a perverse effect, because competing claims can arise when this reserve is used, not necessarily in conformity with the budgeted appropriations.

Directions for Further Improvement

Actions already initiated need to be pursued. All accounts, including foreign exchange accounts, should be integrated in the TSA. Banking arrangements for revenue collection should be reviewed. In particular, there should be strict requirements for processing times within the banks, and penalties should be promptly imposed on any attempts by the banks to create float. The structure of bank accounts should be simplified to facilitate management and ensure effective improvements in transparency, control and efficiency. All government bank accounts should be included in the TSA, including foreign exchange accounts and donor accounts. Special procedures must be designed to manage donor accounts in line with their requirements.

For both financial control and operational performance, actions to modernize procurement and personnel management must be pursued. Further refinement of the procurement systems is needed, including simplification of arbitration procedures, implementation of Procurement Units, development of extensive training program, and amendment to the current legislation to ensure its full compatibility with EU standards. Concerning personnel management, it would be necessary both to strengthen the financial control of personnel expenditures and to set up systems that provide incentives to improve performance.

Improvements in budget preparation and financial control should allow the MOF to abandon some of its practices which are aimed at controlling budget execution, but which present inconveniences for program management. The budget should include a contingency reserve which, except for special circumstances, should also be executed on the basis of the voted appropriations. As improvements become ingrained in the system, the practice of planning cash payments on the basis of 90 percent of budgeted funds, and reviewing the allocation of the remaining funds in the last quarter, can be gradually relaxed and over time, abandoned.

The consolidation of funds into the TSA eliminates the risk that spending units keep idle balances in their bank accounts. Therefore, the cash limits issued weekly by the MOF should be shifted to a monthly basis.

The MOF has the authority to approve the allocation of capital expenditure, including the itemized lists of projects. If, during the budget year, a first-level spending unit wishes to reallocate budget line items, it must seek permission from the MOF, although the regulation governing this is interpreted in a flexible manner. While internal management should be reinforced, it is important to focus MOF controls on the key issues, and avoid involving the MOF in detailed controls, which are often purely pro forma. Of course, such flexibility should concern only the activities or the projects that meet the same set of objectives. Increasing managerial flexibility should go hand-in-hand with actions to strengthen procurement and personnel management systems and internal financial control.

Line ministries and local governments should participate in the preparation of performance reports, including indicators on the results achieved with a view to providing feedback to decision making, developing within agencies a learning-by-doing process through the monitoring of results and accountability for results.

Bulgaria has established the legal and institutional arrangements for auditing, both internal and external. Regarding the latter, a National Audit Office was established in 1995; it is independent from the executive branch of the government; it reports to the National Assembly; and the National Assembly elects its chairman and members. For internal audit, a Public Agency for Internal Control was established and its role was clarified in the State Internal Financial Control Act, which became effective on January 1, 2001. This Act, which has brought the legal and institutional framework in line with EU accession criteria as specified in Chapter 28 of the "*acquis*," is, however, not yet fully implemented. The director of the agency reports directly to the Minister of Finance and the director oversees the activities of "delegated auditors," which are to be established in each first-line budget unit, including 28 regional level administrations. Whereas the external audit function by the National Audit Office is working, the system of internal audit, which is a crucial element of financial control, is still far from fully staffed and effective. In early January 2002, delegated auditors had only been established in four ministries: Agriculture, Finance, Education, and Health.

Summary of Recommendations

To strengthen control over budget execution:

- pursue the implementation of the Treasury Single Account, and the implementation of the GFMIS;
- strengthen financial control (complete the secondary legislation for financial control, organize internal audit services, etc.);
- complete the staffing and make effective the process of internal audit; and,
- strengthen the role of the NAO, enhancing in particular, its capacity to carry out performance audit.

To improve efficiency in program management:

- release funds on a monthly basis (instead of weekly basis);
- release funds on the basis of the budget, phasing out the 90 percent rule as more efficient financial control practices become strengthened over time; and
- increase the degree of flexibility granted to line ministries but, in parallel, reinforce internal control; require line ministries to report on their operational performance.

Reforming Local Government Finances

The territory of Bulgaria is divided into 263 municipalities and 28 regions. Municipalities are the basic administrative territorial unit at the level of which self-government is practiced. Self-government is regulated at this level through the 1991 Local Government and Local Administration Act. Municipalities are legal persons, entitled to own municipal property, and to have their own budgets. The municipal council and the mayor are directly elected by the citizens. The "regions," on the other hand, are administrative territorial units of the central government. They are entrusted with the conduct of regional policy, the implementation of state policy at the local level, and ensuring the coordination of national and local interests. Each region is headed by a regional governor, who is appointed by the Council of Ministers.

Current Situation

Municipal budgets face serious difficulties. Each year local governments accumulate arrears and must be helped at the end of the year by the central government. In 2000, municipalities required the equivalent of 1 percent of GDP more in central government support than budgeted. The problems arise partly from weak management capacity and financial control within a number of municipalities, but they stem in large part from a mismatch between expenditure and revenue assignments. The Government is currently addressing these issues by developing and implementing a program to reduce and eliminate these arrears in 2003 within the framework of the fiscal decentralization program.

Expenditures.   There is no one best way for deciding which level of government should be responsible for the provision of particular government services. Generally, the efficient provision of government services requires that governments satisfy the needs and preferences of taxpayers as effectively as possible. This is best achieved by the "subsidiarity" principle. According to this principle, responsibility for the provision of services should be at the lowest level of government compatible with the size of "benefit area" associated with those services.

On the whole, the current expenditure assignments would fit this principle. The functions allocated to the central government have a national dimension (for example, defense), while most of the expenditure responsibilities of municipalities involve services with local benefit areas (for example, primary education). Nevertheless, the current expenditure assignment arrangements are not satisfactory, notably because the delimitation of responsibilities between the different levels of government is unclear.

The NAO has estimated that 90 percent or so of municipal expenditures are for services and administrative functions that are mandated by the national government and over which the municipal government exercises very little control. The extensive use of "shared" service mandates is a problem in matching expenditure assignment with revenue authority. Municipalities are responsible for meeting part of the costs of services over which, effectively, they have very limited control. Moreover, service mandates can change from year to year and be unrealistic due to poor coordination among central ministries. For example, for the year 2000 budget, the MOF based its estimates of transfers to municipalities on assumptions about reductions in the number of teachers. However, because the number of teachers in each school dictated by the Ministry of Education was not reduced in time, municipalities were left with unfunded teacher positions. Clearly, local governments need more predictability for the efficient management of their resources.

The need to cut back total expenditure has led sometimes to downloading the budget deficit to local governments through unfunded mandates. In addition, until the fiscal year 2000, the State Budget Act contained a set of priorities for goods and services that municipal governments should cover with their own revenues first, and municipalities were legally limited to spending only 10 percent of their MOF-designated own revenues on additional investment (above the amount of the grant targeted to investment). This arrangement has had perverse impacts. It has created the incentive to drive up current expenditures and increased the lobbying for central government capital subsidies.

At the end of the fiscal year, unused investment appropriations financed by the targeted investment subsidy lapse and cannot be carried over. To avoid losing their subsidy rights, municipalities are often authorized by the MOF to finance current expenditures with the unused portion of the investment subsidy. This leads to increasing current expenditures to the detriment of investment. Carrying-over should be authorized for investment expenditure, subject to MOF approval.

All public services with a regional or inter-municipal dimension are assigned either to the central government (or central government enterprises, for example, in the case of water supply) or to municipalities. Many municipalities pay for facilities that serve the population of surrounding municipalities, particularly schools and social care facilities. The funding for these services does not recognize the nature of the inter-jurisdictional costs. In the health sector, this issue is being addressed by removing most health care expenditures from municipal budgets. However, such distortions will remain for health care facilities still owned by the municipalities after the health care financing reform and in other sectors, notably education.

The subsidiarity principle mentioned above must be balanced with other considerations such as the administrative capacities of local governments, regional equity, and the redistributive responsibilities of the Government. Expenditures undertaken for equity or income equalization reasons, such as social welfare, should be the domain of the central government. Municipalities fund a part of social welfare payments from their own revenues. Funding this mandate creates significant disparities in expenditure needs across municipalities. In 1998, welfare payments ranged from 1.0 percent of municipal revenues in Sofia to 22.9 percent in Straldzha; the national average was 6 percent. Municipalities are often unable to pay the amount required for social assistance benefits. The Government is addressing this problem; the part of social welfare payments financed by municipalities' own revenues has been reduced from 50 percent in 2001 to 25 percent in 2002. This effort should be continued with the objective of funding fully social welfare payments from central government revenues in 2003. Progress in this direction is already taking place as the fiscal decentralization program (see Box 4.1) envisages centralizing the financing of the social assistance program in 2003 while local financing will cover social care services only.

Revenues.   Local governments have three main sources of revenue: (i) taxes shared between the central government and local governments, which consist of the corporate income tax (CIT) and the personal income tax (PIT); (ii) central government subsidies; and (iii) own revenue sources which include local taxes, fees and other revenues. The Government is planning to centralize fully the CIT, leaving only the PIT as a revenue source for the local government starting as early as 2003.

The largest proportion of municipal revenue comes from shared taxes, whose yield is uneven across municipalities. The corporate income tax contributes approximately 30 percent of total municipal revenues and the personal income tax 40 percent. The revenues from the PIT are channeled to local budgets according to the taxpayer's place of work. This poses problems when residents of one municipality work in another, because these people use public services according to their residence but pay taxes to another municipality. Similarly, the current allocation of the CIT is based on the location of company, which results in a windfall to some municipalities and a disadvantage to others, especially those where the workers reside.

Transfers from the central government consist of: (i) targeted grants for investment projects; (ii) special purpose grants for social assistance, which generally cover 50 percent of expenditure needs; and (iii) a general subsidy. The general grant is calculated by a formula that includes equalizing elements. According to the formula used for the budget, this transfer is defined as the algebraic sum of: (i) the costs of the "mandatory budget spending" (salaries, social security and health contributions for the poor and scholarships); (ii) social assistance benefits; *less* (iii) tax revenues of local government; *plus* (iv) a grant calculated by using "objective criteria" such as the number of pupils, classes, size of the municipality, number of patients served in specialized public health facilities, etc.; (v) an equalizing element for guaranteeing a minimum bottom threshold for the financial support of the central government; and (vi) subsidy earmarked for capital expenditure.

The elimination of the non-tax revenues is done with the purpose of limiting government intervention in determining the amount of non-tax revenues and the way they are spent. The municipalities' contribution to the tax revenues is significantly less than to the non-tax revenues. Up to 2000, the methodology for subsidy allocation to municipalities did not provide incentives to municipalities to raise higher non-tax revenues. The higher the own revenues of municipality (tax and non-tax) were expected, the lower was the subsidy provided to municipality. In addition, instead of financing community services by entirely own revenues (garbage fees and property income tax), a greater part of these were used for financing the mandatory expenditures—wages and salaries, social insurance contributions, and social assistance benefits. For the first time in 2001, the formula for intergovernmental transfers excluded half of the municipal non-tax revenues

BOX 4.1 FISCAL DECENTRALIZATION CONCEPT AND PROGRAM, 2002–2005

Following the COM approval of the Fiscal Decentralization Concept in March 2002, a program for its implementation was developed and endorsed by the Government in June 2002. This is the first serious attempt to further the process of decentralization in Bulgaria which would require a number of amendments to existing legislation.

The Fiscal Decentralization Concept sets out the main objectives, principles and areas for reforms, while the Program defines the timeframe for implementation of the reform. The main areas for reform aiming at efficiency and equity in delivery of public services are the following:

1. *Efficiency in public expenditure management*
   - Clear rules for division of expenditure responsibilities agreed between the MOF, line ministries, municipalities, and NAMRB;
   - Standards for staffing levels, average wages and maintenance of public services provided at municipal level (education, health, social protection, and culture);
   - Program for gradual reduction of municipal arrears which makes distinction between arrears accrued on centrally mandated or municipal services;
   - Centralizing social assistance benefits while social care services are to be financed by the municipalities;
   - Improvement in municipal budget planning and execution through a number of legislative changes.
2. *Match revenue allocation with expenditure needs*
   - Change in the current formula for calculating the subsidy granted to municipalities to allow a clearer and more transparent division of revenue and expenditure assignments;
   - Financing centrally mandated services from shared taxes, while revenues from local taxes and fees are to be used for financing the delivery of municipal services;
   - Capital subsidy to be reallocated to financing regional projects under the EU pre-accession funds as well as to municipalities with insufficient revenue bases.
3. *Incentives for better revenue collection*
   - Granting authority to local governments in determining local taxes autonomously, and expanding the scope of local taxes;
   - Retaining a portion of the higher than planned revenues from shared taxes by municipalities.
4. *Fiscal discipline and compliance*
   - Borrowing allowed only for investment purposes with clear rules and procedures for municipal borrowing;
   - Procedures for approval, repayment and writing-off interest-free loans granted to municipalities;
   - Procedures for ensuring the enforcement of fiscal discipline and measures to cope with municipalities in poor financial state.
5. *Other areas*
   - Greater citizens' participation in the planning and execution of municipal budgets;
   - Evaluation of impact of the fiscal decentralization program each year;
   - Criteria for assessment of capacity needs and provision of adequate training;
   - Improvement in information systems and accounting standards;
   - Assessment of the planned legislative changes to ensure consistency with existing legislation;
   - Incentives to encourage the use of good management practices.

subsidy for covering the mandatory expenditures (for municipalities which are also regional centers, all non-tax revenues are excluded).

The next steps will be to set apart municipal activities which would be financed by non-tax revenues entirely, and the Government will not interfere at all in the planning and execution stage for these activities.

The formula annexed to the 2002[34] budget is clearer than the formula used before 2001, and has the advantage of taking into account mandatory expenditures. Nevertheless, further improvements are needed. The provision of funds covering the full amount of wages risks fossilizing the distribution of current spending between wage and non-wage expenditures. The fact that local taxes are negative components in the formula used to calculate the transfer does not induce local governments to take measures to improve revenue collection, since they will be penalized if their revenues increase. However, the framework of the fiscal decentralization concept developed in early 2002 includes an entirely new approach for calculating the state subsidy to municipalities to address these deficiencies. The principles underpinning this new approach aim at simplifying and making more transparent the rules governing inter-governmental finances.

The tax revenues of local governments are based on the revenue forecasts of the budget. The central government gives a compensatory grant to the municipalities to cover the amount by which collected revenues are inferior to budget forecasts. In turn, municipalities have to pay back to the central government tax revenues in excess of budget forecasts. Such a provision runs the risk of favoring unduly the municipalities for which revenues have been overestimated and provides little incentive to increase revenues. The overall "surplus" (tax revenues in excess of budget forcasts) is partly redistributed among the municipalities, but criteria for the redistribution are unclear. The fiscal decentralization program includes measures to address these issues.

The legal framework itself provides little incentive to increase revenues. According to the Constitution, all local taxes must be specified in full detail by statutes voted by Parliament. Therefore, the definition of the taxable object, the permitted exemptions, and the authorized rates are set in national legislation. In addition, a number of fee rates are also centrally determined. As a result, municipalities' own revenues are weak and account for only around 15 percent of total municipal revenues. The Government has indicated its intention to grant more authority to municipalities in determining municipal taxes (see Box 4.1).

Finally, there is little predictability in the system of central government transfers, both for general budget support and for targeted investments, which are set up in the annual budget act and can change from year to year. Such a situation impedes sound expenditure programming at the local level and hampers efficiency in management.

Borrowing and Arrears.   Unpaid bills accounted for 11 percent of municipal revenues at the end of the 1999 budget year. Since then, the stock of unpaid bills has been more or less stable, but the central government has provided additional grants to pay unpaid bills. Such practices do not encourage fiscal discipline, but they inevitably result from the significant mismatch between expenditure assignments and revenues.

The legal framework for municipal borrowing is unclear. The 1991 Local Self-Government and Local Administration Act contains a clear prohibition against borrowing to fund general operating expenses, but the 1998 Municipal Budgets Act authorizes municipalities to borrow up to 10 percent of total revenues to fund a planned budget deficit. This last provision can enable municipalities to borrow for financing current expenditures. In practice, a number of municipalities include borrowing forecasts in their budget without any realistic expectation of contracting such a loan and without capacity to repay. Municipalities that resort to this practice do so in the expectation of converting the "loan" amount into an extraordinary MOF subsidy allocation at year-end. There is at present no clear reporting on the full outstanding debt and contingent liabilities of local governments. The fiscal decentralization framework of the Government envisages clear rules and procedures for municipal borrowing—proposed amendments to the Municipal Budgets Act would rule out borrowing to finance current expenditures.

---

[34] Further changes to the formula were introduced in the 2002 budget. All non-tax revenues of municipalities were excluded from the calculation of the transfer, providing municipalities with additional resources which can be used to finance operations and maintenance of non-mandatory activities.

A number of local governments have created a public-private partnership company to engage in economic activity entirely unrelated to the provision of essential public services. In most of these cases, the municipal equity contribution is made in the form of municipal private property or cash. The commercial risk of losing the municipal equity contribution is usually far greater than the expected profits or dividends (which on average represent 0.1 percent of municipal revenues).

Directions for Reform

Whatever the degree of devolution, for the sake of transparency and efficiency, the following basic principles should be applied:

- There should be a clear assignment of functions among the levels of government, with a corresponding delegation of authority to make decisions over the manner, quality and quantity of services.
- Fiscal and revenue sharing arrangements between the central and local governments should be stable and predictable.
- Revenue assignment should be consistent with expenditure assignment. Downloading the fiscal deficit should not be permitted. Mechanisms for adjusting revenues, when expenditure requirements change, are required.
- Incentives to increase efficiency in delivering services at the local level are needed. Increased flexibility should be granted to local government in allocating resources between investment and current spending. Incentives should be provided to mobilize revenues at the local level.

All municipal activities should be divided into two categories: (i) centrally mandated services; and (ii) services provided at local discretion. Operating costs for centrally mandated services, which include basic municipal services, public education services and social and dependent population service, should be financed at a basic level by central government transfers, whether shared taxes or subsidies. A fiscal decentralization working group has been reviewing the division of activities providing useful input to policy makers. A special protocol which was signed by line ministries, the MOF, and municipalities, including the National Association of Municipalities, commits them to work together to define clearly inter-governmental responsibilities. This is providing momentum for important reforms.

The funding and management of public services with a regional or inter-municipal dimension should be reviewed. The estimates of transfers from the central government must take due account of the costs of these services. There is also a need to assess in some sectors, such as water supply, whether special inter-municipal cooperation arrangements can be set up to provide services with a regional or inter-municipal dimension or to supervise their provision.

Responsibilities for capital infrastructure should be placed with the level of government responsible for operation and maintenance. The responsibilities of municipalities in investment budgeting and programming should be increased for those functions assigned to them. Measures adopted for the 2002 budget go in this direction: 50 percent of the targeted subsidy will be allocated among projects by the municipalities themselves. The capital costs of newly corporatized health services should be transferred to the new entities responsible for those services. Before the transfer of full capital budgeting responsibilities to local government is implemented, it is essential to carry out an extensive training program for local budget officials, covering multi-year budgeting, project appraisal techniques, tendering, and contracting.

The central government should encourage and reward, rather than discourage, local efforts to generate additional revenues for themselves. A certain degree of authority should be granted to municipalities over the definition of the tax base (especially, the power to restrict exemptions and to close loopholes), as well as the rates of local taxes, notably the property tax, the vehicle tax and the patent tax. Municipalities should be able to establish freely the tax rates, but within a range of applicable rates stipulated in a statute. To this end, it will be necessary to amend the legal framework. Municipalities should also be given the authority to determine the services on which they will charge fees, the types of fees to be imposed, the rates, the base, and the collection process. Fee calculations should be based on full cost recovery, where practicable. Detailed recommendations on the reform of the local tax and fees system have already been prepared by the Municipal Finance Project supported by USAID. They provide the basis for drawing up and implementing an action plan to improve local revenues. The fiscal decentralization program of 2002–05 incorporates several of these recommendations (see Box 4.1).

All the above measures are aimed at increasing the responsibilities of local government in budget management. This will require setting up proper systems for accountability and promoting performance. The level of basic services should be defined and monitored. A system of sanctions should be set up in case of misuse of the funds provided to finance the mandated basic services. For example, lessening central government control on capital expenditures could be tied to an effective provision of basic services according to some standards agreed between the State and the municipalities, or the general grant could include a bonus that will be transferred under certain conditions. The Government is developing standards for staffing levels, average salaries and maintenance in education, social assistance, health, and culture.

Financial control and audit must be effective. The territorial offices of the Public Internal Financial Control Agency and the NAO should audit the effectiveness of the internal management control systems within municipalities and make appropriate recommendations.

It should be clearly stipulated that long-term borrowing is authorized only for capital investment, any temporary borrowing for cash management should be repayable within the fiscal year. A number of EU countries have adopted a "golden rule" which stipulates that the current budget of local governments must be balanced. Moreover, in some of these countries a provision for depreciation is included under expenses in calculating the local budget balance in order to make the "golden rule" stronger and ensure that municipalities will have self-financing capacity to renew equipment. The feasibility of implementing a system of sanctions/rewards to induce municipalities to enforce the "golden rule" should be assessed. The proposed approach in Bulgaria rules out borrowing to finance current expenditures providing greater clarity and discipline.

An improved system of public debt reporting is needed to provide more complete information on the outstanding debt (loans and bonds) of municipalities. Municipalities should be required to provide detailed information on each outstanding loan and bond, including amount borrowed or issued, debt stock, and fiscal risks, including those related to participation in private law companies. Within the context of the implementation of the new chart of accounts, municipalities are expected, and should be urged, to report their liabilities effectively. There has been important progress in this area as the fiscal decentralization program already incorporates these best international practice principles.

Summary of Recommendations

In the course of finalizing the PEIR of Bulgaria, the Government has initiated a reform of Bulgaria's intergovernmental relations. Some recommendations presented here have been already reflected in the fiscal decentralization program approved by the COM in mid-2002. The challenges going forward hinge upon the implementation of proposed reforms in a timely and systematic way. To increase efficiency in expenditure management, the reforms and their implementation should remain focused on:

- clarifying expenditure assignment with a view to avoiding fragmentation in management. Shared mandates should be generally eliminated or, at least, based on agreements defining clearly the responsibilities and duties of each actor;
- arranging for full funding of centrally-mandated and social assistance expenditures by the central government;
- rendering fiscal and revenue sharing arrangements between the central and local governments to make them stable and predictable, and specify them in a special legislation; include targeted capital subsidies in the MTBF;
- authorizing carrying over of investment expenditure (subject to MOF approval).

To limit distortions between revenue allocation and expenditure needs:

- review the issues related to the funding and management of public services with a regional or inter-municipal dimension.

To induce local governments to increase revenue collection:

- grant increased authority to local governments over local taxes and fees; implement a comprehensive reform of the local revenue system;
- build tax revenues estimates of local governments on the actual collection, instead of the revenue forecasts in the budget.

To enforce fiscal discipline and compliance:

- streamline the legal framework for borrowing, and strictly enforce the "golden rule" which stipulates that the current budgets of local governments must be balanced;
- put in place a sound reporting system for debt, contingencies and other fiscal risks, including municipalities' liabilities;
- regularly audit and reinforce management control systems within the municipalities.

And to develop expenditure programming and resource allocation:

- enhance the capacity for expenditure programming and management, and in particular for investment, within municipalities. The MOF should prepare proper guidance for project appraisal and investment programming.

CHAPTER 5

CLOSING THOUGHTS: CROSS-CUTTING ISSUES, OVERALL PRIORITIES AND AN AGENDA FOR FUTURE WORK

As noted at the outset of this Report, this is the first PEIR prepared for Bulgaria. The Report is not fully comprehensive, as its sectoral coverage is limited to five key sectors and many important areas have not been examined in detail. In the course of preparing this Report and during the ongoing dialogue with Government officials as the report was prepared, a number of issues arose that merit special attention or further examination. This concluding chapter of the main report attempts to pull these together. First, Section A discusses a number of cross-cutting issues that arise in nearly every sector and where government attention at the center is required to support reform at the sectoral level. Next, Section B discusses several overall priorities that should guide the Government's efforts at reform and which lie at the heart of the public finance challenge. Finally, Section C outlines a number of areas for future work in the ongoing process of expenditure reform. As with any PEIR, there are a number of issues which are not covered or which became important during the process of preparing this report that merit further attention and work. The priorities that this report identified are discussed and it is proposed that the Government, the World Bank and other donors look carefully at these areas in developing future work programs.

Cross-Cutting Issues

Cross-cutting issues as defined here are either specific issues that cut across two or more sectors or general issues that affect several sectors and, therefore, need to be addressed on many fronts. Practically all institutional issues cut across sectors and need not be repeated here. This is especially true of issues concerning budgeting, including programmatic and investment budgeting, the budget-investment link, and inter-governmental (central-local) financial relations. Other cross-cutting issues include:

- **State financial support,** namely, reducing dependence on state financing or stabilizing such financing; simplifying the support by both consolidating the plethora of programs, especially for social protection, and the formula for determining the level of support; choosing the most appropriate form or combination of support, e.g, among price support, income support, indirect support, etc.; and coping with conflicting needs within the same sectors. While there is scope for reducing state support practically in every area, the task is complicated by the coexistence, often, of a demand or need to raise state support for specific groups or undertakings. Typical of this challenge is the situation in the education, health and railway sectors where one encounters, side by side, both surplus capacity and under-investment, both benefits that are too high and benefits that are too low.

- **Role of the state.** The cross-cutting issues include: (i) the role of the different levels of government (central, regional, municipalities) in theory and in practice, i.e., decentralization as shaped by the political setting, capacity and financial constraints, etc.; (ii) the relations between the state and the municipalities, and the power and flexibility of line ministries and municipalities *in practice;* and (iii) efforts to devolve responsibilities to the private sector, to facilitate and induce entry by the private sector, especially in the transport and energy sectors.

- **Effectiveness of targeting.** Aside from the cost of targeting, the problems and challenges encountered in every sector include: (i) are the right groups targeted; (ii) are the individual households or people within the targeted groups (the poor, the vulnerable) properly identified; (iii) do the subsidies reach those households and people, do they help, are there abuses; (iv) are the levels of the assistance appropriate; and (v) are there problems in reaching the minorities, especially the Roma.

- **Service delivery.** The issues in common concern: (i) service quality; (ii) efficiency of delivery; and (iii) the variability of access and quality by region or municipality. The specific issues in each area depend on the sector and were identified in the individual sectoral discussions in Chapter 3.

- **EU accession requirements** Span a wide range of issue—legal, institutional, administrative and investment. In large part, government actions to meet EU accession criteria are non-controversial since there is a strong consensus behind the objective. However, addressing these issues will involve a considerable effort in nearly all sectors of the economy. In most cases, this effort will divert and dilute the resources available to undertake initiatives in other areas. This implies that the Government needs to examine existing programs carefully with a view towards eliminating unproductive ones and transferring responsibilities to the private sector where appropriate.

- **The special issue of investments.** Investments are a special case because while the issues are cross-cutting, they need to be addressed at both the central and the sector levels. While the problem is the overwhelming evidence of under-investment, the issues and obstacles concern: (i) the gross lack of knowledge of the state of infrastructure in several sectors, especially education, health and railway transport, i.e., of the impact of deferred maintenance for nearly a decade; (ii) the absence of a programmatic approach to investments—extending beyond the near-term; (iii) insufficient knowledge on the execution of the few ongoing investments; (iv) shortcomings of the investment selection process, insufficiently grounded on cost benefit analysis built on economic criteria; and (v) weak capacity in many areas.

In closing, one *caveat* is in order. The preponderance of cross-cutting issues does not imply that there is a proportionately large role for the central government to play in addressing them. On the contrary, many of the problems and issues highlighted arose because central government policies were designed and applied without sufficient attention to local conditions and preferences, and sector needs and constraints. What the issues point to, rather, is that municipalities should be given greater autonomy and flexibility in both decision making and expenditure allocation.

Overall Priorities

The overall or cross-cutting priorities include:

Completion of reforms that have already been initiated. As discussed throughout this Report, Bulgaria is in the midst of implementing major reforms in a number of areas, for example, pensions, education, health care, railways, the energy sector, privatization, the banking sector. To realize the full benefits of these reforms, and to ensure the intended impact on financial sustainability and improvements in the quality of services, these reforms need to be continued, continuously monitored, refined as needed, and completed. Otherwise, the benefits will not be realized and the situation in these sectors is likely to revert to the pre-reform situation. The large agenda of already initiated reforms implies that the Government needs to be very parsimonious about initiating new reforms; at this point, it seems advisable to work on completing ongoing reforms before opening new areas which would spread more thinly decision makers' attention and government implementation capacity.

Actions aimed at enhancing and demonstrating the benefits of reforms. In many areas, steps need to be taken to monitor the impact of reforms, improve the targeting of benefits and inform the public of the intentions of the reform effort. One example is the recent survey by the National Institute of Public Health on the impact of reforms in the health sector (see para. 7.49), which provides feedback on public perceptions of the health reform program. These types of surveys need to be continuously undertaken to monitor and calibrate next steps. The full benefits of reforms will only be felt when there are concomitant changes in governance that improve service delivery. Another priority is to improve the targeting of expenditures, for which there is scope in many areas. This should include measures to help ensure the equitable distribution of education and health opportunities.

Meeting EU accession requirements. These requirements cut across virtually all sectors of the economy. Estimates, which were prepared by the previous government, show the need for roughly 3–4 percent of GDP in central government expenditures for meeting EU accession requirements over the next few years. The priorities for these expenditures are outlined in the Government's National Program for Adopting the Acquis[35] and also in the Bank's recent country economic memorandum on EU accession.[36] According to the analysis in the first chapter of this Report, these expenditures would need to be accommodated without a rise in the expenditure to GDP ratio, implying the need for prioritization across the expenditure envelope. In addition, there are a number of legal and regulatory requirements that need to be met, and this will require a reorganization and strengthening of public administration across the entire public sector.

Priorities for Further Work

Given the broad agenda that the government has been following and the fact that this is the first review of public expenditures, there are a number of areas related to public expenditures, directly or indirectly, where further work needs to be carried out by the government, the Bank and other donors in close cooperation with each other.

- **Investment requirements.** It is clear from the analysis in all the sectors covered in this Report that investment has been neglected in the economy and this is having an adverse effect on the climate for private sector development. The first priority is to close the knowledge gap concerning maintenance, rehabilitation and investment requirements, by sector. This should be done on the basis of the situation or the ground (state of assets, execution of ongoing projects, etc.), EU accession requirements, available project proposals, but taking into account the overall budget constraint. It should be undertaken by the line

---

[35] See, *Expenditure Policies Towards EU Accession*, World Bank, draft, 2002.

[36] See, *Bulgaria: The Dual Challenge of Transition and Accession,* op. cit.

ministries. It should also be informed by a dialogue with the private sector, as infrastructure constraints are seen to be a major impediment to investment. Since there are several other challenges concerning investment (for example, regarding evaluation and programming processes and capacity), the preparation of a PIP may still be required, but any investment planning exercise would also need to be thoroughly integrated into the overall budget process and the expenditure programs of the various ministries.

- **Fiscal Decentralization and Intergovernmental Fiscal Issues.** Throughout this Report, a number of issues have arisen regarding intergovernmental fiscal and administrative arrangements. The recently approved fiscal decentralization program by the Council of Ministers is a welcome step forward in this area. Building on this important achievement and as the program is implemented, a more systematic analysis of intergovernmental issues is needed to keep the reform momentum moving forward. Issues regarding the rationalization of schools, teachers and hospitals, the administration of social protection expenditures, fiscal pressures arising from arrears in municipal finances, all call for a more systematic analysis of intergovernmental issues, in coordination with the ongoing work, supported by USAID, the EU and others.

- **Capacity Assessment and Public Administration Reform.** In most of the analysis on sectors covered in this Report, the issue of capacity constraints and the need for further public administration reform has arisen. This is also a key issue in the governance challenge facing Bulgaria. Further study in the context of the Bank's program of programmatic lending would help identify key capacity constraints to budget planning and management, which are systemic across ministries and levels of government.

- **Roads.** This Report concentrated solely on transport issues in the railway sector, because the Government is in the midst of a major reform and restructuring of this sub-sector. Nevertheless, there are important issues in the road sector, where the stock is in bad shape and as shown earlier in this Report, entrepreneurs perceive the need for improvements. The road network is also a key priority for EU accession and there will be important trade-offs between expenditures for the Trans-European Network and the national roads program. Similarly, there are tradeoffs between operations and maintenance and new investments. Further work on road transport is, therefore, a priority in future public expenditure work.

- **Higher Education.** This Report and the Government's program in the education sector calls for a rationalization of schools and teachers at the primary and secondary level, especially in rural areas. During the preparation of the Report, issues of excess capacity, equity, access and cost recovery also arose in the higher education sector. Bulgaria has a large number of public universities for its population size and there seems to be rigidities in university financing that violate the principle of "money follows the student." Equity throughout the education system, therefore, calls for greater scrutiny and analysis at the higher education level.

- **Defense and Security Expenditures.** This Report has shown that defense and security expenditures are the highest among EU accession candidates, many of which face the same spending pressures as Bulgaria as a result of joining the NATO and border issues for an expanded EU. While these issues are beyond the scope of this Report, it is clear that a thorough review of these expenditures would be beneficial to the overall expenditure reform effort.

Finally, this Report has identified a number of short-term and medium-term reforms in public expenditure policies in five key sectors of the Budget. For these selected sectors, we have illustrated the range and complexity of issues that confront Bulgarian policymakers as they prepare the budget, evaluate the effectiveness of ongoing programs, and reallocate spending across sectors. However, the Report does not provide a fully detailed, comprehensive reform blueprint. This can only be achieved, not by a one-shot exercise such as this Report, but by a thorough, comprehensive review of the overall expenditure program as a continuous ongoing process.

PART TWO:
SECTORAL BACKGROUND
PAPERS

CHAPTER 6

EDUCATION STRUCTURE, QUALITY AND FINANCING

This chapter describes how public resources are allocated and used in the education sector, how the level and pattern of financing affect the coverage and quality of education, and what changes might lead to better performance of the education system in the future. The questions of how efficiently resources are used and how adequately services are provided in the education sector depend crucially upon the definition of roles and responsibilities of central government and municipal governments, and the financing formula which stipulates how public revenues flow to the center, and back to the originating municipalities. For that reason, much of the chapter concerns itself with the roles of the central and municipal governments in financing and managing education programs.

The Education System: Structure, Coverage, and Quality

Structure and Cost Recovery

Bulgaria's education system consists of: (i) optional pre-school education; (ii) an eight year primary cycle; (iii) a secondary cycle which, starting in the 1999/2000 school year, was extended from three years to four years;[37] and (iv) various higher education programs. Pre-school education is offered from age 3 through age 7, the normal starting age for primary school. Primary education is offered either in eight-year primary schools, or in a combination of "junior school," covering the first four grades, and "middle school," covering grades 5 through 8. Secondary education is offered in several forms—either as general education or as vocational education in a large num-

---

[37] The new four-year secondary structure is being applied starting with the students who entered secondary school in September, 1999. The new fourth year of secondary school will go into operation for these students starting in September, 2002. New curricula, educational materials and teacher training for the new four-year secondary program are being developed under the Education Modernization Project financed by the World Bank.

ber of specializations.[38] Attendance at school is compulsory from age 7 to 16—usually coinciding with the end of the first year of secondary schooling.

Higher education at the start of the transition was organized in a rigid Soviet model, in which 37 higher education institutes (including seven higher military schools) produced the cadres required by the state administration and the command economy. Scientific research was carried out in autonomous academies and research institutes. This system has been restructured since the start of the transition to respond to the needs of the market economy. Higher education programs are now offered in the form of Bachelor's, Master's, and PhD programs, as well as short programs of specialized training.

Primary and secondary education are offered in schools of diverse duration and specialization. Urban areas tend to have large schools offering the complete primary or secondary cycle-sometimes, both cycles in a single school. Small rural communities often have separate four-year junior and middle schools, with few students in each grade. Because of their low student/teacher ratios, these small schools have high unit costs. Wherever possible, the Ministry of Education and Science (MES) aims to keep these small rural schools in operation only for the first four grades, and to bus students to larger, better equipped schools for the higher grades. School consolidation of this type typically reduces recurrent expenditures, since savings in teacher salaries usually exceed the recurrent cost of transporting students to larger schools.

Private primary and secondary education is quite limited, accounting for less than 1 percent of enrollments. There are, in addition, five private universities and five private colleges covering 13 percent of higher education enrollments.

Parents of children in public pre-school pay annual fees for school meals and other services which range from 150 to 300 *leva*. These cover less than a third of the average cost of pre-school provision. There are no fees for attendance at public primary and secondary schools, but students are required to purchase educational materials and textbooks (except for the first grade, where the Ministry continues to provide textbooks at no charge). Cost recovery through tuition in higher education was introduced on a discriminatory basis in 1991. Highly qualified students with entry scores above a specified threshold attended free of charge, while students with entry scores below that level were required to pay a relatively high tuition (ranging from 600 to 700 *leva* per year). Many of the fee-paying students were from low-income households, resulting in part from the fact that poorer households cannot afford tutoring for their children. This policy contributed to cost recovery, but led to an unacceptable dualism in the quality of higher education students and programs. In 1999, the discriminatory cost recovery policy was replaced by a uniform policy under which all students pay tuition but at more modest levels, ranging from 160 to 350 *leva* per year, depending on the specialization. The 1999 higher education legislation stipulates that tuition levels cannot exceed 30 percent of actual per-student costs in individual programs. Current tuition levels are set well below that threshold. Total tuition receipts under this new formula are approximately the same as under the former two-tiered formula.

Education Coverage

Official Enrollments. The evolution of official enrollments by level is presented in Table 6.1. Since the start of the transition, enrollments have declined significantly at all levels except higher education. Enrollments in higher education increased through 1998/99, and have fallen since then-an aberration by comparison with other countries in the region. The sharp decline in enrollments in primary schools suggests a further decline in secondary level enrollments, although there was an upturn in secondary enrollments in 2001/2002.

Enrollment Ratios. In spite of these declines in absolute enrollments for primary and secondary education, the proportion of young people enrolled in each cycle of education as measured by the

---

[38] These are in the process of being collapsed to 18 occupational families.

net enrollment ratio has increased over the same period. The increase over the past seven years for each level of the education system is shown in Table 6.2.

Demographic Impacts. The improvement in official enrollment ratios in spite of the pronounced absolute decline in enrollments results from the unusually sharp contraction of population which has occurred in each of the school-age cohorts since the start of the transition-particularly, in the youngest age cohort (Figure 6.1). Bulgaria was the only Europe and Central Asian (ECA) country with negative population growth in the 1980s, averaging −0.2 percent per year throughout the decade.[39] There was, in addition, an exodus of from 300,000 to 400,000 Bulgarian Turks in 1984 and 1985. The rate of population shrinkage in Bulgaria accelerated during the 1990s to an average of −0.7 percent between 1990 and 1999. Of all the ECA countries, only Latvia and Estonia experienced greater shrinkage of population during the 1990s. The total fertility rate in Bulgaria remains at 1.20. This is just over half the level required to maintain a constant population size in the long term. Population size has been eroded further by net out-migration. Net out-migration was estimated at 8 percent of the population in 1989. Although

TABLE 6.1: ENROLLMENTS BY LEVEL, 1990/91 THROUGH 2001/02

	PRE-SCHOOL	PRIMARY	SECONDARY	HIGHER
1990/91	303,779	975,095	391,832	188,479
1991/92	258,995	934,662	384,100	185,914
1992/93	263,004	890,705	374,793	195,447
1993/94	247,472	853,314	363,436	206,179
1994/95	246,608	839,200	371,388	223,030
1995/96	254,234	821,917	368,558	250,336
1996/97	247,015	808,467	356,685	262,757
1997/98	220,177	797,042	340,103	260,487
1998/99	218,525	779,235	332,448	270,077
1999/00	211,943	759,931	329,018	261,321
2000/01	200,449	740,408	329,427	247,006
2001/02	199,206	708,092	334,813	228,394
% change	−34.4%	−27.4%	−14.6%	21.2%

Note: Figures for secondary education for 1995/96 and 1996/97 include students enrolled in post-secondary vocational training programs.

Source: National Statistical Institute.

---

[39] Between the two population censuses (1992 and 2001) Bulgaria's population declined by 8.5 percent.

TABLE 6.2: NET ENROLLMENT RATIOS BY LEVEL, 1994/95 THROUGH 2001/02

(IN PERCENT)	1994/95	1995/96	1996/97	1997/98	1998/99	1999/00	2000/01	2001/02
Pre-school education	59.7	64.5	66.2	62.1	65.2	66.4	66.9	70.6
Primary education (grades 1–4)	92.8	94.9	95.5	96.0	96.8	96.4	96.3	96.4
Junior high education (grades 5–8)	79.0	78.0	78.4	79.1	80.2	81.4	82.4	84.2
Secondary education (grades 9–12)	61.4	61.5	61.5	61.3	62.1	63.1	64.7	68.3
Higher education	22.1	23.7	24.4	25.1	26.0	26.1	25.8	n.a.

Note: Figures for 2001/02 are calculated on the basis of the preliminary 2001 census data and take into account out-migration flows.

Source: National Statistical Institute.

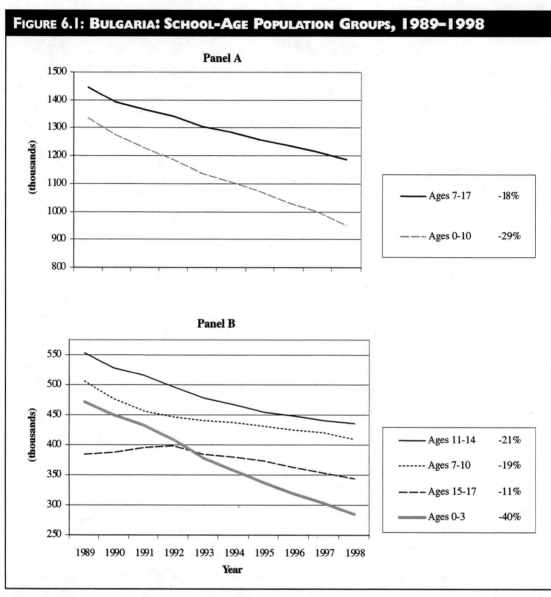

FIGURE 6.1: BULGARIA: SCHOOL-AGE POPULATION GROUPS, 1989–1998

Source: Douglas L. Adkins, *School Finance in Bulgaria in an Era of Education Reform,* June 1999.

this was probably a peak year for out-migration, population loss from this source has continued throughout the 1990s.[40] Based on the numbers already born, it is clear that the school-age population will continue to decline at least through the middle of the current decade. The primary-school age group (ages 7 through 10) in 2005 will be at least 27 percent smaller than in 1998, with similar declines in prospect for other school-age groups.[41]

School Attendance.   Although the net enrollment data show a sizeable improvement in coverage for all levels of education, household survey data on actual school attendance tell quite a different

---

[40] The preliminary results of the March, 2001 population census implied net departures of about 180,000 people between 1992 and 2001.

[41] World Bank population projection, SIMA database.

story. Table 6.3 summarizes the findings of the Bulgarian Integrated Household Survey on school attendance by level for the years 1995, 1997, and 2001. These figures show that:

- school attendance for pre-school education declined by 50 percent between 1995 and 2001, and stands at just 22 percent in 2001/2002-far below the level reported in official statistics;
- school attendance for primary education improved slightly, at rates that are broadly consistent with official enrollment data; for the poor and Roma population, basic education school attendance improved significantly over the past six years;
- school attendance for secondary education fluctuated around an average which is much lower than official enrollment statistics indicate; for the rural population and the poor, secondary school attendance declined sharply over the past six years;
- girls' school attendance rates are higher than boys' in pre-school education, and virtually the same as boys' in basic and secondary education;
- school attendance rates are lower for the rural population than for the urban population, especially for secondary education (where remoteness of schools is often a constraint); secondary school attendance in rural areas has declined alarmingly in the last four years;
- school attendance rates for the poor are much lower than for the non-poor at all levels of education;
- Bulgarian ethnic Turks have lower rates of school attendance than ethnic Bulgarians in pre-school and secondary education (but not primary education); and
- Roma have much lower rates of school attendance than either ethnic Bulgarians or Bulgarian ethnic Turks for all levels of education.

As shown in Table 6.4, school attendance rises with family income for all levels of education. This is especially true for secondary education, where income has become a more serious constraint over the past six years. Currently, children of first-quintile households are only one-quarter as likely to attend secondary school as children from the highest income quintile.

Why are these survey findings on school attendance so much lower than the administrative data on school enrollments? Administrative data on enrollments tend to overstate actual coverage of the education system for several reasons. As in many countries, there is an incentive to over-register enrollments as a means of maintaining existing schools and teaching positions. More fundamentally, administrative data on enrollments do not reflect the number of children actually benefiting from education to the extent that children who are officially enrolled in school do not

TABLE 6.3: RATES OF SCHOOL ATTENDANCE BY LEVEL, 1995, 1997, AND 2001

	PRE-SCHOOL EDUCATION			PRIMARY EDUCATION			SECONDARY EDUCATION		
	1995	1997	2001	1995	1997	2001	1995	1997	2001
Total Population	44	14	22	87	88	90	47	55	46
Males	42	12	21	88	88	90	49	54	46
Females	46	15	24	85	88	89	45	56	46
Urban	46	13	24	88	90	92	52	63	53
Rural	40	14	20	83	84	84	31	32	22
Non-Poor	47	16	26	89	93	94	49	60	52
Poor	8	11	10	54	81	70	20	46	13
Bulgarians	44	15	26	90	93	94	55	66	56
Turks	53	10	19	88	93	90	10	30	34
Roma	25	5	16	55	58	71	3	5	6

Source: Bulgaria Integrated Household Survey, 1995, 1997, 2001 data.

TABLE 6.4: RATES OF SCHOOL ATTENDANCE BY INCOME QUINTILE AND LEVEL, 1995, 1997, AND 2001

	PRE-SCHOOL			PRIMARY EDUCATION			SECONDARY		
	1995	1997	2001	1995	1997	2001	1995	1997	2001
Quintile 1	33	12	17	74	75	77	23	38	14
Quintile 2	35	7	17	92	92	94	49	55	53
Quintile 3	44	22	32	90	95	94	51	60	50
Quintile 4	56	19	28	91	92	91	46	60	63
Quintile 5	60	12	23	89	90	97	63	65	56
Total Population	44	14	22	87	88	90	47	55	46

Source: Bulgarian Integrated Household Surveys, 1995,1997, and 2001.

actually attend school. Non-attendance can take various forms. A pattern that is common in other countries at similar levels of income is that a small number of children—some in urban areas, but more typically in rural areas—never start school at all. More commonly, children may start school but not stay in school through the end of the compulsory cycle. In some rural areas, children who are enrolled in school miss a crucial part of the school year at the beginning and end of the school year because they participate in the autumn harvest and spring planting.

Declining school attendance is a particular problem for households in rural areas, where incomes are low to begin with and schools are generally of inferior quality. In rural areas, school attendance beyond the initial grades may require either an extended school day (because of the need to commute to a school outside the village) or relocation to attend boarding school. Many rural parents are reluctant to send their children outside the village to continue their education. But for some parents, the economic attraction of boarding schools—where their children receive free school uniforms, textbooks, and meals, as well as a stipend which many children share with their families—may overcome that reluctance. Boarding schools may be a low-cost option for some families, even though they are a very high-cost option for the Government in view of their high unit costs. The problems of school attendance in rural areas are compounded by problems of low quality in most rural schools, which reflect these schools' lack of the right materials and support for functioning more effectively. Rural schools also attract the least experienced teachers, but present teaching challenges calling for the skills of the most experienced teachers in the system.

Regional Differences.   There are also significant differences in education coverage by region, even in the age groups where education is compulsory. Some of the gaps are detectable in region level data on official enrollments. The data presented in Table 6.5 indicate that, in some regions, significant numbers of children of compulsory school age are not enrolled in school. In Kurdjali, for example, which has a high proportion of ethnic Turks (62.5 percent of the total population in the region), the primary school enrollment ratio is 76.1 percent, implying a serious deficit of enrollments in the compulsory age group. The persistence of low enrollment rates in a region such as Kurdjali in a situation of shrinking school-age population implies that the main reason for low enrollments is a demand constraint rather than a supply constraint involving insufficient teachers and classrooms. Improving enrollments in this situation does not require more teachers and more classrooms. It requires, rather, special initiatives such as outreach programs to parents of children who are not attending school.

The Plight of Roma Children.   An important dimension of the poverty problem which lies behind these figures is the widespread problem of low school attendance among Roma children through-

TABLE 6.5: OFFICIAL ENROLLMENTS AND GROSS ENROLLMENT RATIOS BY REGION, 2000–01

REGION	TOTAL	ENROLLMENTS			GROSS ENROLLMENT RATIO		
		PRE-SCHOOL	PRIMARY	SECONDARY	PRE-SCHOOL	PRIMARY	SECONDARY
Total	1,275,395	200,449	740,408	334,538	70.8	95.5	76.1
Blagoevgrad	63,505	10,568	37,244	15,693	80.4	95.9	73.0
Bourgas	70,704	12,116	41,432	17,156	72.4	96.9	70.2
Varna	72,680	11,487	41,929	19,264	72.0	104.4	81.7
Veliko Tarnovo	44,065	6,558	25,115	12,392	71.8	97.8	80.9
Vidin	18,790	3,093	11,128	4,569	70.4	96.6	73.3
Vratza	40,068	6,930	24,125	9,013	74.5	97.2	68.9
Gabrovo	20,530	3,021	11,867	5,642	69.3	95.0	78.5
Dobrich	36,559	6,314	21,856	8,389	77.6	94.7	64.3
Kurdjali	30,321	4,917	18,474	6,930	66.9	76.1	50.3
Kiustendil	25,631	4,129	14,862	6,640	75.9	99.1	76.5
Lovech	25,853	4,067	15,086	6,700	65.7	95.5	78.6
Montana	28,096	4,298	16,797	7,001	70.1	99.1	73.0
Pazardjik	52,713	7,148	32,459	13,106	58.9	93.8	68.2
Pernik	22,223	3,066	12,798	6,359	73.3	98.1	82.5
Pleven	49,023	7,828	28,889	12,306	71.7	98.1	76.1
Plovdiv	111,747	17,551	65,252	28,944	71.9	98.8	75.6
Razgrad	27,104	5,255	16,238	5,611	78.8	90.9	58.8
Rousse	42,197	6,567	23,526	12,104	75.5	97.0	84.6
Silistra	22,564	3,660	13,805	5,099	68.1	87.1	58.3
Sliven	36,104	5,219	21,913	8,972	53.0	86.3	63.5
Smolian	25,797	3,358	14,829	7,610	72.4	94.9	80.3
Sofia-City	180,889	27,994	92,924	59,971	73.1	93.0	106.5
Sofia	40,508	6,741	25,479	8,288	79.5	106.8	62.7
Stara Zagora	60,203	9,028	34,982	16,193	67.0	95.4	77.1
Targovishte	23,307	4,024	14,866	4,417	66.8	98.3	53.2
Haskovo	43,482	6,311	25,875	11,296	62.2	93.1	68.3
Shoumen	35,112	5,390	21,520	8,202	66.3	97.4	66.0
Yambol	25,620	3,811	15,138	6,671	69.1	94.6	71.6

Source: National Statistical Institute.

out the country. Roma children often start school, but drop out during the initial grades of primary schooling, mainly due to economic reasons. Language is another problem that Roma children face in school. An important feature of education in Bulgaria is minority language instruction. Under the Constitution, all linguistic minority groups have the right to mother-tongue education, in addition to instruction in the Bulgarian language. Minority-language education is a positive feature of education in Bulgaria, but Roma students do not benefit from this program, because there is no consensus on the appropriate version of the Romany language.

In addition to the linguistic problem, Roma children face other handicaps that contribute to low school attendance. Parents are often illiterate and do not appreciate the importance of education. Low income makes it difficult for most Roma households to purchase the textbooks and other school supplies that parents are expected to provide. Roma children often work in the informal sector to supplement their meager family income. Many Roma children do not have a reasonable command of any of the languages of instruction in schools. Roma often marry and start childbearing at a very early age—as early as age 12. Of those Roma children who do complete primary school, few attend secondary school or go on to university. Data from the 1997 Bulgaria Integrated Household Survey show that among low-income Roma households, only 45 percent of children aged 6 through 14 attended school.[42] The data presented in Table 6.3 show low but improving rates of primary school attendance for Roma children, and extremely low school attendance by Roma in secondary education. This pattern of school participation, combined with the fact that a relatively high proportion of the Roma population is in the primary school age group, suggests that there are may be as many as 70,000 Roma children of primary school age in Bulgaria who are not attending school. The few Roma children who do attend primary school are often stigmatized by being assigned to schools for the handicapped, because of their lack of command of the Bulgarian language and other educational handicaps resulting from their environment rather than from innate limitations.

Education Quality

Student assessment provides the best indication of education quality in terms of the objective of education—student learning. The most inclusive source of internationally comparable data on what students learn is the TIMSS international science and math assessment which was carried out for a nationally representative sample of eighth-grade students in 24 countries in 1995 and 39 countries in 1999. Together with eight other accession countries, Bulgaria participated in the 1995 and 1999 surveys. As shown in Table 6.6, Bulgaria scored above the international average in 1995, but below it in 1999. The decline in Bulgaria's mathematics score was exceeded only by the Czech Republic. Its science score in the TIMSS assessment fell more than any other country's score.

The decline in assessment results reflects the pressures of a severely strained education system. For at least the past fifteen years, investments have not been made to maintain the system—let alone improve it. Moreover, the changes in education financing which are described in the following section have led to systematic neglect of some of the most key inputs to the education process,

---

[42] Roma and the Transition in Central and Eastern Europe: Trends and Challenges, Dena Ringold, World Bank, 2000.

TABLE 6.6: TIMSS 8TH GRADE STUDENT ASSESSMENT RESULTS FOR SCIENCE AND MATH, 1995 AND 1999

	MATHEMATICS		SCIENCE	
	1995 MEAN SCORE	1999 MEAN SCORE	1995 MEAN SCORE	1999 MEAN SCORE
Czech Republic	546	520	555	539
Slovak Republic	534	534	532	535
Slovenia	531	530	541	533
Hungary	527	532	537	552
Bulgaria	527	511	545	518
International Average	519	521	518	521
Latvia	488	505	476	503
Romania	474	472	471	472
Lithuania	472	482	464	488

Source: TIMSS 1999: International Mathematics Report, International Association for the Evaluation of International Achievement, December, 2000, and TIMSS 1999: International Science Report, International Association for the Evaluation of International Achievement, December, 2000.

including textbooks and other teaching and learning materials. Teacher salaries have also plummeted in real terms, leading to a serious problem of motivation, and inducing many teachers to take additional jobs in order to support their families. Although there are no formal assessments to document changes in quality of higher education, it is clear that the quality of higher education has also declined during the past decade. This is apparent both from the severe budgetary limitations, and from the rapid increase which has taken place in enrollments without corresponding growth of staff and other inputs.

Resources for Education

Public Expenditures for Education

Like other countries in the region, Bulgaria responded to falling output and declining public revenue early in the transition by reducing expenditures and diversifying financing for education. Financing was diversified through five actions: (i) decentralizing the responsibility for financing and managing most education programs from central to regional and local governments; (ii) requiring parents to purchase textbooks and other educational materials which had formerly been provided free by schools; (iii) expanding private education; (iv) instituting student fees and other charges for cost recovery in specialized secondary education and higher education; and (v) allowing schools to raise and retain funds through such actions as rental or sale of unneeded facilities and provision of extracurricular courses.

These actions to diversify financing did not prevent a deep fall in expenditures for education. As shown in Table 6.7, real outlays for education fell more precipitously in Bulgaria than in any of the other accession countries during the 1990s. By 2000, they were only 40 percent of their level in 1990. Public budget allocations reinforced the effect of falling GDP and declining public revenues. Falling levels of financing and diversification of sources of financing for education entailed several types of consequences. The sharp fall in financing inevitably contributed to the decline in quality described above. The shifting of financing responsibilities to households for textbooks and other educational inputs which were formerly provided free has also led to financial hardship for some households. These may have contributed to the declines in coverage that were observed for

TABLE 6.7: REAL CHANGES IN GDP AND PUBLIC EXPENDITURES ON EDUCATION, 1990-2000

	REAL GDP IN 2000 (AS PERCENT OF 1990 GDP)	REAL EXPENDITURES ON EDUCATION (AS PERCENT OF 1990 LEVEL)	
		1995	2000
Bulgaria	82.1	52.6	40.3
Czech Republic	99.9	118.3	96.0
Estonia	86.1	91.2	108.5
Hungary	108.0	93.5	98.6
Latvia	62.3	86.5	116.1
Lithuania	68.4	69.1	70.1
Poland	143.2	154.6	211.0
Romania	82.9	154.8	128.9
Slovak Republic	105.1	90.1	81.3
Slovenia	120.1	117.8	139.5

Note. Expenditure figures refer to consolidated general budget.

Source: World Bank database.

TABLE 6.8: EVOLUTION OF EDUCATION EXPENDITURES

	EDUCATION EXPENDITURES (AS % OF GDP)	EDUCATION EXPENDITURES (AS % OF TOTAL PUBLIC EXPENDITURES)
1992	6.1	13.7
1993	5.7	11.4
1994	4.5	10.0
1995	4.0	9.2
1996	3.2	7.3
1997	3.9	10.2
1998	3.9	10.0
1999	4.2	10.0
2000	4.2	10.0
2001	4.0	9.9
2002	4.1	10.0

Source: National Statistical Institute and Ministry of Finance. Figures for 2002 are preliminary projections

primary and secondary education in Bulgaria.

Total expenditures on public education-from both municipalities' own resources and from the state budget-have fallen over the past decade, both as a share of GDP, and as a share of total public expenditures (Table 6.8). Since 1997, public expenditures on education have stabilized at about 4 percent of GDP and 10 percent of total spending. The share of education expenditures as a percentage of projected GDP on Bulgaria is strikingly low in relation to the Organization for Economic Cooperation and Development (OECD) average, as shown in Table 6.9. It is comparatively lower than in some of the first-tier EU accession countries, like Poland and Hungary. The Budget Acts for 2001 and 2002 named education as a priority sector, and provided additional resources to municipalities to spend on education. Even so, it will take years to make up for the long-term erosion of expenditures on education. The budget neglect of the past decade is visible throughout the education system in the form of deferred maintenance on school facilities. Of even greater concern is the deprivation of educational materials for effective teaching in many classrooms throughout the country (particularly in the smaller municipalities), the lack of resources to maintain laboratory and library resources in higher education, and the serious decline in teacher salaries. Significant investments are needed to re-equip schools, to modernize the curriculum and teaching materials, to maintain the school infrastructure, and to rationalize the school network and provide for long-term recurrent budget savings.

TABLE 6.9: PUBLIC EDUCATION EXPENDITURES, BULGARIA AND SELECTED COMPARATORS, 2000

	PERCENT OF GDP	PERCENT OF TOTAL PUBLIC EXPENDITURES
Bulgaria	4.1	10.0
Canada	5.4	13.0
Czech Republic	4.5	12.3
France	5.8	11.1
Germany	4.5	9.8
Hungary	4.5	15.2
New Zealand	6.1	18.8
Norway	6.6	17.4
Poland	5.8	22.1
United Kingdom	4.6	12.0
United States	5.2	16.0
OECD average	5.1	14.0

Source: Data for Bulgaria from National Statistical Institute and Ministry of Finance. Data for other countries from OECD Education at a Glance, 2000.

As shown in Table 6.10, the proportion of municipalities' expenditures devoted to education fell from 33.0 percent in 1997 to 29.7 percent in 1998, and recovered gradually after 1999. In

2002, they are projected to increase by close to 39 percent of municipal spending. The share of central government expenditures on education has remained stable since 1998.

Table 6.11 shows the actual categories of expenditures on education for the year 2000, by spending authority. It is particularly striking that over 85 percent of municipalities' total educational expenditures, including capital expenditures, is spent on staff salaries and benefits, and fuel and energy. Expenditures for library materials, which should play an important role in upgrading the quality of education, account for less than one-tenth of a percent of municipalities' expenditures on education. Expenditures on staff salaries and benefits and utilities are treated as non-discretionary, and have crowded out expenditures on educational materials and equipment which are vital to improving the quality of education.

Budget and expenditure data do not distinguish among allocations for pre-school, primary, and secondary education. Thus, it is necessary to infer the budget amounts for those levels. Because salary and other personnel costs constitute such a high proportion of expenditures, and because the distribution of other categories of

TABLE 6.10: EVOLUTION OF EXPENDITURE SHARES ON EDUCATION BY SPENDING AUTHORITY, 1997 THROUGH 2001

(IN MILLIONS OF LEVA)

	MUNICIPALITIES	CENTRAL GOVERNMENT
1997		
Education expenditures	327.6	356.8
Total expenditures	989.9	5,741.5
Education share (%)	33.0	6.2
1998		
Education expenditures	493.4	372.7
Total expenditures	1,658.9	7,030.3
Education share (%)	29.7	5.3
1999		
Education expenditures	571.7	417.6
Total expenditures	1,864.3	8,047.9
Education share (%)	30.7	5.2
2000		
Education expenditures	626.2	503.7
Total expenditures	2,004.9	9,329.4
Education share (%)	31.2	5.4
2001		
Education expenditures	654.7	537.6
Total expenditures	1970.2	10224.7
Education share (%)	33.2	5.3
2002[a]		
Education expenditures	733.5	537.8
Total expenditures	1,904.6	10,816.2
Education share (%)	38.5	5.0

[a] Data for 2002 are preliminary projections.

Source: Ministry of Finance.

expenditures by level of education is presumably correlated with personnel expenditures, we use the distribution of education staff by level to infer the pattern of expenditures by level of education. This distribution is provided in Table 6.11 and Table 6.12. This pattern of expenditures that emerges is extremely compressed by international standards. This suggests, first, that higher education programs are being seriously under-funded, and second, that there is significant room for improved efficiency in pre-school, primary, and secondary education.

Efficiency in Use of Resources

The prolonged decline in school-age population is a remarkable opportunity for Bulgaria. It should reduce the cost of improving coverage, and in the process should release resources to start the long-overdue process of raising education quality and modernizing the content of education programs. Unfortunately, this has been a missed opportunity thus far. The system did not streamline

TABLE 6.11: EXPENDITURES ON EDUCATION BY CATEGORY OF EXPENDITURE, LEVEL, AND SPENDING AUTHORITY, 2000 BUDGET YEAR

(IN MILLIONS OF CURRENT LEVA)

EXPENDITURE CATEGORY	PRE-SCHOOL, PRIMARY & SECONDARY EDUCATION[a]		HIGHER EDUCATION
	STATE-MANAGED SCHOOLS	MUNICIPALITY-MANAGED SCHOOLS	
Recurrent			
Salaries & contributions	146.9	463.4	147.5
Scholarships	6.7	7.5	12.7
Fuel & energy	42.1	71.7	33.1
Library materials	1.0	0.6	5.7
Boarding costs	6.5	31.2	5.3
External services	5.2	22.2	18.1
Repair	1.7	10.4	5.3
Other recurrent	14.5	11.2	9.6
Investment			
Major repairs	1.8	3.0	4.0
New construction	3.3	4.9	13.0
Total	229.7	626.1	254.3

Source: Ministry of Finance (excludes extra-budgetary accounts of 19.5 million leva).

education resources in primary and secondary education as enrollments declined, thereby raising unit costs of education provision without getting in exchange any benefits of improved quality. The evolution of enrollments and resources over the decade is summarized in Table 6.13. Preschool is the only level at which the decline in enrollments was matched by an equivalent decline in resources (schools and teachers). In primary education, the number of teachers and schools declined, but by considerably less than the decline in enrollments. In secondary education, the number of teachers and schools actually increased, in spite of the sizable decline in enrollments. In higher education, the number of teaching staff declined, while enrollments increased. The number of schools increased to a lesser extent.

These changes are reflected in student/teacher ratios-by far the most important determinant of education unit costs. As shown in Table 6.14, average student/teacher ratios at all levels are far

TABLE 6.12: ESTIMATED PUBLIC EXPENDITURES BY LEVEL OF EDUCATION, 2000

	PRE-SCHOOL	PRIMARY	SECONDARY	HIGHER
Student/Teacher Ratios	10.7	13.7	11.0	10.6
Enrollments	200,449	740,408	329,427	247,006
Education Expenditures (estimated, millions of current leva)	174.6	415.1	266.2	254.3
Per-Student Expenditures (estimated, in current leva)	871	561	808	1,030

Source: NSI and World Bank staff estimates.

TABLE 6.13: CHANGES IN ENROLLMENTS, TEACHERS, AND SCHOOLS, 1990/91–2000/01

	PRE-SCHOOL	PRIMARY	SECONDARY	HIGHER
Enrollments				
1990/1991	303,779	975,095	391,832	188,479
2000/2001	199,206	708,092	334,813	228,394
% change	−34.4%	−27.4%	−14.6%	+21.2%
Teachers				
1990/1991	28,776	64,798	27,384	23,663
2000/2001	18,693	53,868	29,866	23,329
% change	−35.0%	−16.9%	+9.1%	−1.4%
Schools				
1990/1991	4,590	3,403[1]	678[2]	84
2000/2001	3,249	2,770[1]	726[2]	88
% change	−29.4%	−19.3%	+4.6%	+7.1%
Student/Teacher Ratio				
1990/1991	10.6	15.0	14.3	8.0
2000/2001	10.7	13.1	11.2	9.8

[1] Includes schools offering both primary and secondary education (grades1–13).

[2] Includes schools offering junior high and secondary education (grades 5–13).

Source: National Statistical Institute.

below OECD comparators, indicating significant room for improved efficiency. Remarkably, the national average student/teacher ratios for each level of education are below the *minimum* permissible class sizes under prevailing class size norms (Table 6.15). This implies two things: (i) that many exceptions are granted in allowing smaller class sizes than allowed under the minimum class size norms; and (ii) that teaching staff are inefficiently deployed across and within schools, such that many teachers receive a full salary but teach less than full time. A major program of school rationalization, and shedding and redeployment of redundant teaching staff needs to be undertaken to correct this situation.

Because of regional differences in evolution of school-age population, the scope for improved efficiency in education resource use varies by locality. Most municipalities have experienced significant shrinkage of school-age population for all levels of education; many have recorded a reduction of 40 percent to 65 percent in the size of the age 7 (grade 1) cohort over the past 15 years. But in a few munici-

TABLE 6.14: AVERAGE STUDENT/TEACHER RATIOS BY LEVEL OF EDUCATION, BULGARIA AND SELECTED COMPARATORS

	STUDENT/TEACHER RATIO		
	PRIMARY	SECONDARY	HIGHER
Bulgaria	13.1	11.2	9.8
Canada	21.0	22.1	14.5
New Zealand	24.7	21.0	14.8
United Kingdom	22.0	16.7	18.5
United States	16.5	15.9	14.0
Spain	16.0	12.1	16.4
France	21.0	15.2	12.3
OECD Average	18.0	14.6	15.3

Source: OECD, *Education at a Glance, 2001.* Data for Bulgaria from the Bulgarian National Statistical Institute. Primary education in Bulgaria covers grades 1–8.

TABLE 6.15: CLASS SIZE NORMS BY LEVEL AND TYPE OF EDUCATION		
	MINIMUM	MAXIMUM
Pre-school	12	22
Boarding pre-school	12	18
Pre-school for children with disabilities	3–12*	5–18*
Grades 1 through 4	16	22
Grades 5 through 8	18	26
Grades 9 through 12 (general secondary)	18	26
Secondary vocational	18	26
Secondary vocational evening	18	30
Secondary vocational apprenticeship	15	35
Specialized schools	2–15*	3–20*

*Depending on nature of the disability or specialization.

Source: Ministry of Education and Science.

palities, immigration has more than offset reduced fertility, such that the size of the age 7 cohort and other school-age groups has actually increased. This diversity of experiences implies a wide range of needs for the rationalization and consolidation of school facilities and staff. Whereas most municipalities have experienced a major loss of enrollments and need to consolidate schools and streamline teaching and non-teaching staff, others have experienced enrollment growth, and may need to expand facilities or redeploy students from crowded schools. For reasons described in the following section, the decentralization formula does not provide incentives to consolidate primary and secondary schools and shed unneeded teachers. In the few cases where there have been proposals to close schools and dismiss teachers to improve efficiency, there has been strong opposition from local governments and teachers' unions. There is also a major need for improved efficiency in resource use in higher education. Although the student/teacher ratio for higher education increased slightly over the past decade, it remains very low by international comparison. Many classes in individual faculties have fewer than five students.

Finance and Management of Education

Current Process

The responsibility for education finance and management is divided between the central government and municipalities. There are 263 municipalities in Bulgaria, with mayors and municipal councils elected for a four-year term.[43] Mayors and municipal councils are accountable to the electorate of the respective municipalities. In addition to the municipalities, there are 28 *oblasts* or administrative regions which facilitate the provision of centrally-mandated services. Regional officials and staff are appointed by, and accountable to, the central government. Regional government is thus an instrument for providing deconcentrated central services.

The Ministry of Education and Science (MES) is responsible for educational content, quality control, staff policy, appointment of principals for all public schools, and licensing of private schools. The Ministry must also approve all requests by municipalities for school closure, school creation, or other changes in the coverage of schools. The main instruments of quality control are enforcement of central norms for class size and required teaching hours, reporting, and school inspection. These activities are carried out by MES staff and school inspectors who are based in the 28 regions. The Ministry is also developing student assessment as an additional instrument of quality control, with the support of the World-Bank-financed Education Modernization Project.

---

[43] Mayors in the smallest municipalities are appointed.

Primary and Secondary Education.   There are two categories of public primary and secondary schools, which operate under different management and financing mechanisms. These separate mechanisms are described below.

State-Managed Schools.   About 1,000 primary and secondary schools are designated as "national interest schools", and are financed entirely by the state budget.[44] These include about 400 second-ary vocational schools which are managed by the MES, about 100 vocational schools which are managed by the Ministry of Agriculture and Forestry, and about 25 schools of the arts and performing arts which are managed by the Ministry of Culture. Also included are over 400 schools managed by the Ministry of Education and Science for students with special needs-including orphans, juvenile delinquents, and students with infectious diseases-and specialized sports training. Many of these are boarding schools that serve students from throughout the country. Budgets for the "national interest schools" are negotiated by the Ministry of Finance with each of the host ministries. The Ministries of Education and Science, Agriculture and Forestry, and Culture prepare an annual budget proposal for each of the schools that they manage, and these proposals are then negotiated with the Ministry of Finance on the basis of available resources and the Ministry of Finance's stated priories: first, debt service payments; second, salaries, social and health contributions, free medicines, social benefits, and student stipends; third, food, heating, electricity, and maintenance of social, health and education establishments; and fourth, capital expenditure.

Municipality-Managed Schools.   The other public primary and secondary schools-numbering about 2,500-are managed by the 263 democratically elected municipalities, and financed primarily by the municipalities. Municipalities whose revenues are not sufficient to cover the cost of local civil-service salaries and benefits receive transfers from the state budget under a subsidy formula (described below). In general, this formula provides for subsidies to the smallest municipalities, whose revenue base is too small to meet even the staff costs of education and other municipal services. Most of the larger municipalities are able to meet these expenditures from their own revenues, and thus receive no subsidy from the state budget. The current budget allocation formula for municipalities evolved on an *ad hoc* basis during the 1990s, with modifications each year to meet observed deficiencies of the prior year's allocation formula.

As explained in Chapter 4, the budgets of the 263 municipalities combine revenues collected and retained at the municipality level, and subsidies from the state budget. Education currently accounts for 33 percent of municipality expenditures. The bulk of this is spent for the salaries and social and health contributions of teachers and other pre-school, primary, and secondary school staff, who account for 56 percent of the staff of municipalities. Capital expenditures for education are provided through earmarked subsidies on an *ad hoc* basis. In the situation of a shrinking national budget and shrinking school-age population and enrollments, they are all but non-existent.

The general subsidy to municipalities is calculated through an allocation formula which estimates for each municipality the staff costs of providing the services-including public pre-school, primary, and secondary education-for which municipalities are responsible, net of municipalities' potential own revenues. For the budget year 2002, the general subsidy is calculated essentially according to the formula described in Chapter 4.

If the subsidy formula leads to a positive balance for a given municipality, the municipality receives that amount in the form of a block grant.[45] The municipality is, in principle, free to spend its general subsidy as it wishes. But for most municipalities which receive the subsidy, there is, in

---

[44] These schools are defined in COM Decree RD 14-18 of April 8, 1999.

[45] The more prosperous municipalities, such as Sofia, do not receive a general subsidy.

fact, little discretion in how these funds are spent, since virtually the entire amount is needed to pay the salaries and benefits of the existing staff of schools and other public facilities in the municipality. Even for municipalities which do not receive the general subsidy, there are constraints on how municipalities spend their own revenues. Municipalities' discretion to manage education resources-and, in particular, to reduce school staffing-is circumscribed by centrally mandated norms which specify for each level and type of course the minimum and maximum permissible class sizes (Table 6.15) and the minimum and maximum number of teaching hours per teacher,[46] and by the requirement that the MES approve any proposals for teacher dismissals, school closure or school consolidation. For municipality-managed primary and secondary schools, budget proposals are sent directly to the Ministry of Finance, which reviews the proposals for conformity with the norms. For each municipality's budget proposal, class sizes and teaching loads must fall within the range stipulated in the norms. For state-run primary and secondary schools, the MES collates budget proposals from schools, confirms that the proposals comply with the class size and teaching-load norms, and transmits them to the Ministry of Finance for review and approval.

School-Based Management.   One management innovation in education which has received considerable attention recently is the "delegated budget" model which was developed under a PHARE-financed pilot project, and covers one hundred primary and secondary schools in four municipalities. Under this approach, school principals receive their own budgets to manage themselves, rather than having expenditures made on their behalf by their respective municipalities. Unlike conventional schools, which are not allowed to transfer funds from one budget category to another or to retain savings from budgeted allocations, the delegated budget schools are allowed to reallocate budgets across categories, and to retain budget savings, together with any additional funds that they are able to mobilize. The Ministry plans to extend the delegated budget model to an additional twenty schools under the World Bank-financed Education Modernization Project, and to extend the model to all schools by 2009.

Higher Education.   Higher education institutions are managed autonomously under the higher education act, subject to financing constraints defined in the Budget Act for each year. The bulk of their financing is provided by the state budget. Less than a third of their financing comes from student fees and own revenues (paragraph 6.6). Currently, the MES negotiates enrollment limits for each higher education institution (including private higher education institutions), based upon historical enrollments, projected skill demands, and available budget resources, and an overall enrollment limit established by the Council of Ministers. Once those limits are set, each institution establishes its own entry criteria consistent with those limits. In consequence of the rapid expansion of higher education enrollments during the past decade and the continued shrinkage of the age cohort, a much higher (60 percent) proportion of secondary education graduates enters higher education than in most of the neighboring countries. In place of the former negotiated budgets, the MES and the Ministry of Finance have just introduced a new capitation formula under which each higher education institution receives a fixed amount per student, under a schedule of unit cost norms established for groups of specializations. These differentiated unit costs range from 634 *leva* in pedagogy, economics, management, and tourism to 3,933 leva in medicine, dental studies, pharmacology, public health, physical therapy, and sports.

Issues in Finance and Management

Lack of Efficiency Incentives.   In principle, municipalities finance municipality-managed schools from their own resources. This should provide compelling incentives for municipalities to provide

---

[46] These are described, respectively, in Ordinance No. 8 of December 12, 1999, and Ordinance No. 4 of August 14, 1996, as amended on June 27, 1997.

education through the most cost-effective means. But this incentive is undermined in many munic-ipalities because the general subsidy treats existing teacher costs as non-discretionary and hence legitimates what may be an inefficient delivery of education. The subsidy effectively makes up the difference between teacher salary costs and the municipality's own revenues, as long as class sizes and teaching loads in each school conform to the norms. As shown in Table 6.15, the class size norms for primary and secondary education stipulate maximum and minimum class sizes with significant spread between them. These broad bands allow for much larger average class sizes than most schools have and much larger student/teacher ratios than the system-wide averages shown in Table 6.14. The maximum class sizes for general education—22 students per class in the first four grades, and 26 students per class in grades 5 through 12—are not unreasonable. But actual aver-age class sizes are about half this level, as the student/teacher ratios in Table 6.14 imply.[47] Schools in large and growing urban areas often have average class sizes near the maximum provided in the norms. Rural schools and schools in smaller towns typically have much smaller class sizes.

The problem with this model is that the range between the minimum and maximum class sizes specified in the norms is very broad, and the current budget process provides no incentive for municipality education departments with very small average class sizes to reconfigure classes within schools or to consolidate schools in order to provide more cost-effective education. Many urban schools are constrained by the class size maximum. Many rural schools are either constrained by the class size minimum, or are granted exceptions to allow even smaller class sizes. The municipalities with small average class sizes tend to also have very modest revenues, and thus are dependent on the general subsidy. There is no incentive for these municipalities to move towards larger class sizes because the current formula does not allow them to keep any of the salary savings that this would generate. (Their general subsidy would be reduced by the full amount of the savings.) On the contrary, moving towards larger class sizes is likely to involve teacher layoffs which would create problems with teachers' unions. For this reason-and also because of the shrinkage of the school-age cohort-schools in rural areas and small towns tend to maintain the minimum permissible class size. The situation for the larger urban areas with growing population is the reverse. Here, classes tend to stick to the maximum permissible size because limited classroom capacity and the lack of investment budget resources to build new schools does not allow the luxury of smaller class sizes.

Teacher Redeployment Plans. For the 2002/03 school year, the Government plans to implement a redeployment plan for teachers. This plan, which is currently under consideration by the Council of Ministers, is expected to reduce the overcapacity in the education sector through attrition and rationalization of teaching staff in urban areas, and consolidation of schools. These measures have already been incorporated into the 2002 Budget Act. In the medium term, it will be preferable to bring about further efficiency improvements through incentives in the budget process itself, rather than through manipulated changes. The simplest means of doing this is through a capitation sys-tem, in which financing is based on the number of students, not on specific education inputs.

Limited Benefits of the Delegated-budget Pilot. The innovations which are being piloted under the delegated-budget model begin to establish incentives for more efficient use of resources within the school. There have been significant economies in use of some inputs-particularly for utilities, where expenditures in many of the schools have fallen by as much as 30 percent. But the current budget situation, in which financing is essentially limited to salaries and utilities, allows little scope for further improvements unless schools are able to achieve staffing economies. Staffing economies under the pilot have been minimal because system rationalization in the form of school consolida-tion needs to be undertaken at a higher level of aggregation-across schools. Some of the delegated

---

[47] Student/teacher ratios exceed average class size to the extent that teachers teach less than full time or work in non-teaching tasks.

budget schools could have achieved further economies through shedding of unneeded teachers, but principals have tended to feel solidarity with their communities and have been reluctant to impose hardship on teachers and the community.

Higher Education.   The new differentiated unit-cost model is, in principle, an improvement over the former negotiated budgets because it provides a demand-driven basis of financing which should provide incentives for improved efficiency. Nevertheless, there are several concerns about the policy:

(a) **Streamlining the existing system.** The existing higher education system is characterized by too many institutions of widely varying quality and efficiency. There is an urgent need for selective use of public resources to finance higher education programs which meet quality and efficiency standards. Unless it is preceded by a centrally mandated streamlining of higher education programs, the unit-cost financing policy will do little to address this problem.

(b) **The basis for cost differentiation.** The differentiation of unit costs tends to legitimize the existing cost structure, whether or not delivery in individual programs was efficient.

(c) **Flexible admissions.** One of the main benefits of a demand-driven financing model is that it helps guide the setting of priorities for which program to expand and which programs to shrink. The new capitation financing policy will not yield the full benefits unless it is combined with more flexible admission policy. The new demand-driven financing model is fundamentally incompatible with an administered system of admission limits. Instead of the Government setting limits, the demands of students and parents should determine which programs expand and which contract. Individual programs should be free to set their own quality standards. Public financing for higher education should encourage the growth of centers of excellence. This should be based on improved information for users on the career implications of alternative program options.

(d) **Increasing enrollments and declining quality.** Tension has emerged in most higher education institutions between the goal of maintaining teaching staff, and the goal of maintaining quality, since admitting more students often requires lowering admission requirements. Some institutions have resisted the pressure to lower standards, and have not admitted as many students as they were allowed. Although many higher education institutions are expected to adopt the results of the new grade 12 *matura* examination in place of their own entry examinations, the most prestigious universities have announced that they intend to maintain their own entrance examinations.

(e) **Increased cost recovery.** Subsidized higher education leads to excessive consumption of higher education. One symptom of excessive consumption is that students stay in programs longer than necessary. (On average, students spend over seven years to complete a four-year undergraduate program.) Currently, student fees are meant to recover only 30 percent of the cost of higher education. In fact, fee levels have been set so low that they recover much less than that. Improved cost recovery would help limit student demand and would also help generate additional resources for much-needed improvements in quality of higher education programs.

Recommended Policy Directions

A number of policy actions are recommended to address the issues raised above. These are summarized as follows:

Streamline Higher Education

Several actions are needed to improve efficiency and accountability of higher education programs and institutions, beyond the capitation financing that is proposed. A first measure should be to limit budget financing for each institution to reasonable staffing levels-to be agreed in discussion between the Ministries of Education and Finance.

Raise Higher Education Fees

Student fees need to be increased, both as a means of mobilizing resources to help finance quality improvements, and to reduce excessive consumption of higher education—especially in the form of repetition. An appropriate short-term target would be to achieve an overall cost recovery to 30 percent, as the current law foresees. In the medium term, fees should be increased further, combined with a student loan scheme with subsidized interest rates for low-income students. To further discourage repetition, a differentiated fee schedule might be considered, with higher fees for repeated classes. Higher fees should not lead to problems of access for qualified students from low-income households because the Government is developing a means-tested scholarship program and a student loan scheme under the Education Modernization Project.

Introduce Selectivity in Higher Education

In the medium term, public financing of higher education should be limited to programs and institutions which meet agreed standards of quality and efficiency (in terms of resource use and student completion). Programs and institutions which fail to meet these standards could continue operation as self-financing private institutions. Work should begin immediately to develop a system of professional accreditation to define quality and efficiency standards for higher education.

Use the Savings from Higher Education to Improve Quality and Coverage in Primary Education

The savings from these measures should be used to finance measures to improve primary education coverage and quality. Less-than-full coverage of primary education results from lack of demand rather than lack of supply. Raising enrollments and school attendance will require a multi-faceted approach, targeted to the poor, Roma, and other groups with low school attendance rates. Among the interventions that should be considered are the following:

- **Provide free textbooks to children in need.**
- **Provide free school lunches in schools with low school attendance.** Free school lunches have been found in many other settings to be a cost-effective intervention to raise school attendance among the poor.
- **Support targeted, free pre-school programs in areas with high primary-school dropout rates.** Pre-school education has been found to be an effective tool for reducing dropout rates and improving learning achievement in primary schooling. Whereas early dropouts are principally a problem in low-income (often rural) households, conventional pre-school programs predominately benefit the children of more affluent, urban families that are able to afford pre-school fees. Virtually all existing preschools are in urban areas. In order to be effective as an instrument for raising primary school attendance and performance, new forms of pre-school delivery will need to be developed. These should be targeted to at-risk groups, should be offered free of charge, and should be offered in a flexible format in areas where no free-standing pre-schools exist—using, for example, existing primary schools or outreach programs with mothers.
- **For incomplete rural primary schools without nearby continuation schools, either add capacity through complete primary education, or contract for student transport to closest complete primary schools.** Extending school capacity can be cost-effective even in small rural settlements through approaches such as multi-grade teaching, and deployment of teachers across several schools-in effect, bussing teachers rather than students. Multi-grade education is sometimes seen as an inferior form of education. But the results from other countries have shown that, with the right teacher preparation and the right instructional materials, multi-grade teaching can lead to very good educational results.

- **Encourage local solutions to raise school attendance.** Local communities should be encouraged to take initiatives to improve educational results-in terms of both attendance and quality. Where child inputs to seasonal agricultural labor are contributing to attendance problems at the beginning and end of the school year, local communities should be encouraged to alter the school calendar to accommodate theses needs, and thereby raise attendance.
- **Monitor school attendance and evaluate the causes of low attendance.** In Bulgaria, as in most countries, registration focuses on formal enrollments. But children learn only when they are attending school. The large gaps between formal enrollments and actual school attendance indicate the importance of monitoring actual school attendance, as well as registered enrollments. This monitoring should be the basis of evaluative and early corrective action when abnormally high non-attendance is detected.
- **Carry out programs targeted to the Roma and other high-risk groups** to raise demand for schooling. There are a number of NGO-supported programs which offer a range of interventions to help overcome these educational handicaps and to prepare Roma children for successful school participation. These include pre-school education in the Romany language or in a multi-lingual environment, parental education, and other interventions. The experience with Roma-targeted programs in other countries in the region shows that this holistic approach offers the best prospects of raising school participation and school performance among the Roma population—especially when it involves child-centered learning methodologies and the commitment of the Roma community. Other successful measures to improve Roma school attendance and educational performance include: provision of financial incentives to schools which attract and retain Roma students; catch-up classes for Roma drop-outs and tutoring for Roma students; special training for teachers of Roma children and provision of linguistic and cultural mediators in schools with Roma students; optional Romany language and culture classes; and provision of free breakfast and lunch at school. The same holistic approach should be applied to raise school attendance in other groups and regions with low attendance. Measures to improve quality should focus on teacher training and provision of textbooks, library books, and other educational materials.

Finance Primary and Secondary Education Centrally, Manage Locally

Basic education generates benefits for society that transcend the local community. Financing such services locally leads to sub-optimal provision. For that reason, teacher salaries, textbooks, and other essential inputs to basic education should be financed centrally, even if these programs are managed locally.

Strengthen Incentives for Efficient Delivery

Incentives need to be strengthened for efficient delivery of education. One basic approach for doing this is to ensure that schools and municipalities are able to keep at least part of any savings they are able to achieve. Another is to move from input-based financing to output-based financing. The simplest form of output-based financing is capitation-based financing, which determines the amount of a local government's educational subsidy based on the number of students it is educating at each level—differentiated to reflect different costs of different programs of education, and possibly other sources of cost variation. This approach is preferred for two reasons: first, because the basis of financing enrolled students is much closer to the educational objective than are inputs such as numbers of classrooms and teachers, and, second, because it provides an incentive for providers to rearrange inputs in order to provide education more efficiently. But the capitation approach is not perfect. It does not, by itself, provide safeguards to ensure education quality or teaching effectiveness. Neither does it reflect cost differences among different programs, place-specific cost factors, or cost differences arising from special learning needs of students. Finally, it does not provide for improvements in curriculum, teaching materials, and teaching practices—all of which are urgently needed.

Table 6.16 shows how a composite financing formula can provide for all of these needs. The most advanced applications of this approach are in the Anglo-Saxon countries: the United States, Canada, England, Wales, Australia, and New Zealand.[48] Per-student allocations should be differentiated to reflect intrinsic differences in the cost of education delivery, such as the higher cost of technical specializations, and greater population dispersion in rural areas. Great care needs to be taken in designing this differentiation to reflect the unavoidable differences in cost of education provision due to factors such as population dispersion and climate differences. It is essential that the financing formula reflect these differences in order not to impose further hardship on the districts which experience higher costs. But if financing formulas simply mirror the current unit costs of different localities, the resulting schedule of coefficients will legitimate an inefficient delivery model. The same considerations apply to differentiation of costs for different programs of studies. Whereas unit investment cost differences among specializations primarily reflect the facilities

---

[48] *Needs-Based Resource Allocation in Education via Formula Funding of Schools,* edited by Kenneth Ross and Rosalind Levačić, International Institute for Education Planning, UNESCO, Paris, 1999.

TABLE 6.16: A COMPOSITE FORMULA FOR EDUCATION FINANCE

COMPONENT	DIMENSIONS	INDICATORS
Basic Per-Student Allocation	total enrollment, differentiated by grade and program	Full-time equivalent (FTE) enrollments by grade and type of program
School Site Needs	school size	Primary <200 FTE Secondary <600 FTE
	school remoteness operations and maintenance costs	Kilometers to town of 50,000+ persons Interior area of school in square meters
Student Supplementary Educational Needs	socio-economic hardship	percent of students from households receiving social assistance
	low educational achievement	number of students below 20th percentile assessment results
	non-fluency in national language	percent of students below cut-off score in national language test
	disabilities and special learning needs	number of students formally assessed with special learning needs
Educational Quality Improvement	specialized curriculum	FTE enrolled in specialized program
	specialized school	Total FTE (if special curriculum school)

Adapted from *"Principles for Designing Needs-Based School Funding Formulae",* Rosalind Levačić, and Kenneth Ross, in *Needs-Based Resource Allocation in Education via Formula Funding of Schools,* edited by Kenneth Ross and Rosalind Levačić, International Institute for Education Planning, UNESCO, Paris, 1999.

requirements of the specialization, recurrent costs differ largely as a function of class size and teaching loads. Some of the specialized secondary programs have very high unit costs as a result of too-small class sizes. The financing formula for specialized secondary and higher education programs should encourage these institutions to rationalize course offerings. This could take the form of moving towards more affordable class sizes, or reconfiguring course offerings, for example, by providing art education as one of several options in comprehensive secondary schools rather than in free-standing art schools. Adopting a relatively narrow spread of unit costs encourages more efficient delivery of the specializations with the highest historical costs. Because any additional costs would need to be financed from own sources, it also encourages the managing authorities to consider very carefully whether technical education programs which cost more than this amount are providing good value to the community.

A still more advanced approach to formula financing of education is to finance educational results rather than enrollments. Some of the charter school contracts in the United States, for example, condition the payment to private education providers on the achievement of agreed educational targets in terms of learning achievement. This approach is likely to grow in use as the tools for assessing school performance improve.

Eliminate Inconsistencies in Decentralization Roles

The potential benefits of decentralized education management have been frustrated by the inconsistency of responsibilities and resources of local governments under decentralization. Local governments are meant to be accountable to the local community for managing basic education effectively and efficiently. Yet they lack the authority to do so because the bulk of financing—for teachers' salaries and benefits—remains centrally controlled (or guaranteed), and because the MES retains control over key decisions affecting education delivery. The MES is responsible for curricula, recruitment, evaluation, training, and promotion of school principals and teachers, and establishment of norms governing minimum and maximum class size and teaching hours. These constraints make it impossible for local governments to carry out actions to improve efficiency—such as school consolidation—unless the Ministry of Education agrees. In addition, the MES must approve any proposals for teacher dismissals, school closure or school consolidation. In designing the decentralization legislation, Parliament retained these functions for the MES as a means of education quality assurance, but the experience of the past decade has shown that these input controls are not effective instruments for quality assurance. The decentralization formula should be changed in order to align responsibilities and accountabilities for managing primary and secondary education. This means empowering local authorities to carry out actions such as staff reduction and school consolidation that are necessary for improved efficiency. Quality assurance should be carried out through assessment of teaching practices and classroom results, rather than relying exclusively on normatives and staffing controls.

Manage Education at an Efficient Level of Aggregation

Most municipalities are of a suitable size to make the appropriate decisions about educations system rationalization, but some are too small to do so. There are a number of very small municipalities with as few as 3,000 residents, only a few primary schools, and no secondary schools. Students from these municipalities attend schools in adjacent areas. Where individual municipalities are too small to capture the economies of scale, decisions about rationalization of the education system need to be made by a group of municipalities—possibly at regional centers or the regional level. One of the reasons often given for managing education delivery at the municipal rather than the regional level is that regional officials are appointed, not elected, and thus lack the accountability of municipal councils. Nonetheless, voluntary associations of small municipalities could be formed under existing legislation, and this could contribute to efficiency in the management of education delivery.

Expand the Delegated-Budget Model

Although the results of the delegated-budget school management pilot have been modest to date, the approach embodies important principles of allowing school managers to retain any savings achieved through improved efficiency, and allowing expenditure flexibility across budget categories. These should be part of the broader reform of financing and management proposed above.

Let Student Demand Drive Higher-Education Offerings

The current managed quotas for enrollments in each higher education institution and program are an anachronism, and are inconsistent with the demand-driven model that the Government envisages. As higher fees are instituted, this managed process should be abandoned, and replaced with a fully demand-driven model in which institutions set their own admission standards consistent with their quality standards and aspirations. Doing this under Board of Trustees management for each institution would help ensure responsiveness to local, regional and national needs and aspirations.

Plan Capital Expenditures More Objectively

The current earmarked subsidy for capital expenditures should be replaced with a more objective mechanism—ideally, one that is based upon well-documented feasibility studies and involves significant cost-sharing by local governments. So far, the investment decisions depend merely on the availability of financing, usually through grants from the European Union.

CHAPTER 7

HEALTH IN TRANSITION

Poor health status, comparatively low levels of health spending, and inefficient use of resources (as manifested through excess capacity) have led the Government of Bulgaria to embark on wholesale reform of the health sector. The primary focus of this reform, the central component of which is the National Health Insurance Fund, has been organizational and financial. The hope is that the move to an insurance-based system, with contractual relationships between purchasers and providers, coupled with consumer choice, will improve the effectiveness of Bulgarian health expenditures and lead to improvements in the health status of Bulgaria's people.

The transition to a leaner, more efficient health care system is ongoing. Its successful implementation will require painful decisions, particularly with regard to the rationalization of hospital capacity. Some refocusing of the labor force has already been achieved—there are fewer doctors now than there were five years ago, and the role of the general practitioner has attained a high degree of prominence through specific retraining programs. The process of capacity reduction must, however, continue and be matched with investment in the surviving facilities in order to transform the system to one that provides truly modern health care.

Sector Overview

Bulgaria's health system was relatively neglected during the first years of transition as the Government addressed problems of macroeconomic stabilization and labor market and enterprise reform. Nonetheless, a number of laws were passed to allow private provision of health services; professional associations were re-established in the sector; and devolution of health care responsibilities to municipalities was undertaken in reaction to central planning. Still, as recently as 1999, the system was described as "mainly based upon the Soviet Shemashko model of public sector provision, tax-based financing, weighted towards hospital care, and with few incentives for providers to improve the effectiveness and efficiency of health care."[49] More recently, the Government has

---

[49] European Observatory, 1999.

embarked on a wide-ranging reform of the sector, using the social insurance model of Western Europe that has been adopted by many other Central and Eastern European countries over the past 10 years. These reforms are meant to strengthen the financial and operational performance of the system and to improve both allocative and technical efficiency, while maintaining universal and equitable access and coverage.

Health Indicators

Health indicators in Bulgaria have shown little improvement—and have in some cases deteriorated—over the transition period. Life expectancy at birth, which was one of the highest among the Central and Eastern European countries in the 1980s, has remained almost unchanged through the last decade, while most other countries (apart from Romania) have seen longevity increase (Figure 7.1). The incidence of new cases of tuberculosis has risen steadily over the transition, and while not of the same magnitude as Romania's problem, continues to be high compared to other CEE countries. The incidence of another important infectious disease, hepatitis, in Bulgaria, though similar to that of other countries in Eastern Europe, stubbornly remains four to five times the level in Central European transition economies. A similar pattern is displayed by rates of maternal mortality across the region.

Bulgaria was one of the few countries in Central and Eastern Europe to show a sustained drop in immunization coverage. The proportion of children under two immunized against DPT at the beginning of the transition was virtually universal, but by 2000, it had fallen to 68 percent. Immunization against polio has evolved similarly (Table 7.1).

Against this background, the reforms initiated in 1999 are aimed at improving health indicators while providing incentives for providers and consumers to use resources more efficiently. A National Health Insurance Fund undertakes the roles of pooling risks and purchasing medical care, through the use of contracts signed with individual physicians, group practices, and hospitals. Anecdotal evidence shows that nominal incomes of primary care physicians have increased dramatically since the introduction of the health insurance (by a factor of about five[50]) and are now about eight to ten times the average salary in the country. These gross wages must now cover office expenses and the wages of auxiliary staff (nurses, etc.); so, the increase in net wages has been somewhat smaller. However, there appear to be nursing shortages, suggesting relatively low wage offers for auxiliary staff. Thus, although definitive figures are not available, the increase in net general practitioner (GP) compensation has almost

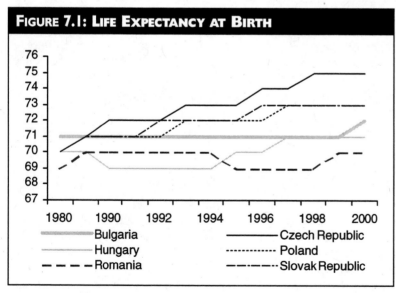

FIGURE 7.1: LIFE EXPECTANCY AT BIRTH

Bulgaria — Czech Republic
Hungary ············· Poland
– – – Romania —·—·— Slovak Republic

Source: TransMONEE.

---

[50] Bulgarian Medical Association.

TABLE 7.1: POLIO IMMUNIZATION RATE

COUNTRY	(PERCENT OF CHILDREN UNDER TWO IMMUNIZED)											
	1989	1990	1991	1992	1993	1994	1995	1996	1997	1998	1999	2000
Bulgaria	99.7	99.7	99	98.8	97	93.9	96.8	95.4	95.9	96.5	97.2	94.4
Czech Republic	99.0	99.0	99.0	99.0	99.0	98.0	98.0	98.0	97.0	97.0	97.0	97.4
Hungary	98.5	98.6	98.6	98.6	99.9	99.9	99.9	99.8	99.7	99.9	99.7	99.8
Poland	—	90.1	88.6	87.9	88.9	89.3	90.4	91.6	93.2	94.1	94.6	94.8
Romania	89.4	80.5	83.5	92.3	90.7	91.0	94.2	96.8	97.1	97.6	97.4	96.3
Slovak Republic	98.8	99	99.2	98.6	98.6	98.6	98.6	—	—	—	—	—

Source: TransMONEE.

certainly been high. Incomes of hospital specialists are expected to increase similarly in the near future.

Higher incomes and more discretion will make members of the medical profession considerably better off than they were previously. However, in the absence of direct control, additional incentives will be required to induce providers to pursue socially desirable but privately unrewarding goals, such as locating in remote areas and serving disadvantaged populations, including minorities. Offering sufficient incentives to providers to serve some populations may be expensive. Indeed, additional fees have been allocated for GPs locating in remote areas (for example, as measured by the conditions of roads and communications), but policies directed specifically at ethnic minorities have been more difficult to formulate and implement. The increased payments have been instrumental in reducing the number of vacant GP practices, but the cost of reaching the truly disadvantaged may be significantly higher.

Level and Structure of Health Expenditures

Total public expenditures in the health sector were at about 1.2 billion leva in 2001, or some 4 percent of GDP. The share of GDP devoted to public expenditure in the health sector has remained between 3.6 and 4 percent over the past five years (Table 7.2). However, an undetermined level of private spending—either legitimately for services outside the public sector or unofficially—is known to take place. Bulgaria's health expenditure as a percentage of GDP has been amongst the lowest in Central and Eastern Europe during the transition period, and well below the average for Western European countries (around 8 percent). Accounting for the level of per capita income, however, one finds that the share of GDP devoted to health care expenditure is only "somewhat" less than in comparable countries. The sector faces important challenges in adjusting to demographics and to higher efficiency and quality standards.

Under the unreformed health system, all public expenditures in the sector were allocated through the Ministry of Health and other ministries, either directly or via grant-financed activities of the municipalities. As a result of decentralization and the establishment of the National Health Insurance Fund (NHIF), the flow of funds is now more complex. Figure 7.2 shows the institutional composition of health expenditures from 1997 through 2001. Over this period, the share of the state budget in health spending has remained approximately constant: between 33 and 40 percent. However, the advent of the NHIF has been associated with a sharp reduction in the share of municipality spending: from about 50 percent in 1997–2000, to 15 percent in 2001. As the NHIF appropriates more responsibility for expenditures, particularly in the hospital sector, its share will likely increase above its current 36 percent level. In 2001, about 551 million leva, or 46 percent of the total, is channeled though line ministries, and most of it (85 percent) through

TABLE 7.2: COMPOSITION OF PUBLIC HEALTH EXPENDITURES

	1997	1998	1999	2000	2001
			Millions of Leva		
Current:	585.3	753.0	818.9	896.8	1114.0
Wages	239.7	373.2	418.3	317.2	132.9
Drugs	161.5	193.7	189.0	140.7	53.4
Other Current	184.1	186.1	211.6	438.9	927.8
Capital	46.8	56.6	114.0	81.0	82.0
Total	**632.1**	**809.6**	**932.9**	**977.8**	**1196.0**
			Percent of Total		
Current:	93	93	88	92	93
Wages	38	46	45	32	11
Drugs	26	24	20	14	4
Other Current	29	23	23	45	78
Capital	7	7	12	8	7
	100	100	100	100	100
Total Health Expenditures as percent of GDP	**3.6**	**3.6**	**3.9**	**3.7**	**4.0**

Source: Ministry of Health.

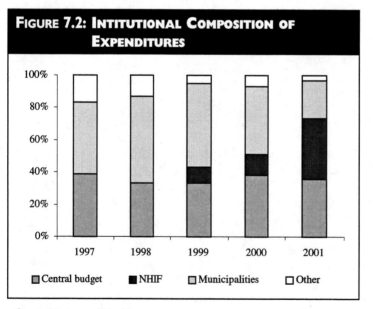

FIGURE 7.2: INTITUTIONAL COMPOSITION OF EXPENDITURES

Legend: Central budget · NHIF · Municipalities · Other

Source: Ministry of Health.

the Ministry of Health.[51] The NHIF accounts for about 428 million leva (excluding the reserve fund of some 29 million leva), while municipalities spend 183 million leva (23 percent), some of which is financed by transfers from the central budget.[52]

From 1997 to 2000, between 32 and 46 percent of health expenditures were devoted to wage costs (including social security contributions). Over this period, the share of spending on drugs fell from 26 percent to 14 percent, and capital spending accounted for about 8 percent of the total. In 2001, with

---

[51] The Ministries of Transport and Communications, Defense and Labor and Social Policy, plus the Council of Ministers, incur some health expenditures directly.

[52] In principle, inter-governmental grants are not tied, but in practice municipalities must adhere to certain guidelines in the use of grants. For example, priority must be given to covering recurrent costs (mostly wages); the "appropriate" level of such costs is negotiated between the central government and the municipalities.

General Practitioners fully funded by the NHIF and hospitals estimated to receive 20 percent of their funding from this source, the share of wage costs in total spending is estimated at 11 percent. In 2001, spending on drugs fell to 9 percent, just half the share of two years ago, and capital spending shrank to 7 percent of total health spending. These developments suggest a general shift in funding from suppliers of material medical inputs to health care providers, and from future to current consumption.

Health Care Capacity

The relatively poor health status of the Bulgarian population suggests either an inadequate level of quality medical care or greater than normal health reducing activities (for example, smoking and lower prevention), or both. This section examines indicators of the availability of medical care—facilities and labor—and the extent to which it is used.

Commonly used measures of health care capacity include the number of hospital beds per capita and the number of physicians per capita. Figure 7.3 shows indicators of the first measure for six transition economies in Central and Eastern Europe. Bulgaria has moved from having the highest number of hospital beds to having about the same number as Romania, and slightly fewer than Hungary. It is relevant, of course, to examine also utilization rates, as measured, for example, by the bed occupancy rate. Less data are available for this indicator, especially for countries in Eastern Europe, but the figure does suggest that at least in the mid-1990s, Bulgaria's large capacity of hospital beds was under-utilized. Even by 1999, the National Center for Health Information reported an average bed occupancy rate of only 67 percent, despite the elimination of some 26 percent of beds between 1997 and 1999.

Low-occupancy rates masked an even lower real rate of utilization of resources, as the average length of stay in a hospital bed was 11.9 days. This is virtually twice the time that a patient stays in hospital in Western Europe, and one and a half times that for an average patient in the Czech Republic. Thus, many hospital beds are empty much of the time and even when they are occupied, they are used inefficiently. The introduction of day surgery and more efficient management processes should reduce average lengths of stay considerably. In contrast, the rate of out-patient contacts per person in Bulgaria in 1999 (5.4 per person) was approximately equal to the average for OECD countries, which ranged from 2.7 in Sweden to 12.7 in Japan (although these are 1985 data).

In terms of labor inputs, Bulgaria faces a similar problem of surplus. Until 1998, it had more doctors per capita than any other Central or Eastern European country, except Hungary, and nearly twice as many as Romania. Consistent with this pattern, Bulgaria has had a much lower ratio of nurses to physicians than other countries in the

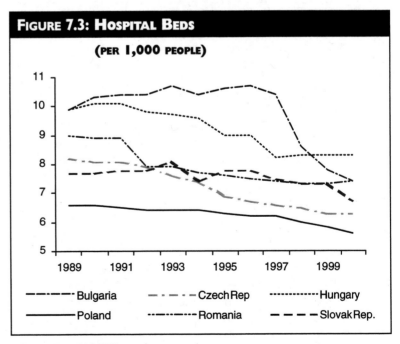

FIGURE 7.3: HOSPITAL BEDS

(PER 1,000 PEOPLE)

Legend: Bulgaria; Czech Rep; Hungary; Poland; Romania; Slovak Rep.

Source: TransMONEE.

region, again except for Hungary. Anecdotal evidence from interviews with officials suggests that, particularly in the primary care sub-sector, the supply of nurses remains low.

Organization of the Health Care Market

Under the old system, most health care was delivered through polyclinics and hospitals. The reformed system has introduced the concept of a General Practitioner (GP) as the first point of entry into the health system for most non-emergency cases. GPs are self-employed and can operate singly or in group practices.[53] Unlike in some other countries, specialist physicians work either in hospitals or on an out-patient basis, but rarely both. Out-patient specialists (including dentists) are also self-employed, while hospital specialists have employment contracts.

All physicians are permitted to provide care privately and to charge patients a negotiated fee. However, to earn income from the NHIF, GPs must have a list of registered patients on the basis of which they are paid, as explained below. A GP is permitted to sign a contract with the NHIF only if the list contains at least 800 people. This feature represents an obvious barrier to entry for physicians who want to enter geographically new markets, although it can be circumvented by joining a group practice. There are good reasons to support a minimum practice size (for example, maintaining skills), but this requirement should be imposed on practices after they have had some time to build up their clientele, but not for new practices.

The transformation from polyclinic care to private family GPs, while aimed at changing the incentives of providers and patients, has not involved drastic actions. Some evidence for this is that the physical structures in which polyclinics operated have been "privatized" simply by giving them to physicians (for example, in Pleven municipality). The physicians were not required to purchase the assets, nor were they charged any meaningful rent for their use.[54]

There are about 300 hospitals in Bulgaria, two-thirds owned by the state, and one-third by municipal governments.[55] Until now, these have been funded directly by the Ministry of Health and municipal governments. In 1991, most state hospitals were "commercialized" in the sense that they were converted to joint stock companies, although they remain state-owned.[56] The hospitals are managed by a Board of Directors, which collectively sign a management contract with the Ministry of Health. This Board, acting through the executive director, can choose the size and structure of the hospital's labor force, having the rights to both *hire* and *fire*, and receives guidelines from the Ministry of Health on remuneration levels.

The number of hospital beds has been reduced by 30 percent since 1997 but, as noted earlier, utilization rates still remain low. Some officials suggest that further reductions of beds (as many as 12,000 of the current 62,000 beds) need to be effected, especially if out-patient surgery practices are adopted, implying that further difficult decisions will be required. At hospitals visited in both Sofia and Pleven, bed reductions were effected by reducing the number of beds per room. The primary effect of this is probably to improve quality levels, but the impact on costs is likely to be relatively small: staff costs change little, as do heating and other utility costs.

Hospitals are beginning to respond to the new environment, reporting the need to attract patients (this will be particularly true once the new NHIF payment mechanisms are introduced), and exercising more autonomy in their management decisions. Guidelines continue to be set by the central Ministry of Health regarding such items as wages and employment, but management is afforded some discretion over these and other decisions, including investments. While investment plans must still be submitted to the central ministry, hospitals have greater incentives to assess

---

[53] Indeed, some polyclinics have been transformed into GP group practices.

[54] A four-story building with dental equipment was rented for the equivalent of about US$170 per month.

[55] A Constitutional Court ruling stated that regional hospitals, in which the MoH kept a controlling interest, legally belonged to the municipalities.

[56] Twenty-five regional hospitals were commercialized, but their equity was split between the MoH and the relevant municipality in a ratio of 51:49.

investment needs more carefully than they did previously, primarily because such investments can either reduce costs (for example, for heating) and thereby free up resources for quality improvement, or because they can improve quality directly.[57] As only 25 percent of hospital funding derives from contractual arrangements with the NHIF for a narrow set of procedures, most capital costs are financed by state and municipal budgets. However, as the financing role of the NHIF expands, prices paid for services should begin to incorporate explicit capital charges to cover depreciation. In the absence of such an explicit recognition of capital needs in the provider contract rates, necessary capital improvements will have to be funded through operating savings or reductions in necessary operating expenditure. This represents a major challenge in achieving and maintaining a sustainable level of investment for the health sector.

The Insurance-Based Reform

Organization of the Insurance Market

Private health insurance in Bulgaria is very limited, and there is little data on its extent or nature. Private insurance companies are permitted to operate, and it is possible that as medical care providers are given more autonomy and freedom, alliances between providers and private insurers could develop. At present, however, the main source of insurance is the public sector.

By granting physicians and hospitals some decision making authority, and by engaging them on a contractual basis, the Government is moving towards a system of publicly administered insurance, implemented through the private provision of care. The primary role of the NHIF is to perform the administrative functions of an insurance provider, acting as a pooling mechanism to spread risks, and as a purchaser of services on behalf of the consumers. Contributions to the NHIF (see below) are mandatory, and are not related to expected costs of care. The package of covered services is uniform across the population, although quality is likely to vary.

There are 28 Regional Health Insurance Funds that act as administrative units of the National Fund. Regional funds are not self-financing; they are merely offices of the NHIF. Insurance contributions are collected by the NSSI and channeled to the NHIF. The central fund, in turn, allocates them to the regional funds. The primary role of the regional funds is to implement the purchasing function. Local providers sign contracts with, and are paid by, their regional fund, although each fund has little authority to alter the parameters of the contract. The regional funds also appear to have little discretion over which hospitals they sign contracts with. They are not involved in the accreditation process by which hospitals are granted eligibility to contract with the NHIF, this process being carried out by the Accreditation Council, a specialized body for accreditation of hospitals.

Contributions to the National Health Insurance Fund

The NHIF is funded primarily from payroll-based contributions made by working individuals, and general revenues, from which contributions are paid on behalf of the non-working population. Currently, the contribution rate is 6 percent of wages up to 870 leva per month, thus putting a ceiling on contributions. Employees make 75 percent of the payment, and employers 25 percent.[58] The contribution rate is the same for those at minimum wage jobs and those making 10 times the minimum, making the scheme somewhat regressive, and a potential barrier for the working poor. Since the current minimum wage of 100 leva per month is below the "subsistence minimum" level of income, even minimal health insurance payments and provider co-payments will reduce the resources available for food and other basic living expenses. This is a potential access issue that needs to be addressed in the overall financing regime.

---

[57] Fuel costs reportedly fell by 50 percent after commercialization of the Pleven University Hospital. Telephone charges similarly fell, while the average length of stay dropped from 12.5 days in the first quarter of 2000 to 10.2 days in the same period of 2001.

[58] By 2007, the split will be 50/50.

Self-employed individuals are required to pay to the Fund 6 percent of their incomes, which are assumed for tax purposes to be at least twice the minimum wage. There are a further 13 categories of contributors, including pensioners, whose contributions are paid for by the state budget, and those receiving unemployment benefits, whose contributions are financed by municipal budgets. The insurance contribution for these people is based on 70 percent of the minimum monthly wage for most groups. The result of this is that the average government contribution per person for those who are not working is around 36 percent of that of the working individuals. The level of government contributions for these "non-working" groups may need reconsideration in terms of equity and revenue generation/sustainability.

Health insurance contributions are collected by the NSSI in conjunction with pension contributions. Compliance rates for NHIF contributions appear to be better than for pensions, because younger individuals tend to be concerned more about current health risks than future income needs. While this is probably true (despite the fact that insurance demand by the young is often low also), it assumes that individuals are able to report different taxable incomes for the different contributions. If this is so, it suggests that full integration of the contributions at the collection stage should be considered.[59] Indeed, the Government envisages to establish a Unified Revenue Agency (URA).

Projections of future expenditures by the NHIF suggest that adjustments to the contribution rate will be necessary. Table 7.3 shows projected revenues and expenditures of the Fund until 2005, with an initial surplus converting to a deficit by 2003. Over the six-year period, the undiscounted surplus is projected to reach 525 million leva. However, the long-term financial sustainability of the Fund will require additional revenue mobilization if projected deficits continue into the future, unless there are changes to the costs to be covered out of the NHIF budget.

Although the current surpluses of the NHIF can be used to finance future health care costs, it is important to examine the total impact of public spending in the health sector, and indeed across sectors. One concern of the Government is that the interest rate available on NHIF reserves, which are deposited in the central bank, is much lower than the rate at which the Government can borrow to finance its deficit. This financing cost must be weighed against the potential efficiency improvements of the new institutional arrangements. However, it is important to remember that these reserves have accumulated on a one-time basis, and result from conscious decisions to delay the health insurance implementation in an attempt to improve the chances of a smoother implementation process. Once the NHIF reaches a "steady state" of operations, the cash reserves are likely to be quite modest. This underscores the need to move to a steady state situation as soon as possible, with predictable revenue and expenditure streams. If such a steady state situation can be achieved fairly soon, the remaining accumulated reserve fund presents a unique opportunity for

---

[59] This could have the adverse effect of *reducing* health contributions, instead of increasing pension contributions.

TABLE 7.3: REVENUES AND EXPENDITURES OF THE NHIF

(MILLION LEVA)	2000	2001	2002	2003	2004	2005
Revenues	549	614	686	764	855	926
Expenditures	127	428	549	900	1048	1178
O/w: claims	97	404	487	791	934	1111
Surplus/Deficit	422	186	137	−136	−193	−252
Accumulated Surplus	422	609	716	854	718	525

Source: NHIF.

the Government to make priority investments in rationalizing the service delivery system and renovating and re-equipping the remaining facilities. Together with specific capital funding and reimbursement policies, these initiatives can ensure a sustainable long-run capital investment and replacement regime.

Provider Payment Mechanisms

The NHIF has been contracting with physicians for out-patient (or pre-hospital) care since July 1, 2000, and began contracting with hospitals for in-patient care starting on July 1, 2001. Most elements of these contractual arrangements are determined within the National Framework Contract, negotiated annually between the Fund, the Ministry of Finance, the Ministry of Health, the Bulgarian Medical Association, and the Bulgarian Dental Surgeons' Association. Currently, out-patient services are paid differently, depending on the type of provider.

General practitioners, who have only existed in their current status for less than two years, are paid on a capitation basis. Contributing individuals are required to register with a GP of their choice, to whom a monthly capitation fee is paid from the NHIF. In 2000, the capitation payment was based solely on the patient's age: it ranged from 2.19 BGN for children up to three years to 0.55 BGN for people in the 18-34 age group. This schedule was revised in 2001 in two ways: first, the number of age categories was reduced; and second, GPs began to receive additional capitation payments for patients with chronic diseases, such as heart disease, lung disease, diabetes, psychiatric conditions, and cancer. GPs are entitled to charge a co-payment equal to one percent of the monthly minimum wage, amounting to 0.85 leva in 2001. These payment mechanisms have led to gross annual GP incomes of approximately 18,000 leva. Even accounting for the recurrent costs of running a GP practice, compared with the average annual income of polyclinic physicians in 1990 of about 2,400 leva (in current leva), it is far more rewarding to be a doctor now than in the past.

In many countries, additional payments are made to GPs for the provision of high-priority services, such as immunizations, through a mix of prospective (for example, capitation) and retrospective (fee-for-service) payments. Retrospective payments are generally not used in Bulgaria; however, the prospective component responds to expected costs in two ways: patients of different ages attract different capitation rates; and GPs are compensated for enrolling patients with certain chronic diseases (for example, heart disease, diabetes, etc.). These payments reduce the incentive of physicians to sign up low-cost patients.

In order to guarantee access to medical care, the Ministry of Health composes a "health map" of the country, identifying areas with a less than adequate number of GPs and health care. In order to induce GPs to locate in remote areas, the National Framework Contract allows a lump-sum payment of 300 leva, plus an additional 100 leva per month. This represents approximately a 15 percent premium on monthly income earned in less remote areas (not accounting for income from private sources, which may be significant in urban areas).

Specialists like GPs, are also permitted to charge a co-payment but, in contrast to GPs, they are paid on a per visit basis, receiving 8 leva for an initial visit, and 4 leva for a subsequent visit. Further visits associated with the same episode of illness or any visits that are not referred by a GP (or in some cases another specialist) are not reimbursed by the NHIF, but specialists are permitted to charge a fee, which is negotiated directly with the patient. Specialists are only allowed to claim payment for up to 400 visits per month; assuming half of these are new visits, and that the physician reaches the quota, this amounts to an annual income of approximately 29,000 leva, or 10 times the average wage.[60] In practice, however, few out-patient specialists reach the limit on the number of allowed visits.

---

[60] The average annual wage in 2001 is estimated at 2,980 leva.

The payment of **dentists** is similar to that of specialists, except that they are paid not according to the number of visits, but on an hourly basis (at the rate of 26 leva per hour). One substantive difference with the payment of specialists is that payments for dental visits are more responsive to underlying costs (because different procedures are accorded different time allotments whereas specialist visits are subject to the same fee schedule). A second difference reflects the apparently large oversupply of dentists in the country: dentists are limited to claim payment for at most 21 hours per month, implying a maximum annual income of a little over 6,500 leva. There is a widespread belief, although there are no data to confirm this, that many dentists charge additional fees to supplement their incomes.

Laboratory services, provided by either independent or in-house laboratories, are paid on a fee-for-service basis, but without limits on the number of tests they can perform. Finally, there is a list of about 1,200 pharmaceutical products whose costs are reimbursed at varying rates by the NHIF. The reimbursement rate varies between 20 and 100 percent for drugs on the list; for others it is zero.

On July 1, 2001, the NHIF began financing a part of hospital recurrent costs. Initially, hospitals are paid by the Fund for each of 30 "pathways". [61] In 2001, the NHIF payments amounted to 20 percent of hospital budgets, and 25 percent in 2002. Until 2004, the number of services covered and the reimbursement rates will be increased. This pattern is expected to continue until the Fund covers about half of hospital expenditures, the remaining funds coming from either state or municipal budgets, and own sources.

Administrative Costs

As the NHIF is still in the phase-in stage, it is difficult to judge its performance in terms of administrative costs. Estimates from the NHIF show that as the Fund takes on further responsibility for paying medical claims, its administrative costs of 3.2 percent of current revenues in 2001 would increase to 3.8 percent by 2005 (Figure 7.4).

One aspect of the system that will keep the administrative costs of the insurance fund down is the monopoly position of the Fund. Other countries that have instituted competitive insurance systems, such as Chile, have found that marketing and sales costs have added significantly to non-medical expenses, causing administrative costs to rise to more than 15 percent of revenues. Absent the discipline of the market, however, alternative mechanisms are required to ensure cost-efficient insurance provision. The legal limit on administrative costs is such a mechanism, but it will need to be backed up by appropriate sanctions in the event of cost over-runs.

An important component of administrative costs consists of those borne directly by physicians. There is a perception that GPs especially work harder than before, now spending "half their time filling in forms." Under the old system, physicians recorded in a single sentence the diagnosis, treatment, and medication of each patient. Now a GP fills in a long form for each visit, three copies of which are sent to three different offices. These documents, which are not electronically transmitted, are meant to provide the inputs for a monitoring system, but many physicians do not submit them, and those that are submitted are often not examined. In Sofia, 18 clerks examine about 50 forms per day, leading to an increasing backlog. A current World Bank health project is supporting the development of information systems at both the NHIF and health providers to reduce the overhead costs and increase timeliness and accuracy.

Investment Programming

The transition to the new institutional arrangements for financing and delivering health care has meant that some planning procedures have become less than transparent. This is simply a result

---

[61] A pathway is a set of procedures, comprising, for example, diagnosis, admission, acute care, surgery, and recovery, deemed appropriate for particular conditions.

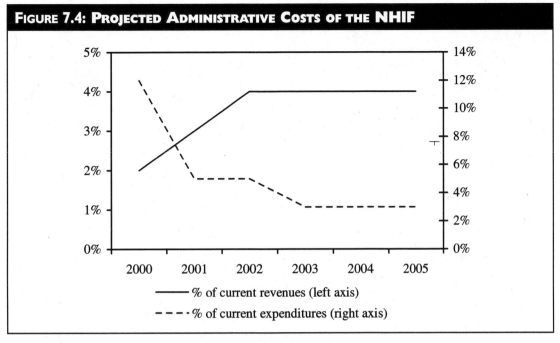

FIGURE 7.4: PROJECTED ADMINISTRATIVE COSTS OF THE NHIF

——— % of current revenues (left axis)

- - - - % of current expenditures (right axis)

Source: NHIF.

of the creation of the NHIF with considerable financial resources and authority, and the associated need to coordinate policy and planning decisions, particularly with regard to investment plans, both in terms of the acquisition of new equipment, and the repair and maintenance of buildings and other structures. This fact, along with the sketchy information available on the quality of the existing capital stock, makes it difficult to assess both investment needs and the adequacy of proposed spending in this area.

An obvious response to the lack of complete and accurate data on the existing capital stock is to undertake a careful inventory of medical equipment and structures, possibly on the basis of a random survey of establishments, as opposed to carrying out an exhaustive census. Ideally, such data should be complemented by existing (or newly collected) indicators of need, such as local demographic and epidemiological measures, so that both the level and distribution of capital goods can be evaluated. It is important to include in such an undertaking estimates of capital availability not just in public hospitals and NHIF-affiliated physician offices, but also in private establishments that operate outside the public system.

In the absence of such data, a very rough estimate of the adequacy of investment spending in the health sector can be derived by comparing Bulgaria's expenditure levels with those of other countries. Table 7.4 suggests that mature market economies allocate, on average, 3 to 4 percent of health spending to investment.[62] In Poland (the only transition economy for which data were available), however, capital spending amounted to about 10.5 percent of current health spending. The share of capital health spending in Bulgaria is about 7 percent, with only one peak in 1999, attributable to the set-up costs associated with the establishment of the NHIF. It would seem imprudent at this transitional phase, during which significant restructuring and modernization is

---

[62] This figure must be interpreted with caution. As medical care becomes increasingly more capital intensive, investment augments the capital stock, so this level of expenditure cannot be seen as the steady state level required to cover depreciation, thus maintaining the existing level of capital. Nonetheless, it provides a basis for judging the adequacy of capital spending.

TABLE 7.4: RATIO OF CAPITAL TO CURRENT PUBLIC HEALTH EXPENDITURES, 1998	
(SELECTED OECD COUNTRIES)	
	CAPITAL SPENDING RATIO (PERCENT)
Austria	3.6
Canada	3.1
Denmark	3.0
France	2.8
Iceland	3.0
Korea	4.5
Poland	10.5
U.K.	3.7

Source: TransMONEE Database, UNICEF.

required, to adopt something approaching the steady-state level of investment in Western Europe. By controlling the level of physician compensation (which, as has been indicated, has increased substantially over the last two years), capital funding could amount to levels of the order of 8–10 percent of current health expenditures. This round of new investment should focus on medical equipment and structures, instead of administrative facilities and computers for the NHIF and its branches.

New investment in out-patient facilities, particularly GPs' offices, has been financed through a World Bank loan. However, the hospital sector appears to be in need of significant refurbishment and replacement of key diagnostic and therapeutic equipment. Some of the costs of the required investment could be financed from capacity reductions within the sector. However, the cost savings from such closures are uncertain at best. For example, one hospital in Sofia had reduced bed capacity by nearly one half, but primarily through a reduction in the number of beds per room. Since utilization rates were low beforehand, and utility costs were essentially unaffected by the change, cost savings are likely to have been minimal. It is clear that closures of whole wards or even complete facilities, as well as the amalgamation of facilities to reduce administrative overhead, will be required if any significant efficiencies are to be achieved.

At the same time as mobilizing sufficient resources to cover investment needs, the institutional environment within which investment choices are made needs to be clarified. If the NHIF is to contribute only 50 percent of hospital funding on a continuing basis, with the balance coming from state and municipal budgets, there is a possibility that each funding institution will leave it to the other to cover investment costs. In principle, this free-rider problem can be averted at the time when the National Framework Contract is negotiated, when all relevant parties are represented. If capital costs are to be financed from the insurance fund, then at a minimum the reimbursement rates offered to hospitals will need to include a depreciation allowance and perhaps other capital charges. Alternatively, the fund might be seen as financing only current costs, with investment and depreciation covered by the Ministry of Health, or municipalities.

One advantage of financing capital costs through NHIF service fees is that hospitals may be able to borrow, or issue equity, against these future revenues. This could represent an attractive source of additional funds, given the Government's limited access to capital markets, although it would require that creditors perceive the underlying pricing policies as credible and sustainable. Regardless of the approach chosen, it is clear that a concrete policy direction must be established soon, together with the appropriate legal, financial, funding and policy framework.

Initial Impact of the Reform

Aggregate public spending in the health sector, as a proportion of GDP, is not expected to change significantly in the near future, although some increase is planned. Of greater interest is the change in the way in which this expenditure is channeled to end users, primarily as a result of the health insurance reforms. Since these reforms are in their infancy, there is little objective and representative data available at this stage with which to judge their impact.

There is anecdotal evidence that hospitals and physicians are beginning to alter their behavior. Bed numbers have been reduced and some hospitals have merged; some facilities report that average lengths of stay have fallen and that patient turnover rates have increased; and the mix of services from high-level curative care to primary care has been significant. One regional health insurance fund reported an increase between the first half of 1999 and the corresponding period of 2000 in the number of non-hospital consultations, while payments to providers remained mostly unchanged.

These apparent—though statistically unconfirmed—improvements in technical efficiency have occurred in tandem with some negative developments regarding access. Members of Romani Baht, a non-governmental organization serving the Roma community, have voiced concern over the closure of some facilities in Roma neighborhoods, particularly in Sofia. This has stemmed from the greater autonomy given physicians, who previously could be assigned to posts. The Government thus needs to recognize that when providers are given more discretion, the financial cost of providing services to some communities may be much higher than others. The Government has initiated a project aimed at training Roma nurses (it is believed that there are currently few, if any, registered Roma doctors, although data on the ethnic breakdown of the country's physicians is not officially maintained): whether this strategy is more productive than paying nurses (and doctors), regardless of their ethnic background, a high enough wage to induce them to work in minority communities is difficult to say. The European Union has committed funds (1.1 million Euro) to a project aimed at improving the health status and medical services of Roma communities. It includes rehabilitation and equipment of medical practices in rural areas with predominantly Roma and other ethnic minorities. In addition, training of GPs, nurses and informal leaders of Roma communities is envisaged. A new World Bank project has specific emphasis on ensuring access, especially by the poor and ethnic minorities.

Consumer satisfaction with the reforms so far has been mixed. A survey conducted by the National Institute of Public Health found that more than 50 percent of respondents were not satisfied with the new system. However, 70 percent of individuals were happy with their choice of GP. There was evidence that GPs were more attentive to patient needs and desires, and also more competent. On the other hand, more than 20 percent of respondents reported that GPs prescribed very expensive drugs, and that waiting times for GPs were too long.

The Road Ahead

Bulgaria has embarked on a fundamental transformation of its health care system in the hope of improving its relatively poor health status indicators and using the available resources more efficiently. The focal point of the reforms is the National Health Insurance Fund, which undertakes both risk pooling and medical care purchasing functions on behalf of the population. This institution, while exercising autonomy from the Ministry of Health, remains a part of the public sector: the principal rationale for its existence seems to be that creating a new institution was likely to be politically easier than fundamentally reforming an old one (the Ministry of Health).

Tax-financed universal health insurance has been adopted by many countries, although the extent to which the *provision* of services has been allocated to the private sector has varied. Bulgaria has adopted a middle of the road approach, choosing to treat medical care providers (including doctors and hospitals) as regulated private agents, while publicly operating the insurance function. In contrast, some countries, for example, Chile and the Czech Republic, have moved further towards private provision of insurance, as well as medical care.

The "single payer" nature of the public health insurance system has some advantages, particularly with regard to avoiding the marketing costs of a competitive insurance industry, which can be high. However, it will be important for the Government to maintain the incentives of the monopoly insurer to be cost-conscious, to ensure equitable access to care, and to induce continued quality improvements on the part of physicians and hospitals. Maintaining these incentives will require a clear separation of the roles of the National and Regional Health Insurance Funds vis-à-vis the medical profession.

Another mechanism by which incentives can be provided to the NHIF might be via the discipline of a fringe of private insurance companies. This industry is in its infancy and, at this stage, probably cannot be relied upon to represent a significant competitive element, primarily because most people cannot afford to purchase private coverage. Over the medium term, the Government will need to trade off the competitive benefits of a private insurance sector against the need to maintain the quality of, and political support for, a universally available system.

The large increase in the share of health expenditures devoted to physician incomes needs to be monitored closely. In particular, it will be important to ensure adequate maintenance of existing capital assets, as well as investment in new equipment and facilities, so that the quality of care does not suffer. As noted above, the current accumulated surplus provides a unique opportunity to establish and partially fund the introduction of a sustainable capital improvement and maintenance system. Regardless of whether this surplus is used, the reimbursement and financing policies of the NHIF need to be revised explicitly to take into account the potential sources of capital financing (including the private sector) and the uses of capital assets in health care delivery (including capital charges and depreciation).

Proper incentives for medical personnel are essential if the focus of providers is to be reoriented towards patients. However, the primary channel by which incentives are provided is through the *way* in which doctors are paid, not the *amount* they receive. The reforms have changed both of these margins, moving from a salary-based system to a capitation-based one (for GPs), as well as increasing income levels. But the over-supply of doctors inherited from the central planning system suggests that previous income levels were not so low as to discourage entry into the medical profession. This implies that the main mechanism for improving incentives should be the change in *how*, not *how much*, doctors are paid. If medical care facilities are consequently starved of investment funds, the main outcome of the reforms could be simply a transfer of wealth from taxpayers in general to the medical profession, with little improvement in the quality of care or the efficiency with which it is delivered. The recent reforms have, however, led to important changes in the medical marketplace. Since July, 2000 up to mid-2001, 800 physicians and over 4,000 other medical personnel have been let go from previously secure government jobs in the health sector, and over 2,000, including 191 doctors and dentists, are currently collecting unemployment benefits.

At an institutional level, the functions of the NHIF, the Ministry of Health, and the municipalities, should be clearly delineated. Each of these institutions will continue to play important roles, although their scope and scale will change as the NHIF assumes greater responsibility for hospital financing. The Ministry of Finance will need to act in a coordinating capacity, to ensure that changing responsibilities are matched by corresponding changes in resource flows. There is a pressing need to develop the parameters of a "steady state" health financing system, including the long-term division of responsibilities and revenue sources between the MOH and the NHIF.

Over the coming years, the resources of the NHIF will need to be augmented as it expands its financing role. One option is to increase the rate of the payroll tax. If this is offset by a reduction in payroll taxes earmarked for pensions, then the revenue problem will just be shifted to the pension system. If there is no offset, the increased tax burden on wages will have further undesirable effects on labor supply and costs of private business. An alternative is to increase contributions to the NHIF made by the state on behalf on non-working individuals. Since these contributions are financed from general revenues, the net effect (including any tax increase or expenditure reduction) could be determined, based on a judgment of the capacity of the overall tax system. Clearly, different combinations of payroll contribution increases and additional general revenues would yield different additional resources for the health sector, with different distributional and efficiency effects. The NHIF needs to consider the introduction of a more graduated premium payment approach to ensure access to those at the lower end of the income spectrum. This could include reductions in both the premium rate and the level of co-payment for the "working poor", as well as those with minimal income who are not working or covered by other premium exclusions. Although this will entail some initial administrative costs and procedures, these features could be incorporated into the new NHIF computer system to be financed under the World Bank loan, and this could have a positive impact on the level of access to health services by the poor.

CHAPTER 8

SOCIAL PROTECTION: ISSUES AND RECOMMENDATIONS

Bulgaria has a comprehensive social protection system consisting of a mix of programs inherited from the socialist period, such as family benefits, as well as new programs, initiated during the 1990s to address the social outcomes of economic reforms, including unemployment programs and social assistance. Prior to 1991, guaranteed employment served as the main social protection mechanism in the country. Social assistance had a relatively small role, with limited programs for those who were not able to work, such as the elderly and the disabled. With the economic restructuring and reforms of the late 1990s, the social protection system has expanded to encompass welfare programs that explicitly help households to cope with the new risks of poverty and unemployment.

Over the past decade, Bulgaria has been quite successful in completing a first phase of substantial post-socialist social protection reforms, including establishing the legislative and institutional framework for labor market and social assistance systems, and laying the ground for pension reform, based on a diversified multi-pillar model. The second phase of reforms involves steps to address new challenges, including unemployment growth, particularly long-term unemployment, the changing nature of poverty, and upcoming shocks to households, such as the planned increase in domestic energy prices. The road ahead entails important challenges to improve the sustainability of social protection mechanisms, and to strengthen the targeting and effectiveness of programs.

This chapter starts with an overview of the overall expenditure envelope for social protection, the coverage of the system, and the poverty alleviation impact. The rest of the chapter discusses issues related to the social protection system at large, as well as specific policy issues within the three subsectors: pensions, labor markets and social assistance. It also presents analyses of the incidence and effectiveness of programs, based on three nationally representative household surveys conducted in 1995, 1997 and 2001.[63]

---

[63] The chapter draws upon a forthcoming report by Cornelia Tesliuc, prepared as background for both the PEIR and the Poverty Assessment Update, entitled "Social Protection and Poverty Reduction in Bulgaria."

Overview of Social Protection

Expenditures

Over the 1990s, social protection financing in Bulgaria averaged 12 percent of GDP, peaking at 15 percent in 1993, and dropping to a low of 9.3 percent of GDP during the crisis of 1996. Social protection spending increased at the outset of the transition period with the growth of unemployment and the influx of early retirees into the pension system. Real social expenditures started to decline in 1992 alongside inflationary financing and as a consequence of the 1996/97 crisis it fell to a record low of 36 percent of 1991 levels by 1997. After 1997, social protection spending grew alongside GDP, attaining 13.6 percent of GDP in 2001, and has been gradually recovering its purchasing power (Figures 8.1 and 8.2). As a share of total consolidated government expenditures, social protection expenditures increased from 21 percent in 1996 to 33 percent in 2001—and these are projected to reach 35 percent in 2002.

The composition of social protection spending has changed as follows in the 1990s. Family benefits have declined relative to other benefits, as the main benefit, child allowance, has been frozen in nominal terms since 1997. Social assistance benefits, including the two main targeted cash benefit programs for low income households-the Guaranteed Minimum Income (GMI) and energy benefit programs-have increased as a share of GDP. Pensions, after falling to 6 percent of GDP during the crisis in 1996/1997, account for 9.1 percent of GDP in 2001.

Old age pensions comprised almost 55 percent of total social protection spending in 2001 (Table 8.1). Another 11 programs account for more than 30 percent of spending: the larger ones are the unemployment benefit (5 percent), disability pensions (5 percent), child allowances for children of insured parents, and sickness benefits (3 percent each). The remaining 22 programs account for 4 percent of social protection spending. The major ones are described in Sections B through E.

Coverage

Social protection programs in Bulgaria have wide coverage within the population. Over 80 percent of Bulgarians received at least one type of benefit in 2001 (Table 8.2)—however, only one-third

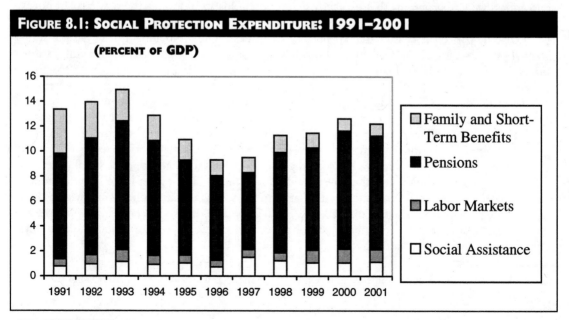

FIGURE 8.1: SOCIAL PROTECTION EXPENDITURE: 1991–2001

(PERCENT OF GDP)

Legend:
☐ Family and Short-Term Benefits
■ Pensions
▨ Labor Markets
☐ Social Assistance

Source: MOLSP, MOF.

FIGURE 8.2: SOCIAL PROTECTION SPENDING AND GDP DYNAMICS IN REAL TERMS (1991=1)

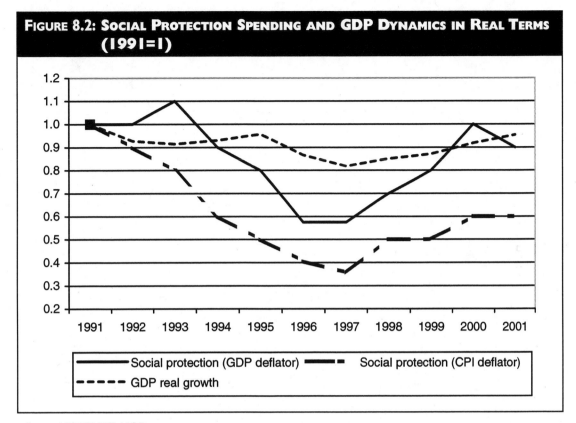

Source: MOLSP, NSI, MOF.

of the population is of retirement age or poor. At the aggregate level, this has remained stable since 1995. At the program level, however, there have been significant increases in coverage, namely for unemployment benefits, child allowances, and social assistance, including the extended GMI program (a combination of cash and in-kind means-tested programs which comprise the main safety net program). By and large, social protection programs have become more pro-poor since the mid-1990s. In 1995, the share of poor and non-poor households receiving benefits was nearly identical.[64] Pensions and unemployment benefits had similar outreach among poor and non-poor households. Child allowances were received more frequently by the non-poor than the poor and, as expected, social assistance programs had a higher outreach among the poor. The pro-poor orientation of all social protection programs-with the exception of pensions-increased in 1997, and further in 2001. The share of poor households receiving all types of social assistance programs nearly doubled, from 26 percent in 1995 to 49 percent in 2001.

The outreach of social protection programs is higher among the poor and in rural areas where poverty is concentrated. Various social protection programs have different outreach. Pensions have the largest incidence; almost half of the population live in households receiving an old age, disability or survivor pension. Old age pensions are the most widespread, benefiting 25 percent of Bulgarians. The coverage of pension benefits extends further within the population; 50 percent of the population live in households where at least one household member receives an old age pension.

---

[64] Throughout this paper "poor" households refer to those households which fall below two-thirds mean 1997 per capita consumption (Box 8.1). This is the line used in the forthcoming Poverty Assessment Update.

TABLE 8.1: MAIN SOCIAL PROTECTION PROGRAMS BY LEVEL OF EXPENDITURES, 2001

	RANK	EXPENDITURES (MIL. LEVA)	SHARE IN TOTAL SOCIAL PROTECTION EXPENDITURES (PERCENT)
Old Age Pensions	1	2205	55
Unemployment benefits	2	212	5
Disability pensions	3	220	5
Child allowances, insured parents	4	106	3
Sickness benefits	5	102	3
Occasional and monthly means-tested benefits	6	90	2
Energy subsidy	7	75	2
Social pensions, means-tested	8	73	2
Farmers pensions	9	60	1
Maternity and child benefits, uninsured parents	10	47	1
Child care benefits, insured parents	11	45	1
Social care services and institutions	12	39	1
Other programs	13–34	148	4
Administrative costs		607	15
Total, including administrative costs		4,026	100

Note: The heading "Other programs" refers to the remaining 22 programs from both social insurance and social assistance category.

Source: MOLSP, MOF.

TABLE 8.2: COVERAGE OF SOCIAL PROTECTION PROGRAMS: 1995, 1997 AND 2001

(AS PERCENT OF PERSONS RECEIVING BENEFITS[1])

	TOTAL			BY POVERTY STATUS OF THE RECIPIENT					
				1995		1997		2001	
	1995	1997	2001	NON-POOR	POOR	NON-POOR	POOR	NON-POOR	POOR
Total social protection	80.4	79.4	83.6	80.4	82.1	76.9	83.8	82.5	92.0
Pensions	52.7	52.3	53.8	52.4	57.4	47.9	60.3	54.6	47.7
Unemployment benefit	6.0	6.4	13.4	5.7	11.7	5.1	8.7	11.4	28.3
Child allowance	33.7	36.9	40.5	34.6	19.2	36.6	37.5	39.4	48.4
Social Assistance	12.8	11.1	19.1	12.1	25.5	8.7	15.2	15.2	48.8
Extended GMI	2.6	6.3	7.1	2.3	7.0	5.0	8.8	4.3	28.5
Maternity and childcare	6.6	3.8	6.6	6.1	14.8	2.9	5.5	5.3	17.0

[1] Beneficiary households weighted by household size.

Source: BIHS 1995, 1997, 2001.

The Impact on Poverty

Poverty levels have been reduced dramatically in Bulgaria since the 1997 crisis (Box 8.1), helped by social protection programs, particularly pensions, which have a substantial impact on living conditions and protect households from falling into poverty. Analysis of the 2001 household survey data found that the poverty rate would be 18 percentage points higher in the absence of social protection programs (Table 8.3). Even though the main objective of pension benefits is not poverty relief, these benefits are largely responsible for the reduction in poverty. Without non-pension benefits (for example, unemployment and social assistance), the poverty rate would be two percentage points higher.

BOX 8.1: RECENT POVERTY TRENDS AND THE POVERTY GAP

The 2001 poverty profile for Bulgaria shows a dramatic rebound of living standards since the 1997 crisis. Poverty escalated to 36 percent of the population in 1997, according to the household survey for that year. Since then, poverty rates have declined, as consumption levels have recovered from the crisis. Using poverty lines updated from 1997, poverty fell by nearly two-thirds to 12.8 percent, and the depth and severity of poverty have also improved (see Table below)[a] In order to compare trends over time, the relative poverty lines from 1997—two-thirds of per capita income (high) and one-half per capita income (low)—were fixed in real terms.

Poverty and Inequality Trends

| | 1995 | | 1997 | | 2001 | |
POVERTY ESTIMATES	HIGH	LOW	HIGH	LOW	HIGH	LOW
Headcount ratio	5.5	2.9	36.0	20.2	12.8	7.5
Poverty Gap	1.7	0.9	11.4	5.9	4.2	2.2
Poverty Depth	0.8	0.4	5.3	2.7	1.9	0.9
Aver. per capita consumption (June 1997 BGL)	117,208		62,604		99,035	

Source: Poverty Assessment Update, The World Bank (forthcoming), 2002. BIHS 1995, 1997, 2001.

Despite the improvements since 1997, poverty remains at twice the levels of 1995. In addition, recent improvements in welfare have not been equally distributed across the population. There are "pockets of poverty" among certain groups, particularly the unemployed, ethnic minorities, most notably Roma, and families with more than four children. Poverty also has a significant rural dimension. Urban areas have experienced a more significant drop in poverty levels, from 34 to 6 percent, while in rural areas, poverty rates were less than halved, from 41 percent to 24 percent.

The poverty gap has also fallen since 1997, but it remains more than double 1995 levels at 4.2 in 2001. The poverty gap measures the amount by which the mean consumption of the poor, on average, falls below the poverty line. In 2001, the poverty gap amounted to 0.2 billion leva, or 0.7 percent of 2001 GDP. This implies that-under conditions of perfect targeting and zero administrative costs-eliminating poverty would cost 0.7 percent of GDP. As these assumptions are unrealistic, the true cost is likely to be higher, perhaps as high as 2.1 percent of GDP.

[a] The poverty line is set at two-thirds mean 1997 per capita consumption, adjusted to 1995 and 2001 prices. In other words, the relative poverty line from 1997 is held constant to function as an absolute poverty line.

TABLE 8.3: POVERTY LEVELS WITH AND WITHOUT SOCIAL PROTECTION BENEFITS, 1995, 1997 AND 2001

(PERCENT)

	RECIPIENT 1995			RECIPIENT 1997			RECIPIENT 2001		
	YES	NO	TOTAL	YES	NO	TOTAL	YES	NO	TOTAL
POP. SHARE:	80	20	100	79	21	100	84	16	100
Poverty Headcount									
without	24.2	5.0	20.5	52.7	28.4	47.7	35.1	6.4	29.9
with	5.6	5.0	5.5	38.0	28.4	36.0	12.8	6.4	11.7
Poverty gap									
without	12.5	2.3	10.5	23.6	9.0	20.6	19.9	2.4	16.8
with	1.6	2.3	1.7	12.1	9.0	11.5	3.8	2.4	3.6
Poverty severity									
without	10.1	1.2	8.4	15.0	4.5	12.8	17.4	1.2	14.5
with	0.7	1.2	0.8	5.5	4.5	5.3	1.8	1.2	1.7

Source: BIHS 1995, 1997, 2001.

Estimates indicated that social protection programs combined reduced the overall poverty headcount from 29.9 to 11.7 percent in 2001. Among those benefit recipients, the poverty headcount fell from a high of 35.1 percent before benefits (ex ante), to a low of 12.8 percent after benefits (ex post). In relative terms, ex post poverty is 61 percent lower than ex ante (as a weighted average of a 64 percent reduction among beneficiaries and 0 percent reduction among non-beneficiaries).

The reduction in poverty headcount provides only a partial picture of the impact of social spending. The poverty headcount does not take into account the reduction in poverty among those poor who are not lifted out of poverty by social protection programs. This can be addressed by examining the "poverty gap" and "poverty severity" measures, which are more distributionally sensitive. Social protection programs as a whole succeeded in reducing the poverty gap by 79 percent from its ex ante estimate, and poverty severity by 89 percent. In 2001, non-pension social protection programs had a modest impact in reducing the overall headcount rate from 13 to 12 percent, the poverty gap from 4.7 to 3.6, and the poverty severity measure from 2.6 to 1.7.

The aggregate impact of social protection on poverty reduction hides considerable diversity among programs. The following sections discuss the effectiveness of individual programs in terms of targeting, coverage and adequacy in more detail.

Pensions

The pension program constitutes the largest expenditure within the social protection scheme, having reached 9.1 percent of GDP in 2001 (see Table 2.5). It provides old age, disability and survivor pensions for 2.4 million beneficiaries. Hitherto, the program was primarily based on a pay-as-you-go (PAYG) scheme financed from payroll taxes, with a few minor programs financed from general revenues. The contributory scheme suffered a severe shock during the transition period: a sharp decline in the number of contributors per pensioner, rising payroll taxes, and low and highly volatile value of benefits. By the end of the 1990s, the system faced a severe crisis of public confidence that could only be addressed with a far reaching reform. In 1999, Parliament approved a comprehensive legislative package providing the basis for a more financially sustainable pension system. The implementation of the new system has progressed in several steps starting in 2000. As of early 2002, the universal pension pillar, an essential pillar within the new framework, came into effect. Although the implementation of the reform has been largely on track thus far, the reform is not yet consolidated and faces significant challenges.

Structure and Financing in the 1990s

At the outset of the transition, Bulgaria inherited a state mandatory contributory pension system covering old age, survivor, disability, work injury risks, and maternity benefits. Nearly 90 percent of the system's beneficiaries received an old age or a survivor pension. Female and male participants had a right to a full pension at age 55 and 60, respectively. Although the statutory retirement age was already low, special occupations enjoyed the option to retire 3 to 8 years earlier. In addition, early in the transition, a new policy was instituted offering early retirement to workers laid off by firms undergoing restructuring, causing a surge in the number of retirees. The reversal of this policy in 1993 stabilized the number of retirees and even led to some modest declines in the second half of the decade (Figure 8.3).

While the overall stock of pensioners rose, the number of insured persons shrank, mirroring the collapse in employment. The number of contributors started to recover towards 1996 but registered important declines again in the aftermath of the 1997 crisis, as unemployment continued to rise. As a consequence of these unfavorable economic trends, the system dependency ratio (ratio of contributors to beneficiaries) moved from an already high level of 53 percent in 1989 to 108 in 2001.[65]

To manage the financial pressures created by the shrinking contribution base and the higher number of pensioners, successive governments resorted to discretionary indexation of benefits and an overall compression of pensions. As a consequence, the average pension as percent of the average

---

[65] The old-age dependency ratio (measured as the ratio of the population over 60 to those within the 18–59 age rate) shows a modest increase during this period, rising from 36 percent in 1990 to 39 percent in 1999.

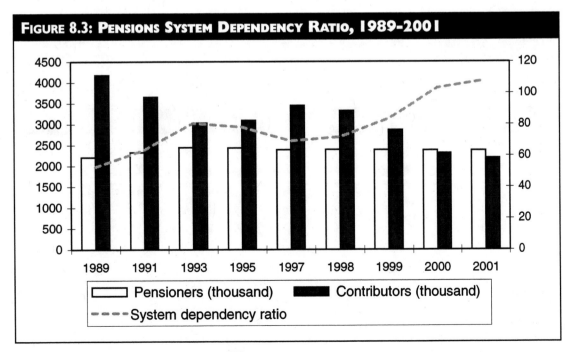

FIGURE 8.3: PENSIONS SYSTEM DEPENDENCY RATIO, 1989-2001

Legend: Pensioners (thousand) — Contributors (thousand) — System dependency ratio

Source: National Social Security Institute (NSSI).

wage suffered important cuts, from 44 percent in 1991 to 38.4 percent in 2001, bottoming at 29.1 percent in the midst of the 1997 economic crisis. In addition to sharp cuts in benefits, the contribution rate was increased several times. The traditional flat payroll tax of 28 percent rose to 37 percent for employees entitled to normal retirement, 47 percent for those entitled to retire three years early, and 52 percent (on average) for those entitled to retire from 5 to 8 years early.[66] Table 8.4 shows the continued volatility in the system's revenues and expenditures throughout the 1990s.[67]

Besides the main contributory scheme, the pension system encompassed special schemes financed from general tax revenues that covered, *inter alia,* benefits for war veterans, merit pensions, and social pensions. These groups comprised close to 6 percent of the total number of pensioners by the end of the decade.

The overall performance of the pension system during this period created a crisis of public confidence in the pension system. The dramatic decline in pension benefits generated political pressures from pensioners, while workers' incentives to contribute, particularly for the self-employed, were weakening and exacerbating the system's problems. Additional raises in payroll taxes were not feasible since they would only compound the contribution problem and foster higher unemployment. Prospects for a further shrinking and aging of the population undermined even more the credibility of the system among younger workers.

The New System

The Mandatory Social Insurance Code and the Supplementary Voluntary Pension Insurance Act, approved in 1999, laid the legal foundations for a new multi-pillar pension framework. The main objectives of the new system are to improve the financial sustainability of the public scheme, diversify the sources of retirement income between funded and non-funded plans, enhance the transparency of social subsidies, and generally treat all participants more fairly. The reformed system comprises three pillars: (i) the PAYG; (ii) mandatory universal and occupational pension plans; and (iii) supplementary plans. The last two pillars are to be fully funded and managed by the private sector.

---

[66] These rates also cover short-term benefits.

[67] Pension expenditures also include social pensions and special state supplements, since these were not disaggregated historically.

TABLE 8.4: FINANCIAL PERFORMANCE OF THE PUBLIC PILLAR 1991–2001

(PERCENT OF GDP)	1991	1993	1995	1997	1998	1999	2000	2001
Revenues	9.1	10.7	8.4	7.7	9.4	9.3	8.7	8.1
Expenditures	9.8	11.6	8.4	7.0	9.3	9.5	9.8	9.7
Pensions*	8.4	10.3	7.5	6.3	8.4	8.6	8.8	9.0
Short-term benefits**	1.3	1.2	0.8	0.6	0.8	0.8	0.8	0.6
Administrative costs and other	0.0	0.1	0.1	0.1	0.1	0.1	0.2	0.2
Balance	−0.7	−1.0	−0.1	0.7	0.1	−0.2	−1.1	−1.6

* Excludes social pensions and other state benefits.
** Excludes benefits under the Birth Promotion Act.
Source: NSSI and World Bank estimates.

Public Pillar.   The first pillar, effective since 2000, is based on a more rationalized PAYG. Its main characteristics are:

- creation of three separate funds[68] for the insurance coverage of pensions, short-term benefits, and general sickness and work injury and a decline of 3 percentage points in the overall contribution rate to finance these three funds;[69]
- clear separation of social programs, such as social pensions and supplemental benefits to pensioners, from contributory programs, and financing of the former by the State;
- an increase in the retirement age from 55/60 to 60/63 years for female/male over a 10/6 year period and an even faster rise in the minimum length of service;
- the establishment of a transparent system that defines closer linkages between contributions and benefits;
- a dramatic rationalization of Categories I and II workers[70] that enjoyed early retirement provisions from more than 20 percent of contributors in 1998 to 6 percent by early 2001,[71] and a parallel increase in their minimum retirement age;
- introduction of separate "occupational pension plans" to bridge early retirement pensions of Categories I and II until they reach the statutory minimum retirement age of the PAYG; and
- increase in the minimum retirement age of social pensions, which became a means-tested benefit.

The increase in the statutory retirement age and the funding of occupational privileges will contribute towards the improved financial performance of the public pillar in the medium and long term. The structure of the new benefit formula is also more transparent and in line with the overall financial capacity of the public system. The formula breaks with the practices of the past decade of *ad hoc* changes which made benefits highly unpredictable; only pension indexation rules remain unclear in the legislation and subject to discretion. The reformed system is able to merge financial with social objectives but makes the cost of these social undertakings (i.e., social pensions and other supplements) more transparent by segregating them from the public pension pillar and financing them from the state budget.

Mandatory Universal Pension Plans.   The mandatory component of the pension system will complement the public pillar with two additional funded pillars: universal plans, mandatory for all workers born after 1959 and effective since early 2002, and occupational pension plans, compulsory for workers benefiting from special early retirement provisions and effective since early 2001. The establishment of universal pension plans will lead to better diversification of retirement income for younger workers, since labor and capital market risks influencing the performance of the PAYG and the funded pillar are not perfectly correlated. The funded pillar also creates an opportunity for workers to realize a more adequate replacement rate during their old age, as the rate of return in the funded pillar is bound to surpass growth in the average wage, a major determinant factor of the PAYG implicit rate of return. The legislation, however, did not prescribe the contribution rates to the public and private pillars, and the share of diversification between the two pillars remains uncertain.[72]

---

[68] The new unemployment insurance fund became effective in January 2002.

[69] The overall payroll tax for these three funds was cut from 37 percent to 34 percent, including 29 percent for the pension system. However, these rates are determined on a yearly basis during the fund's budget approval by Parliament rather than in the legislation.

[70] Including military staff and workers working in hazardous conditions.

[71] Categories I and II now constitute 1 and 5 percent of total contributors, respectively.

[72] Under the recent agreement with the IMF, the Government has undertaken to increase the contribution rate to 5 percentage points of the social contributions by 2007.

Occupational Pension Plans. The dramatic rationalization of workers under Categories I and II was a major achievement of the reform. The parallel establishment of occupational fully-funded pension plans constitutes an innovative, fair, and transparent way of tackling the problem of special privileges within the pension system. All participants within the PAYG scheme will be treated fairly (except for remaining gender differences). Fully-funded plans will permit a clear assessment of early retirement costs, deterring the resurgence of these costly provisions, as occurred in the 1990s. Poland is following the same approach to address early retirement provisions for special occupations, and Russia is considering this option.

Voluntary Supplementary Pension Plans. Supplementary pension plans constitute the last pillar of the reformed system. Supplementary plans had been operational in Bulgaria since 1994 but had functioned under a highly deficient regulatory framework and no supervision. The reform seeks to correct these major weaknesses. Assets in voluntary plans remain modest at 103.4 million leva (0.3 percent of GDP) in mid-2001.

All private pension plans-universal, occupational, and voluntary-will be supervised by the State Insurance Supervision Agency (SISA) created in mid-2000. Private pension plans will be administered by specialized pension fund administrators established as separate legal entities with minimum capital and other licensing requirements. Each pension fund administrator can manage only one universal fund, one occupational, and one voluntary plan. Assets are held by a custodian bank pre-approved by SISA in coordination with the Bulgarian National Bank. At present, eight pension insurance companies are operating in the market and a ninth company is under liquidation.

During the accumulation stage, pension plans will follow a Defined Contribution (DC) model where contributions and investment returns accrue in individual accounts. On retirement, the three types of plans will offer different options. Savings accumulated in occupational funds will be transformed into phased-withdrawals until the beneficiary reaches the statutory retirement age in the public and universal funds pillars and can start claiming benefits from these pillars. Savings accumulated in the universal funds will be converted to an annuity, although this construction is poorly defined in the legislation. Only universal funds can offer annuities within the mandatory system, excluding life insurance companies from this market which might increase the cost of annuity provision. In the voluntary pillar, individuals can withdraw savings as a lump-sum or convert them into phased-withdrawals or annuities.

Implementation: Challenges and Issues

As the previous section highlighted, the reform constitutes a major leap forward in building a more secure and stable pension system. Although the basic legal and institutional foundations of the new system are already operational, these foundations present some weaknesses that could hinder the successful development of the new system unless they are properly addressed. The structural framework of the new system will also have to evolve along with developments in Bulgaria's broader financial markets and its eventual accession into the European Union. The main outstanding issues and key implementation challenges are presented below within a short- (one to two years), medium- (five additional years) and long-term framework. Simulations of the financial performance of the new pension system over the long term under various assumptions are included in a forthcoming report on Social Protection and Poverty Reduction in Bulgaria.[73]

Short-Term Issues

Enhancing Compliance and Coverage. Preliminary simulations conducted by the NSSI suggest that the system will reach a comfortable financial position by the end of the decade, even after

---

[73] This refers to a forthcoming report by Cornelia Tesliuc, prepared as background for both the PEIR and the Poverty Assessment Update, entitled "Social Protection and Poverty Reduction in Bulgaria"

accounting for transition costs. The simulations assume important improvements in compliance. Special efforts to enhance compliance initiated in 2001 (for example, joint audits with the General Tax Directorate) should continue, and the plan to unify collection of social security contributions and taxes should be reinvigorated, as its completion date has been slipping further into the future. Expansion of the system's coverage merits special attention, as some economic groups have been poorly covered by the system since the early transition days, especially workers in the agricultural sector. Similarly, efforts to enhance revenue and expenditure control on the resources accumulated in or disbursed from the social insurance funds should continue.[74] The amendments to the Mandatory Social Insurance Code introduced in early 2002 increased the coverage of the system: (i) employees working short term (up to five working days per month), previously only insured against disability or work injury, are now insured for old age; and (ii) self-employed, craftsmen, owners, farmers, paying contributions themselves, may be insured also against general sickness risks.

Monitoring and Restraining the Rise in Disability Trends.   The recent changes in legislation entitle beneficiaries with disabilities of more than 70 percent to additional pension disability, calculated at 25 percent of the social pension for disability. This has generated a surge in social claims. The number of new additional social pensions increased to 190,000 in 2001 compared to 82,400 a year earlier. The increase in the expenditure on social pensions is estimated at 0.11 percent of GDP prior to the introduction of this new benefit. The probability of becoming disabled is positively correlated with aging and deteriorating health. It is inevitable that the increase in the statutory retirement age will produce a rise in the overall number of disabled, but the surge observed during 2001 points to a potentially deeper problem. It is recommended that the NSSI closely monitor disability trends and cautiously studies disability regulations and administrative procedures if the abnormal rise in the number of disabled continues over the next year.

Clear Rules for Indexing Pensions.   The new legislative framework set forth clear criteria for determining benefits but failed to define a transparent rule for indexing benefits, retaining a fair amount of policy discretion in this area. Discretion can help control short-term volatility in the system, but it can equally foster inappropriate management of pension expenditures. Beneficiaries will also prefer a more predictable pension indexation provision in order to enjoy a smoother income and consumption pattern rather than confronting *ad hoc* changes. The comfortable financial position achieved by the public pillar by the end of the decade suggests that benefits could be indexed to inflation, plus a modest percentage of real wage growth.

Prompt and Transparent Transfer of Contributions to Private Pension Funds.   A new IT system is already operational at the NSSI to support the collection of social security contributions for the PAYG, as well as the universal and occupational pension funds. The universal pillar, effectively launched on January 1, 2002, will not face the severe disruptions encountered in other European economies at the outset of the multi-pillar reform, for example, in Poland.[75] Nonetheless, 10 percent of contributions from occupational pension plans have not yet been reconciled. These contributions are administered by the BNB and receive a 2 percent nominal interest rate, yielding a negative interest rate and imposing a severe penalty on workers. In addition, an amendment was introduced in late 2001 expanding the period for transferring contributions from 10 to 30 days. It is critical that the NSSI issues transparent procedures for transferring contributions and that this period reverts from 30 to 10 days by the end of 2002. A long transfer period imposes unnecessary inefficiencies and costs on worker savings, equal to the foregone investment returns. The transfer

[74] See The Governance Program of the Government of the Republic of Bulgaria, 2001–2005.

[75] A year after launching private pension funds in Poland, the Social Security Institute (ZUS) had only allocated 10 percent of resources due to private pension funds.

period should be shortened even further in the medium term. Contributions that are not transferred within the stipulated period should obtain a market interest rate, at a minimum the market interest rate on short-term Treasury bills.

Strengthening Supervision of Private Pension Plans. A strong supervisory institution will be central to the sound development of private pension plans.[76] SISA has less than two years of experience and is still learning about its functions. Moreover, progress in the institutional strengthening of SISA in 2001 was very limited. Thus, the institutional strengthening process should receive greater attention and government support. SISA should also intensify and formalize its collaboration with other supervisory agencies to develop joint regulations in areas that cut across different segments of the financial market and to benefit from the longer experience of those agencies. The establishment of the Consultative Committee on Financial Supervision,[77] a separate body of senior officials from all financial services supervisory agencies, is a step forward in that direction.

Over the next two years, SISA will have to monitor closely the performance and financial sustainability of pension insurance companies and their capacity to start recovering the high investments made up-front to establish IT systems and gain market share. The financial and operational capacity of pension insurance companies seems to vary widely, with some of the smaller companies presenting a weaker profile. SISA should prepare itself to closely monitor a market restructuring process (through mergers, acquisitions and possibly even liquidations) that should subsequently result in a stronger sector.

Upgrading Regulations of Private Pension Plans. Regulations concerning accounting and valuation procedures should receive close attention, as they constitute the basis to assess the financial performance of pension plans. New accounting principles in accordance with international practices will become effective in 2003. New valuation procedures were issued in late 2001, but these guidelines continue to permit a fair amount of discretion to the pension insurance companies and could benefit from additional revisions. A regulation should be issued on investments outside Bulgaria (up to 10 percent of a pension fund's assets) and permit some initial and gradual foreign diversification of pension portfolios, a matter that will become even more pressing in the medium term as pension assets build up.

Defining the Contribution Rate for Universal Pension Funds. The universal pension pillar was started in 2002 with a 2 percent contribution rate. The Mandatory Social Insurance Code, however, does not prescribe the contribution rate for the public nor the private pillar-an important vacuum within the legislation. The contribution rate will be defined on a yearly basis when Parliament approves the budget for the public pension fund. At present, workers do not have the capacity to assess what could be their potential retirement income and the share that will emanate from the public and the private pillars. Such a gap and lack of strategic direction for the public and private pillars dents the credibility of the public on the overall reform and renders the pension system more vulnerable to discretionary changes and to potential reversals.[78] Uncertainties on the funded pillar will also hamper efforts by pension insurance companies to formulate adequate business plans in order to analyze their future viability.

---

[76] Even though universal plans and occupational plans offer no explicit state guarantees, weak performance of mandatory private pension funds due to inadequate supervision or regulation could lead to fiscal liabilities in the long run as workers claim compensation for poor supervision of mandatory savings.

[77] The Consultative Committee on Financial Supervision was established in March 2002.

[78] Under the present scheme, contribution rates to the funded pillar could even be interrupted for a few years, or rise one year and decline the following.

It is critical for the Government to outline the roles of the two mandatory pillars, and the contribution rates to finance these benefits. The program should clearly define the path for increasing the contribution rate to the second pillar and be embodied within the legislative framework to prevent reversals.[79] This plan should be accompanied by a new public education campaign, with renewed emphasis on the universal pillar, so workers can acquire a better understanding of the reform and make more educated decisions concerning private pension funds.[80] As an option, the plan could link the increase in the contribution rate diverted to the funded pillar with the financial performance of the public fund. This link would need to be simple and transparent to assure the credibility of key stakeholders and prevent undue interference with the strategic direction of the pension reform. Such a plan would entail a prior definition of a viable pension indexation rule and the overall contribution rate to the mandatory system; such important provisions would need to be prescribed in the Mandatory Social Insurance Code.

Medium-Term Issues[81]

Strengthening the Legal Framework.   In the medium term, the legislative framework of private pension plans should be strengthened, including the governance structure of private pension plans, the authority and independence of the supervisory agency, provisions on the retirement phase, and the liberalization of the investment regime. Amendments to the Voluntary Pension Insurance Act should clarify that voluntary pension plans can offer both phased withdrawals and annuities and define proper reserves accordingly.[82] Pension funds are *de facto* offering annuities despite contradictions in the legislation.

The Mandatory Social Insurance Code, too, displays inconsistencies requiring workers to convert their savings in the universal funds into annuities, seemingly variable annuities. The law prescribes that pension insurance companies should create reserves and bear the life expectancy risk; at the same time, the law allows the heirs to receive the savings remaining in a pensioner's account upon his/her death, an inconsistency that will render the system unviable during the retirement phase. Although the retirement phase in the mandatory pillar will not be initiated for another two decades, it will be preferable to correct this serious flaw along with the introduction of other amendments to the law. Such a deficiency in the legislation could raise doubts on the long-term sustainability of the reform and discourage potential new investors from entering the pension insurance market over coming years.

Moving Towards a More Flexible Investment Regime.   The infant development of Bulgaria's capital markets and cautious public debt financial policies restrict local investments available to pension funds. In the medium term, as pension assets rise relative to the size of the local capital markets, it will be necessary to increase the level of foreign diversification prescribed in the law from 10 percent to at least 25 to 30 percent. Other financial intermediaries already enjoy more liberal foreign investment policies only limited by prudential criteria on foreign exchange risk. The minimum 50 percent requirement on debt guaranteed by the state or bank deposits should be eliminated. Overall, it is

---

[79] The Government has defined that a 5 percent contribution rate will be diverted from the public pillar to the second pillar by 2007. No detailed plan has yet been elaborated on how the second pillar contribution rate will reach 5 percent from its current 2 percent level.

[80] A public education campaign on the general principles of the reform already took place, but general surveys seem to indicate that there is a need for continued public information on the new system.

[81] The Government has formed a working group to address some of the medium-term priorities outlined in the report.

[82] Articles 8 and 82 of the Act contradict each other. The former only allows lump-sum and phased withdrawals, while the latter also permits annuities.

preferable to define a more open investment regime in the legislation but authorize the supervisor to prescribe stricter criteria in the regulation.[83] Such flexibility permits easier changes in the portfolio investment, in accordance with evolving market conditions.

The Government has formed a working group which is carrying out active consultation with stakeholders to develop and propose legislative solutions to address several of the short- and long-term issues discussed in the previous two sub-sections, including clarifying the functions of the SISA, improving the investment regime and management of pension schemes.

Long-Term Issues

Integrating Private Pensions Funds with Other Financial Markets and the EU.   In the long term, the private pension system should be better integrated with the rest of Bulgaria's financial markets and Bulgaria's accession into the European Union. This will imply the elimination of restrictions to foreign diversification; permit pension insurance companies to offer a more diverse set of funds; and allow life insurance companies to provide annuities within the mandatory scheme removing the market segmentation presently envisioned in the legislation.

Increasing the Retirement Age of Women.   The public pillar will also have to adapt to EU regulations eliminating any provisions that discriminate among genders and equalizing the minimum retirement age between men and women. The increase in the retirement age of women from 60 to 63 years should be motivated not only by EU regulations but also to adjust to improvements in life expectancy and by the long-term financial sustainability of the system. Preliminary NSSI actuarial projections on the financial performance of the public pillar incorporate extremely conservative estimates on life expectancy of retirees, compared to other middle income countries. Improved life expectancy over the long term will worsen the system's dependency ratio and the overall financial position of the pension system calling for a higher retirement age, even 63 years remains low compared to the standards of OECD countries.

Labor Market Benefits and Programs

Improving effectiveness of labor market programs and implementing fundamental :labor market reform are critical elements in facing Bulgaria's unemployment challenge. At 17.5 percent in 2001, unemployment in Bulgaria has been rising steadily since 1996, and is among the highest in the region. The labor market is also characterized by low flows out of unemployment into jobs and a high share of discouraged workers-those workers who have stopped looking for a job and drop out of the labor force all together. In 2001, long-term unemployment was 49.3 percent-a disturbing development, as the long-term unemployed face the greatest obstacles in re-entering the labor market. Following the transition, Bulgaria established an unemployment insurance system to assist workers who lost their jobs. In addition to passive cash benefits, Bulgaria provides a set of active measures to promote employment, including public works programs, training, employment subsidies and support for small business development. However, fundamental labor market reform has lagged and growth of employment opportunities remain below its full potential. This section focuses on the analysis of labor market benefits and programs.

Unemployment benefits provide adequate income support to the poor, but appear to be low enough to promote work incentives. A large share of unemployed (for example, long-term unemployed) exhaust unemployment benefits and become eligible for social assistance. Bulgaria has a range of active labor market programs (ALMPs) and is in the process of expanding these programs

---

[83] The legislation could possibly prescribe separate ceilings of 30 percent on investments in equity and in private fixed-income investments, understanding that these are medium-term targets and that regulations will stipulate much lower ceilings in the short term. In developed capital markets, for example the U.S., the allocation of equity in private pension plans usually ranges from 40 to 60 percent.

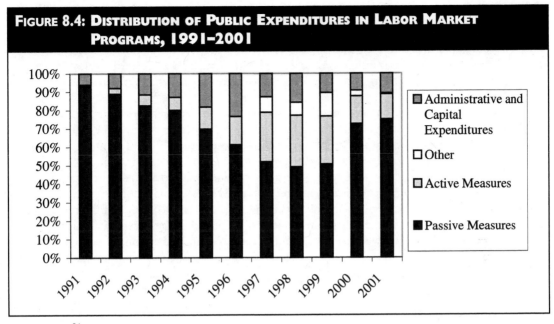

FIGURE 8.4: DISTRIBUTION OF PUBLIC EXPENDITURES IN LABOR MARKET PROGRAMS, 1991–2001

Source: NES.[84]

with the introduction of a social investment fund. A continued evaluation of these measures is essential to ensure their effectiveness and their consistency with fiscal stance. In parallel, the Government is considering fundamental labor market reform—including Labor Code reforms to reduce dismissal costs, promote flexible forms of employment, and improve wage flexibility—to reduce the costs of using labor in the economy and expand employment growth. Labor market programs together with an unemployment insurance and social assistance policies can complement well but can not substitute for a dynamic labor market conducive to expanding employment opportunities. Labor market reform, labor market programs, unemployment insurance, and social assistance policies should complement each other to promote work incentives and employment growth.

Financing

Public expenditures in labor market have doubled from 0.6 percent of GDP in 1991 to 1.1 percent in 2001. The increase has been largely driven by the growth in payments for unemployment benefits, which amounted to 0.7 percent of GDP in 2001. The balance between active and passive measures has shifted during the decade. Active measures were gradually introduced in the early 1990s and were scaled up during the crisis period of 1996-97, particularly the temporary employment program. Since then ALMPs have been scaled back, declining to 14 percent of total labor spending in 2001 (Figure 8.4).

Up to 2001, all unemployment programs were financed through an extrabudgetary fund, the Professional Training and Unemployment Fund (PTUF)[85], which was financed by payroll taxes. The contribution rate for benefits was 4 percent of gross wages, with 0.8 percent paid by the employee and 3.2 percent paid by the employer in 2001.[86] This was reduced from 4.5 percent in 1998. The Government planned to reduce the tax burden further to 3 percent. However, because

---

[84] In 2002, the NES became the Employment Agency.

[85] Starting in 2002, the PTUF has merged into the NSSI budget as the unemployment risk has been added to the risks administered by the NSSI.

[86] In 2002, employers pay 3 percent and employees 1 percent.

of the increase in unemployment, the PTUF has run a deficit for the past two years, and additional reductions have not been possible. Since 1997, the state budget has provided transfers to the PTUF to cover the deficit. State budget transfers were 33 percent of revenues in 2001. However, the fund ended with a surplus amounting to 14.6 million leva, or 5 percent of total revenues. Additional revenues come from fines. The PTUF also makes social insurance contributions to the health and pension funds.

In 2002, the Government implemented important reforms to unemployment benefits. The amendments to the Mandatory Social Insurance Code, which became effective on January 1, 2002, incorporated an unemployment insurance fund which succeeds the PTUF. The unemployment insurance fund is designed to cover the insured social risk of unemployment. The NSSI manages the new unemployment insurance fund. In line with the European Social Insurance Law, the amendments introduced uniform rules to insured social risks and social security system rights by expanding the scope of the State Social Insurance and incorporating coverage of the risk of unemployment. Under this new framework, management is simplified as the necessary information is already captured by NSSI allowing better use of the resources and execution. The unemployment benefit is no longer linked to the minimum monthly wage but instead a minimum and maximum level of assistance will be determined annually in the Law of the Budget of the State Social Insurance. In 2002, the monthly minimum level was set to 70 leva and the maximum to 130 leva.

Program Effectiveness and Main Issues

Unemployment Benefits.   Up to 2001, provisions for regular unemployment benefits were outlined in the 1997 "Unemployment Protection and Employment Incentives Act." Workers were eligible for benefits if they were registered with the local labor office, had been employed for 9 months during the last 15 months, and were willing to accept a job or training, if offered. Benefits ranged from 85 percent to 140 percent of the minimum wage and were paid for 4 to 12 months, depending on the length of prior employment. In 2001, 161,864 unemployed workers received benefits, or approximately 24.2 percent of those registered as unemployed. The coverage rate has fallen dramatically over the past decade with the high growth in long-term unemployment. In 1990, 79 percent of registered unemployed received benefits, while by 1994 this figure had fallen to 27 percent.

Workers who had exhausted unemployment benefits became eligible for unemployment assistance after six months. Unemployment assistance amounted to 60 percent of the minimum wage and was paid for six months. This benefit was introduced at the end of 1997 and replaced a means-tested allowance which lasted six months. Workers who remain unemployed following the expiration of unemployment assistance become eligible for social assistance benefits. In 2001, 22,501 individuals received the allowance, this marked a significant increase over 1999, when 9,003 workers received the benefit.

In line with the trend in other countries of Central and Eastern Europe, the replacement rate for unemployment benefits in Bulgaria has declined over the decade. In 1997, the replacement rate was 0.3, consistent with that of Poland and the Slovak Republic. Benefits appear low enough to provide work incentives; however, further analysis of job search patterns of the unemployed is needed to assess this. Besides, despite the low replacement rates, benefits do appear to provide meaningful income support to poor families. Although a large share of the poor are not eligible for unemployment benefits because they are among the long-term unemployed, the system has been reaching an increasing number of poor households over time. In 2001, over one-third of those receiving benefits were in poor households, and over one-third of the amount spent on benefits was channeled to the poor. Benefits had a significant impact on household consumption for those households which received them; they increased significantly in 2001, when they amounted, in average, to 117 percent of the pre-benefit consumption of the poor.

The targeting of unemployment benefits in Bulgaria was more problematic than that of the main social assistance cash transfer programs, discussed below. In 2001, roughly two-thirds of the benefits went to the non-poor. Despite this, Bulgaria's unemployment benefit is more redistributive than that of other Central and Eastern European countries (Figure 8.5). Only Estonia had a target rate of 31 percent, close to Bulgaria's 33 percent.

Recent Reforms: Eligibility.   The amendments to the Mandatory Social Insurance Code, which became effective on January 1, 2002, introduced important reforms. Workers are now eligible for unemployment benefits if they are registered with the NSSI, have been subject to compulsory social insurance coverage against all social risks covered in the system for at least 9 months during the last 15 months before termination of the social insurance contributions, and are willing to accept a job or training, if offered. In addition, eligibility also requires: (i) to be registered as unemployed at the respective local labor office of the Employment Agency; (ii) to have not obtained the right to pension on account of their record for social insurance purposes and old age, or occupational pension for early retirement; and (iii) to not have performed any work that would be subject to compulsory social insurance. Changes in status on eligibility requirements need to be reported monthly to local labor offices of the NSSI.

Recent Reforms: Benefits.   Under the new framework, cash benefits are 60 percent of the average income reported for social insurance purposes received by the beneficiary during the last 9 months of employment. The 2002 Law of the Budget of the State Social Insurance set the monthly unemployment benefit minimum of 70 leva and a maximum of 130 leva. Benefits are paid for 4 to 12 months according to the period of contributions to the compulsory social insurance coverage (Table 8.5). Other rules governing receipt of unemployment benefits are:

- A minimum of 4 months is applied to eligible unemployed whose participation in the system is terminated with their consent or due to sanction, and to those who become eligible within three years from having received unemployment benefits.

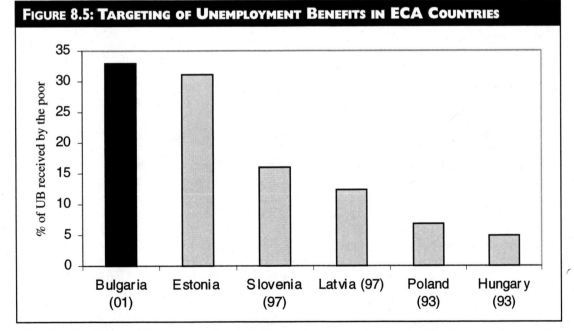

FIGURE 8.5: TARGETING OF UNEMPLOYMENT BENEFITS IN ECA COUNTRIES

Note: Data for Bulgaria refer to ex ante (pre-benefit) targeting of unemployment benefits. The figure for ex post targeting of Bulgaria is 18 percent.

Source: Vodopivec, et al., 2001.

TABLE 8.5: UNEMPLOYMENT BENEFITS

YEARS IN THE COMPULSORY SOCIAL INSURANCE SYSTEM	DURATION OF UNEMPLOYMENT BENEFITS (MONTHS)
Up to 3	4
3 to 5	6
5 to 10	8
10 to 15	9
15 to 20	10
20 to 25	11
Above 25	12

Source: MOLSP.

- Duration of unemployment benefits for part-time workers who become unemployed is determined by the full-time equivalent of time worked-thus the minimum period may be lower than that indicated in Table 8.5.
- The period of unemployment benefits is incorporated in the years in the compulsory insurance system and the beneficiary's contributions for pension and health insurance are covered by the unemployment fund.
- Beneficiaries who are hired part time with a salary lower than the minimum monthly wage set for the country are entitled to 50 percent of the unemployment benefit during the remaining of the eligible period set for unemployment benefits.

Overall, recent reforms are important steps forward since they consolidate unemployment benefits, aim at closing the gap between contributions into and benefits from the social security system, and at improving management of resources. The new framework aims at increasing the participation in the social security system, but it also provides coverage of contributions for pension and health insurance while receiving unemployment benefits and these may be sizable costs. And as in earlier years, after unemployment benefits expire, unemployed workers become eligible for social assistance benefits. It is critical to monitor closely the effects of the new framework together with the social assistance programs and ensure that incentives indeed encourage choosing employment over unemployment and to monitor the fiscal costs of the unemployment fund.

Active Measures

Bulgaria provides a range of employment programs for unemployed workers, including public works, employment services and training. The main programs are the following:

- **Temporary Employment Program.** Provides temporary work for up to 5 months in public or private sector projects.
- **Training/retraining.** Involves professional training organized by the National Employment Service (NES), now the Employment Agency. Participants are paid an allowance of 60 percent of the individual's benefit allowance.
- **Subsidized employment.** Provides support to employers who hire employers hiring young, disabled and long-term unemployed persons.
- **Employment associations.** Provides temporary employment, up to 24 months, for the unemployed in regions severely affected by restructuring. Based on local partnerships.
- **Self-employment program.** Provides financial support to unemployed workers starting their own businesses.

A number of other smaller ALMPs have been implemented, mostly since 1997, including regional employment programs. ALMPs cover a relatively small share of the unemployed. In 2001, 106,780 persons participated in ALMPs and other various programs, about 14 percent of the total registered unemployed. The majority of these participants were enrolled in the temporary

BOX 8.2: LABOR MARKET POLICY: OBJECTIVES AND STRATEGY

The labor market policy and its reform challenges are central to the development prospects of Bulgaria. Labor market reform is needed to face the unemployment challenge—Bulgaria faces a 17.5 percent unemployment rate—to improve competitiveness, and to advance towards the EU accession. In addition, under a Currency Board Arrangement, labor market policy is an essential complement to fiscal policy to adjust to changes in economic conditions. Recognizing the centrality of labor market reform, the Government has defined and is implementing a labor market policy along the following objectives and strategy.

Objectives. The key objectives of labor market policy in Bulgaria are to ensure a well functioning labor market that facilitates a higher rate of employment, to reduce unemployment and poverty, to enhance labor quality to meet labor demand, to provide men and women with equal opportunities for employment and professional growth.

Strategy. The Ministry of Labor and Social Policy is implementing reforms in the following areas:
- Building capacity at the central and local levels for the efficient use of EU pre-accession instruments to reduce the adverse effects of economic restructuring on the labor market;
- Improving the flexibility of the labor market and of employment;
- Reducing and preventing unemployment and social exclusion;
- Maintaining and enhancing the quality of human capital and their employment prospects;
- Improving standards of living.

National Council for Tripartite Cooperation. This tripartite council provides a forum to discuss labor market reform. The council includes representatives of workers, businessmen, and the Government. The Ministry of Labor and Social Protection meets regularly with council members and discusses current conditions and reforms on several areas including industrial relations, incomes, living standards, unemployment, working conditions, and social assistance and social insurance. The council has national, branch, state, and local representation.

National Employment Action Plan 2001. The action plan, endorsed by the Council of Ministers in April 2001, outlines the MOLSP approach to facing Bulgaria's unemployment challenge. The action plan emphasizes active measure programs. The action plan spent about 84 million leva in 2001 (near to 73 percent of total original requirements of the plan).

Law on the Social Investment Fund. This law became effective in April 2001. The fund is designed to support the implementation of priority projects and activities.

The Employment Incentives Act of 2002. This Act, which became effective on January 1, 2002, requires that the Government adopts a national employment action plan every year and to provide full funding for it through the Law on State Budget. This law introduces several changes, including,
- Aiming at enhancing decentralization and regionalization of employment policy and developing the corresponding labor market institutions;
- Promoting development of social partnership at regional and local levels;
- Strengthening the provisions against any discrimination—sex, age, ethnic origin—aimed at assuring full harmonization with the EU guidelines and directives;
- Developing employment promotion measures and assisting in the integration of vulnerable groups in the labor market;
- Ensuring consistency with other pieces of legislation.

Source: World Bank staff based on information provided by MOLSP.

employment program (75,199) and training/retraining programs (11,769). And 29,648 were provided with longer-term employment.

The Bulgarian NES undertook a net impact evaluation of the main active measures in 1998 in order to assess the contribution of ALMPs to improving the re-employment probabilities of participants. The study was based on a representative survey of 6,101 individuals who had participated in the programs, as well as a control group.[87] The study found that all of the programs studied have a positive net impact, and therefore do improve the employment prospects of some groups of participants. However, the study showed that for several programs the impact is minimal. In addition, the results showing a net positive impact need to be treated with caution, as the analysis does not give an indication of the sustainability of the new businesses created. Outcomes should be tracked over a longer period of time, at least two years. These results imply that while ALMPs seem to have a net positive impact, their impact is minimal in several programs, and at present there is no evidence that the positive results are sustainable. They also imply that there is scope for improved targeting of programs.

The positive results of the study for Bulgaria compare favorably with analysis of ALMPs in Central and Eastern Europe and Western Europe. In many countries results are negative. For example, in Poland and Hungary, public employment programs were found to lower the prospects of becoming employed. The outcomes suggest the need to focus on programs which are well targeted, either on equity grounds (for example to the most vulnerable groups, such as ethnic minorities); or on efficiency grounds (for example to groups which benefit the most from program participation). The Government's National Action Plan for Employment 2001 incorporates lessons from the net impact survey.

Social Assistance

Social assistance programs encompass cash benefits and in-kind services. The main benefits include: (i) the Guaranteed Minimum Income (GMI) benefit, a means-tested cash benefit paid to low-income households below an income threshold; (ii) energy benefits, cash benefits paid to low-income households during the winter heating season (November-April); (iii) family benefits paid under the Birth Promotion Act,[88] including child allowances, maternity leave and birth grants for uninsured households; (iv) cash and in-kind benefits for the disabled, including medical and transportation benefits; and (v) social care services and institutions.

The effectiveness of social assistance programs in reaching and addressing the needs of the poor in Bulgaria has improved over the decade (Table.8.6). The two main cash benefit programs, the GMI and energy benefit programs, have high incidence among the poor. In 2001, the "extended GMI" program-encompassing cash and in-kind benefits-channeled 68 percent of resources to the poorest 20 percent of the population, while 53 percent of the energy benefit went to the bottom quintile.

Despite these achievements, there is scope for improving further the effectiveness of social assistance in Bulgaria. Intergovernmental financing mechanisms for most benefits are weak and lead to under-funding in poor municipalities; benefits are frequently paid irregularly or in-kind; and targeting can be further improved to reach poor households which remain outside of the safety net. The following sections discuss the financing for social assistance, and then the main policy issues related to the individual programs.

---

[87] It is important to note that although such studies are useful, they only provide a partial picture. Among other issues, net impact studies refer to the impact of program participation on the *individuals* who participated in the programs, *not* on the impact on unemployment at large. Accordingly, these studies reveal little on "macro" impact of ALMPs. This is because they account only for deadweight loss, but not for substitution/displacement effects. Also, extrapolation of results can be misleading due to diminishing returns to scale. Programs that perform well on a small scale do not necessarily perform well if expanded and run on a larger scale. This is because small scale programs tend to attract both best (most motivated, etc.) unemployed and best program operators.

[88] In April 2002, the Family Benefits Act replaced the Birth Promotion Act.

TABLE 8.6: BENEFIT INCIDENCE BY (EX ANTE) CONSUMPTION QUINTILE[1]

CONSUMPTION QUINTILE	EXTENDED GMI (INCLUDING IN-KIND)			GMI (CASH BENEFITS ONLY)			ENERGY BENEFIT
	1995	1997	2001	1995	1997	2001	2001
1	47.3	18.4	68.3	54.7	20.3	60.5	52.9
2	16.9	18.5	12.4	9.9	7.4	17.6	21.7
3	2.7	11.6	8.2	0.2	17.4	12.4	11.9
4	19.4	26.5	8.5	0.0	38.9	9.3	10.0
5	13.8	25.0	2.5	35.2	16.1	0.3	3.4

[1] Table shows the incidence of the benefit, estimated in the absence of the benefit.

Source: BIHS 1995, 1997, 2001.

Financing

Social assistance expenditures comprised 13.8 percent of total social protection spending, or 1.1 percent of GDP, in 2001. Over the past decade, social assistance spending has shifted from social services and institutions toward cash benefits (Table 8.7). Total spending on the GMI program increased by two and a half times, from 0.13 percent in 1991 to 0.34 percent of GDP, in 2001. GMI expenditures now amount to nearly one-third of total social assistance expenditures. The introduction of the energy benefit program in 1995 and its expansion to nearly 0.3 percent of GDP in 1999 have also shifted the composition of social assistance expenditures toward cash benefits.

Responsibility for funding social assistance benefits was shared equally between the state and municipal budgets.[89] Beginning in 1999, the MOF incorporated earmarked funding for social assistance programs into the system of intergovernmental transfers to municipalities. This financ-

---

[89] In 2002, municipalities finance only 25 percent of the social assistance benefits, the rest is financed by the state. Further changes are expected to be introduced in 2003 (see Box 4.1).

TABLE 8.7: SOCIAL ASSISTANCE BENEFITS: 1991–2001

(PERCENT OF GDP)

	1991	1995	1997	1998	1999	2000	2001
Guaranteed Minimum Income (GMI)	0.13	0.09	0.09	0.14	0.25	0.30	0.34
Benefits under the Birth Promotion Act (of which:)	0.18	0.47	0.21	0.21	0.25	0.28	0.28
Child allowances	0.01	0.07	0.07	0.07	0.09	0.07	0.07
Maternity leave	0.17	0.39	0.13	0.14	0.15	0.19	0.20
Birth grants	0	0.01	0.00	0.00	0.01	0.01	0.01
Cash and in-kind benefits for the disabled	0.06	0.04	0.03	0.03	0.04	0.04	0.04
Energy benefits	—	0.07	0.05	0.17	0.26	0.23	0.25
Social care services and institutions	0.41	0.3	0.20	0.18	0.19	0.13	0.13
Administrative costs of the MOLSP	0	0.07	0.06	0.08	0.08	0.09	0.09
Total	**0.78**	**1.04**	**0.65**	**0.82**	**1.07**	**1.06**	**1.13**

Source: MOLSP, MOF.

ing arrangement covers the GMI program, Birth Promotion Act benefits and additional cash and in-kind benefits for the disabled. While this has improved coverage of the GMI program (as discussed below), many municipalities, particularly the poorest, continue to have difficulty in mobilizing their share. The amount of the state budget transfer required is also consistently underestimated. In 2001, social assistance expenditures were 86 percent of planned need (Figure 8.6). At the end of 2001, there were 14 million leva (14 percent of the 2001 GMI expenditures) of outstanding social assistance payments.

The share of planned social assistance benefits paid on time varied by type of benefit. Local governments have been more likely to pay family benefits under the BPA than other types of benefits, while the GMI program has been consistently the most under-funded program. This implies that poor households are most likely to be affected by local government financing constraints.

The effectiveness of the overall intergovernmental fiscal system needs to be strengthened in order to ensure that local governments have sufficient resources to cover their expenditure obligations, including social assistance. This will require adequate own revenues at the municipal level, as well as a transparent, predictable and equitable system of intergovernmental transfers. The current formula for allocating transfers is excessively complicated and changes annually. In the case of the earmarked transfers for social assistance, the transfers allocated do not cover local needs and, as a result, the central government provides compensating transfers periodically, either in the fiscal year in which the deficits accrue, or afterwards. This considerably limits the capacity of local governments to plan expenditures. The fiscal decentralization program approved in mid-2002 addresses some of these issues.

The 2002 budget law increases the share of funds coming from the central budget to 75 percent (25 percent to come from local budgets) and there are plans to centralize funding of social benefits in 2003. This is a step in the right direction since it would improve *the safety net for the poorest households* and help to assure that a basic safety net is provided to all who qualify. In the absence of centralized financing, the poorest municipalities will still not be able to fully cover social assistance. Local governments will retain the discretion to provide additional benefits on top

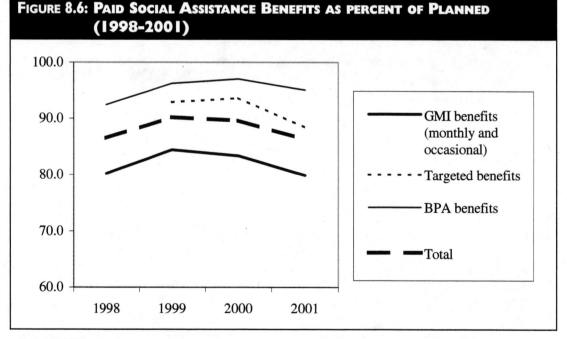

FIGURE 8.6: PAID SOCIAL ASSISTANCE BENEFITS AS PERCENT OF PLANNED (1998-2001)

Source: MOLSP.

of the national programs. The benefits of centralized funding is demonstrated by the energy bene-fit program, another social assistance. It is provided during the November-April heating season, and it is 100 percent financed through central transfers and experiences no delays in payments.

Program Effectiveness and Main Issues

Guaranteed Minimum Income (GMI) Program.   The GMI program is the main national safety net benefit. The effectiveness of the program has improved considerably over the past seven years, in terms of coverage and poverty alleviation impact. In 2001, 31 percent of households receiving the benefit were poor, a significant increase from 11 percent in 1995, and 53 percent of the funds spent on the program went to poor households (Table 8.8). The benefits had a substantial impact on the welfare of recipient households; for the poor, benefits comprised nearly 94 percent of the households' pre-benefit consumption.

These positive results mask a considerable weakness of the GMI program. A large share of beneficiaries receive GMI benefits irregularly or in-kind, substantially reducing the poverty allevia-tion capacity of the program. In 2000, only 16 percent of beneficiaries received regular cash bene-fits, 11 percent received one-time cash benefits, and the remainder received benefits in-kind, such as food or clothing. The payment of benefits in-kind is prompted by the local budget constraints discussed above. In-kind benefits are in general less effective than cash, because they distort con-sumption and reduce welfare. According to the beneficiary, they are also frequently provided in the form of inferior goods and can generate secondary markets if beneficiaries sell or trade the goods. In-kind benefits should be eliminated in favor of the cash GMI benefit.

There is also scope for refining the targeting of benefits to reach the remainder of poor households. Over 70 percent of the poor live in a household that does not receive benefits through the GMI program. Improvements can be made through further strengthening of the administration for social assistance delivery by: (i) training social workers to identify better poor households; (ii) improving information systems to facilitate means-testing and reduce payment of duplicative benefits; and (iii) expanding communication activities to inform beneficiaries about eligibility criteria and application procedures.

Energy Benefits.   The energy benefit program is a cash supplement to the GMI program which is paid during the winter heating season of November-April. For the 2000/2001 winter period, the amount of the benefit was set at 37.4 leva. In 2000, approximately 600,000 families received ben-efits under the program. A strength of the program is its method of financing. As funds are pro-vided directly to municipalities through earmarked transfers from the central budget, the program does not suffer from under-funding or delays in payments which characterize the other social assistance programs which rely on local funding.

TABLE 8.8: EFFECTIVENESS OF THE GUARANTEED MINIMUM INCOME PROGRAM*

	1995	1997	2001
Coverage (percent of households which are poor)	11.1	8.8	31.0
Targeting (percent resources received by poor)	26.9	39.7	53.1
Adequacy (ratio of benefits received by the poor to pre-benefit consumption of the poor)	33.3	0.6	93.7

* GMI includes all benefits (in-kind and cash) paid under means-testing criteria defined in the Social Assistance Act, excluding energy benefits. The poverty rate is 12.8 percent (see Box 4.1).

Source: BIHS 1995, 1997, 2001.

Coverage of the program is high at 28 percent; however, targeting and adequacy are weak compared to the GMI program. Over 65 percent of funds go to non-poor households. This is a result of program design. The energy benefit program has a higher threshold level: the differentiated GMI plus the lev equivalent of 450kwh of electricity. In addition, members of an extended family, although living under the same roof with other family members may claim benefits separately. In fact, the distribution of beneficiaries by family size indicates that nearly 60 percent of those receiving energy benefits are one member 'families,' many of whom are likely to be pensioners living together with other members of the family. *Further efforts are, therefore, needed to revise eligibility criteria to focus the benefit on poor households, and continued public information activities to reach potential beneficiaries.*

Further analysis is needed to determine whether the poor can absorb future price shocks. Once the tariff increase schedules for electricity and district heating have been agreed, priority should be given to determining what additional resources will be needed for the program and to estimating the number of additional beneficiaries.

Child Allowances.[90]   All children in Bulgaria are eligible for child allowances through the age of 16 (18 if a student). Benefits are paid through the NSSI for children whose parents are employed, and through municipal budgets, for children of uninsured parents. Children of the self-employed receive benefits from the NSSI if their parents pay contributions. In 2001 approximately 1.2 million children received child allowances, and total expenditures amounted to 0.7 percent of GDP.[91]

Because of their near universal eligibility, child allowances have high coverage-50 percent of poor households received child allowances in 2001. However, in terms of beneficiaries, only 16 percent of the resources spent went to these households. Benefit levels are also too low to have an impact on poverty. The level of the child allowance has been frozen in real terms, at 8.6 BGN per child per month, since May 1997. Even for poor households, the child benefit amounted to less than 10 percent of pre-consumption household income.

On April 1, 2002, the Law on Family Benefits which aims to improve the adequacy of child benefits and target them to poor households was enacted. Under the new Law, the benefit level would be doubled to 15 leva per child, and benefits would be income tested, such that only households with income under 150 leva per capita per month would receive benefits. The proposed change to the benefit level is too low to have a significant impact on the poverty rate, and the income threshold is too high to effectively concentrate the program on poor families. Under the new law 1.15 million children are expected to receive child allowances, a decrease of 50,000. However, the new Law would cover children who are currently not receiving the benefit, so the reduction in the number of beneficiaries would be greater.

The increased child allowance will contribute to a modest reduction in poverty among households with two or more children, but will have no impact on the consumption distribution of families with one child.

The new Law on Family Benefits is projected to cost an additional 89.7 million leva, or 0.32 percent of 2001 GDP. The administrative burden on the system would also increase, as all households would have to submit income information for the means test. The Government faces a number of options to maximize the impact of these resources on poor households with children:

- Expanding coverage to poor households currently not covered by child allowances. The current system excludes children of the uninsured self-employed, a large share of whom are

---

[90] Although child allowances are short-term benefits, paid both through the social insurance system, and by the MOLSP through social assistance offices, all child benefits are discussed here together as 'social assistance.'

[91] This comprises 0.3 percent of GDP from the MOLSP budget, paid through municipalities, and 0.4 percent paid through employers and financed by the NSSI.

poor. In 2001, 23 percent of the children not receiving benefits were poor, representing 24 percent of poor children in Bulgaria.

- The cost of eliminating the poverty gap among households that do not receive child allowances is approximately 0.37 percent of GDP-indicating the proposed increase under the new Law would be better spent if targeted to a smaller pool of beneficiaries.
- Increasing coverage and raising benefits for households with children through the GMI program. As the GMI program is an effective mechanism for reaching the poor, it can be further built upon to expand coverage for households with children.
- Means-testing child benefits through the income tax system.

Benefits for the Disabled. The 1995 Act on Protection, Rehabilitation and Social Integration of Disabled Persons regulates the rights of the disabled to rehabilitation, social integration, and their protection. It supports the payment of a number of small cash and in-kind benefit programs for the disabled. The 2001 amendments aimed at the creation of conditions enabling social rehabilitation, professional qualification, and employment opportunities in an integrated working environment for the disabled. The Act also specifies the terms and conditions for the provision of technical support appliances for the disabled and for monthly allowances for disabled children. Benefits also include targeted assistance, according to income levels of the respective families, for the refurbishment of the homes of severely disabled persons, for the purchase of passenger motor vehicles, and for companions of blind and deaf persons. Other targeted benefits include, for certain categories of disabled persons with permanent infirmities, payment of rent of municipally-owned premises, use of telephone services and transportation facilities, and balneotherapy. Targeted benefits for the use of communal transport facilities are based on income level of beneficiaries. The 2001 amendments to the regulations transferred the administration of the technical support appliances, mainly medical devices, to the health system.

These benefits amounted to 2 percent of total social assistance expenditures in 2001. Two of the main disability benefits: transportation benefits (for example, vouchers for public transport), and medical benefits (for example, in-kind provision of medical supplies) are not targeted to the poor, and hence are ineffective in terms of their welfare impact and costs. Both programs are regressive in that they target less of their resources to the poor than the share of the poor in the population. Both programs are also expensive in terms of costs. These benefits should be shifted to the health system where possible.

Short-Term Benefits

In addition to pensions, the NSSI provides short-term and family benefits, many of which are provided under the Mandatory Social Insurance Code (MSIC). Short-term benefits are financed out of two extrabudgetary funds managed by the NSSI: the "Work Injury and Occupational Disease Fund" and the "General Sickness and Maternity Fund." These funds grant 12 categories of benefits, including: general sickness, maternity and child care, care for sick children, compensations for work injuries and occupational diseases, wage subsidies for sick persons and pregnant women reentering the labor market, and subsidies for special diets. These funds also cover child allowances (discussed above) and birth grants for insured households, funeral grants, and monthly allowances for disabled children.

Benefits paid out of the "General Sickness and Maternity Fund" are set at 80 percent of gross daily wages, and benefits paid out of the "Work Injury and Occupational Disease Fund" at 90 percent of gross daily wages. All compensations paid in case of temporary incapacity to work are paid to those who have had an insurance record for at least 6 months, with three exceptions: (i) in case of work injury and/or occupational sickness; (ii) in case of maternity leave/benefit; (iii) in the event that the insured person is under the age of 18. All short-term benefits based on social insurance payments are paid by the employer.

TABLE 8.9: SHORT-TERM AND FAMILY BENEFITS

(PERCENT OF GDP)

	1991	1995	1997	1998	1999	2000	2001
Child allowances	2.16	0.76	0.51	0.50	0.43	0.38	0.36
Birth grants	0.01	0.02	0.01	0.01	0.01	0.02	0.02
Sickness benefits	0.53	0.48	0.33	0.46	0.45	0.32	0.31
Care for sick child	0.05	0.05	0.03	0.04	0.04	0.01	0.01
Maternity benefits	0.16	0.08	0.05	0.08	0.08	0.07	0.06
Compensation for work injuries and occupational diseases	0.02	0.02	0.01	0.01	0.01	0.01	0.01
Child care benefits	0.54	0.18	0.10	0.12	0.14	0.15	0.15
Compensation for special diets	0.01	0.02	0.00	0.01	0.01	0.01	0.00
Monthly allowance for disabled children	0.00	0.00	0.00	0.01	0.01	0.01	0.01
Other	0.07	0.20	0.14	0.16	0.41	0.71	0.66
Total	3.54	1.81	1.19	1.38	1.59	1.68	1.59

Source: MOLSP, MOF.

Financing

The "General Sickness and Maternity Fund" is financed through a 3 percent payroll tax shared between employers and employees.[92] The self employed make their own contributions; and the state budget contributes on behalf of civil servants. Contributions to the "Work Injury and Occupational Disease Fund" are paid by the employers only and amount to 0.7 percent of payroll.

Total spending on short-term and family benefits has declined substantially over the decade: from 3.5 percent of GDP in 1991 to 1.6 percent in 2001. This has come about largely because of declining expenditures on child allowances for insured families (child allowances for uninsured households are paid through the social assistance system), which comprise the largest share of spending on short-term benefits. The decline in spending on child allowances has been driven by the demographic decline and increased unemployment, which has shifted recipients of child allowances to the social assistance system.

Program Effectiveness and Main Issues

Sick Leave Benefits.   Sick leave benefits have declined over the decade. The total number of paid work days fell from 25.5 million in 1991 to 10 million in 2001, or from 7 days per person in 1991 to 5 in 2001. This fall reflects the rise in official unemployment and the growth of informal sector activity. In addition, the Mandatory Social Insurance Code, adopted in January 2000, shifted the responsibility for paying the first three days of sick leave to the employer. Prior to this change, the NSSI was responsible for financing all sick leave. Following this change, NSSI expenditures on sick leave fell by 22 percent-from about 0.45 to 0.32 percent of GDP between 1999 and 2000. However, employer payments increased by 35 percent indicating a cumulative increase and, consequently, an increase in the cost of labor for employers. Other countries which introduced employer payment of sick leave, including Poland and Latvia, experienced an increase in payments following the implementation of this approach due to fraud and abuse.

---

[92] Contributions were 80 percent by employers and 20 percent by employees in 2001. According to the new Mandatory Social Insurance Code, employee contributions will increase by 5 percent points each year until contribution rates are equalized in 2007.

Some employers blame the increase in sick leave days on the recent health reform in Bulgaria and the introduction of primary care physicians (GPs). GPs issue sick leave documents and may be more liberal in granting sick leave than the old polyclinics. This may be due to increased liability of physicians and their desire to avoid malpractice claims. Some employers' associations favor a transfer of responsibility for paying sick leave benefits to the National Health Insurance Fund. This would presumably entail an increase in payroll taxes to cover the costs and, therefore, would not lead to a net reduction in labor costs. *The incidence of sick leave should be monitored to ensure that it is applied consistently, and that usage does not escalate, neither fraud nor abuse takes place.*

Maternity and Child Care Benefits.   Bulgaria's child care leave benefits are the most generous, in terms of both benefit level and duration, in the European Union and the OECD. Mothers are eligible first for maternity leave, and then for child care benefits. *Maternity leave* lasts for 135 days-45 days before and 90 days after delivery. Benefits equal 90 percent of their prior wage or the minimum wage-whichever is higher. Women do not need to have a contribution history in order to claim benefits, only a labor contract. Following this period, mothers-or another family member who takes leave to care for the child-are eligible for *child care leave,* equal to the minimum wage, until the child is two years old. If no one in the family takes leave and the mother returns to work, she is eligible for a wage supplement of 50 percent of the child care benefit. After child care benefits expire, mothers can take leave without pay until the child is three years old. For uninsured mothers, maternity and child care benefits are provided for under the Birth Promotion Act. The legislation includes a re-entry guarantee-the mother's job is kept during maternity and child care leave, until the child is 3 years old. If the enterprise closes down while the mother is on leave, the benefit is terminated and can be provided through the unemployment office and social assistance system according to their eligibility criteria.

The duration of maternity benefits in Bulgaria is in line with current EU practices. Benefit duration ranges from 14 weeks in Britain to 28 weeks in Denmark. Compensation levels are also consistent with European countries. Child leave benefits in Bulgaria are longer in duration than similar parental leave programs in EU countries. The most generous programs are currently in Austria, which provides 22 months of paid leave, and Germany, where parents have the option of two years of unpaid leave, following one year of paid leave. Bulgaria is also an outlier in the length and generosity of benefits provided to uninsured mothers.

There is scope for reducing the duration of child care leave and changing benefit design to improve labor market flexibility. Expenditures on benefits are not high as a share of the budget. In 2001, maternity and child care benefits amounted to 0.21 percent of GDP, a substantial decrease from 0.7 percent in 1991. The drop has been due to a decline in the number of eligible mothers as a result of both the low birth rate and falling employment. Despite the low fiscal costs, there are two arguments for reducing the eligibility period for child leave benefits. First, the high cost to employers may potentially deter employers from hiring young women. According to the MSIC, employers are obliged to make social insurance contributions for the entire period of maternity and child leave (for example, up to 3 years). Second, maternity benefits for uninsured mothers have limited targeting and divert resources from poor families.

In order to improve incentives for employers, the duration of child care leave should be reduced to one year. Additional measures should include: (i) eliminating the re-entry guarantee for child care leave; and (ii) transferring responsibility for paying insurance contributions for those on leave to the NSSI, rather than the employer.

Summary of Policy Recommendations

Social protection reforms undertaken in Bulgaria in the 1990s are beginning to have an impact on welfare outcomes. As a whole, benefits substantially reduce poverty, and play a significant role in helping households manage risk. Reforms to the PAYG pension system have improved fiscal sustainability and effectiveness. The introduction of unemployment benefits has provided protection for workers affected by restructuring; and changes in social assistance design, financing and administration have led to expanded coverage and improved targeting.

The agenda ahead entails a second generation of reforms which will further improve the effectiveness and sustainability of the social protection system. This involves attention to cross-cutting issues, such as a strategy to reduce the payroll tax burden which will maintain revenues and improve labor market incentives, and improvement of the intergovernmental fiscal system, which will strengthen the potential of local governments to provide social assistance.

Further sector and program specific interventions are also key. In pensions, the primary issue is to consolidate the multi-pillar reform recently launched by defining in the permanent legislation the contribution rate to the second pillar and enhancing regulation and supervision of private pension plans. Concerning labor markets, desirable objectives include ensuring the fiscal sustainability of unemployment insurance, and improving the effectiveness of active labor market measures. In social assistance, key issues are improving the targeting and fiscal sustainability of the safety net. The effectiveness of the GMI program as a safety net for the poorest households is improving. Further consolidation of benefit programs into the GMI program-as was done with the energy benefit would be desirable to reduce the complexity of the system and administrative costs. For example, the GMI's mean-testing mechanism could be used to target child benefits to poor households. Specific measures are outlined below.

Pensions

In the short term:

- Enhance compliance and coverage of the public pillar, control the rise in social pensions for disabled and define a clear rule for indexing pensions.
- Ensure a prompt and transparent transfer of contributions to private pension plans and proper management of contributions that have not yet been reconciled.
- Strengthen the institutional capacity of SISA and upgrade regulations to foster the sound development of private pension plans.
- Define a transparent plan for the universal pillar to eliminate current uncertainties for its future.

In the medium term:

- Strengthen the legal framework of private pension plans, especially the governance structure of private plans, and the authority and independence of the supervisory agency, and make the investment regime more flexible.

In the long term:

- Seek closer integration of private pension funds with the rest of Bulgaria's financial markets and the EU.
- Harmonize the retirement age of men and women.

Labor Market

- Accelerate fundamental labor market reform that facilitates the net creation of jobs and enhances improvements in productivity.
- Continue the on-going monitoring of ALMPs to ensure the effectiveness and long-term impact of programs to ensure it benefits vulnerable groups.
- Monitor closely the results of the new unemployment fund in terms of the profile of unemployment beneficiaries, including duration of employment before and after having received benefits, share of beneficiaries that return to employment, and costs of the new fund.

- Continue to consolidate the social security system on the whole to lower the compulsory contributions to employees and employers by broadening the base, and by closing the gap between contributions into and benefits from the system.

Social Assistance

- Strengthen the GMI program by fully centralizing funding for the program.[93]
- Improve targeting of social assistance by: (i) training social workers to identify poor households; (ii) improving information systems to facilitate means-testing and reduce payment of duplicative benefits; and (iii) expanding communication activities to inform beneficiaries about eligibility criteria and application procedures.
- Improve targeting of the energy benefit to benefit poor households.
- Target expenditures on child allowances to the poor. Evaluate program design options for expanding coverage to children currently not covered by the benefit.
- Eliminate provision of GMI benefits in-kind.
- Eliminate payment of the regressive medical and transportation benefits.

Short-term Benefits

- Monitor sick leave payments and incentives.
- Reduce period of child care leave benefits to one year.
- Eliminate the job reentry guarantee for mothers on child care leave beyond one year.
- Shift responsibility for paying social insurance contributions for individuals on child care leave from employers to the NSSI.

---

[93] The Government's fiscal decentralization program described in Chapter 4 envisages centralizing social benefits in 2003.

CHAPTER 9

THE STATE RAILWAY—FISCAL BURDEN AND OPTIONS FOR REFORM

Although the Bulgaria State Railway (BDZ) has taken substantial measures in recent years to adjust to its rapidly changing economic environment, it remains in a fragile financial situation and its long-term future is uncertain. The state contribution to the railway has remained steady at about 0.8 percent of GDP since 1999, and no solution seems in sight to put the railway on a sustainable development path. BDZ is at a crossroad and faces important decisions because of several factors: considerable stock of assets inherited from the socialist era which are arriving to the end of their service life; the possibility that capacity bottlenecks affect investors' perceptions of economic opportunities in Bulgaria; the sweeping changes in sector organization being implemented under the new railway law of November 2000;[94] and the major investments in infrastructure being decided upon under concessional funding from the European Union. Within this context, the purpose of this Chapter is to briefly present the railway's financial situation and requirements for state support, discuss the main reasons for the railway's poor performance, outline the likely long-term consequences of the present situation, highlight necessary reforms, and assess the impact of three alternative reform programs on the railway's finances and the requirements for state support.

There are serious issues affecting other modes of transport in Bulgaria, but they are generally not as pressing as those affecting the railway. The other main land transport mode, road transport, has changed drastically in the past 10 years. Road transport enterprises have been privatized and, spurred by deregulation, have restructured. Numerous small owner operators have appeared. As a

---

[94] In accordance with the new law, BDZ has now been split into two separate enterprises, one in charge of infrastructure (National Company Railway Infrastructure-NCRI), and one in charge of railway operations (BDZ EAD). The complexities and opportunities which result from this drastic change will be briefly discussed later. Given this Chapter's focus on strategic issues in the railway sector as a whole, the analysis and the financial projections lump NCRI and BDZ EAD together. The two enterprises are jointly referred to as "BDZ".

result, road transport is today remarkably competitive and efficient. In a survey of road freight transport costs among EU accession countries carried out in 2001 by the International Road Union (IRU), Bulgaria came with the lowest cost at about 60,000 Euros per truck on average, or about 75 percent of the mean value for all countries. In the freight area, road transport, which has a share of about 55 percent of the combined road plus rail market, largely complements rail transport, focusing on shorter distance, higher value, and more time sensitive shipments. In the passenger area, on the contrary, road transport competes aggressively with rail transport and has gained a share of about 70 percent of the intercity transport market. Bulgaria's main road network of about 19,000 km is managed by the Road Executive Agency (REA). Only one-third of these roads are in good condition, which is roughly similar to the average for EU accession countries and notably better than Romania or Poland. REA is financed to a large extent from outside the State budget. Its main sources of revenues are an earmarked tax on the price of gasoline and diesel fuel, transit fees paid by foreign vehicles, and external loans and grants. Main issues in the road and road transport sectors are: (i) REA's weak capacity to assess its priorities and prepare expenditure plans; and (ii) the insufficient allocation of funds to road maintenance (only about 20 percent of expenditures for road works). These issues will need to be addressed at the same time as the railway sector issues.

Maritime/river and air transport are also important for the economy. The key challenge in these sectors is to increase drastically the share of private sector activity. The Government plans to privatize the two main maritime and river transport enterprises in the near future. A sound institutional and regulatory framework also needs to be established to foster private sector involvement in ports and airports under the form of concessions.

Financial Performance and Requirement for State Support

The past financial performance of BDZ is summarized in Table 9.1. This table shows that, in essence, BDZ does not operate as a commercial enterprise; it functions, rather, as a government department. For BDZ, profit maximization has not been a goal. In fact, its net income has been negative since the start of the economic transition. Its deficit reached 124 million leva in 2001, or 21 percent of total cost, even after taking into account operating subsidies provided by the Government. Like a government department, BDZ operates with very little cash and aims only at balancing its revenues and the cash outflows necessary mainly for operations and debt service. In the past few years, BDZ has failed to achieve even this objective because of unexpected circumstances to which it has not been able to adapt rapidly enough, namely, a sharp reduction of demand, high oil prices, and increases in foreign exchange costs, in particular. As a result, BDZ has encountered serious liquidity problems and has accumulated arrears vis-à-vis the State, suppliers, and even its personnel. Constrained by resources, BDZ has also not been able to maintain its assets adequately for many years, with dire effects on the quality of its facilities and equipment and thus on the quality of its services. If proper maintenance had been undertaken, BDZ's financial results would have been considerably worse.

BDZ receives a significant contribution from the State. As shown in Table 9.2, this contribution comes from a large number of sources. One of these sources, the accumulation of arrears to the budget (for non-payment of taxes) and to the social funds, is imposed by BDZ on the State and is evidence of a "soft budget constraint". In total, the State contribution to BDZ is equivalent to about 0.8 of GDP. On average, about half of this amount represents an operating subsidy and the other half an investment. Not counted in Table 9.2 are other forms of state support, such as arrears to state-owned companies (especially, to the electricity supplier, NEK), interest payments on loans from the European Investment Bank, and provision of sovereign guarantees for World Bank and European Bank for Reconstruction and Development (EBRD) loans. Beyond these, the loss of railway assets due to their inadequate maintenance and renewal is an additional important, but implicit, price that the Government pays for railway transport.

TABLE 9.1: BDZ: OPERATIONAL AND FINANCIAL PERFORMANCE

(AMOUNT IN MILLION LEVA)

	ACTUAL		ESTIMATE		FORECAST
	1998	1999	2000	2001	2002
Passenger Traffic - Passenger-km (billion)	4.7	3.8	3.5	3.1	3.1
Freight Traffic - Ton-km (billion)	6.2	5.3	5.5	5.1	5.1
Total Traffic Unit (billion) (pkm + tkm)	10.9	9.1	9.0	8.2	8.2
Revenue (operating + non-operating)	343	307	360	386	415
Costs (incl. depreciation and fin. charges)	454	505	518	586	548
Net income (deficit)	(111)	(198)	(158)	(200)	(134)
Govt. PSO* and operating subsidy	53	79	77	76	61
Net income (deficit), including effect of subsidy	(58)	(119)	(81)	(124)	(72)
Net cash generation from operations	(39)	(32)	12	11	38
Cash at the end of year	11	5	7	7	7
Working Ratio (excluding Govt. PSO subsidy in percent)	106	125	114	125	116
Debt Service Coverage Ratio	2.5	0.6	0.8	0.6	1.2
Current Ratio	1.2	0.7	0.6	0.5	1.0

* Public Service Obligation.

Note: Costs in 2001 include an exceptional 37 million leva interest charge on arrears to the State budget.

Source: BDZ accounts.

Causes of Poor Financial Performance

Uneconomic Services

BDZ operates a large number of services, many of which are not economic. To a large extent, this is a legacy of the past, as economic efficiency was not a prime objective during socialist times, and the railway was given a dominant role in land transport, while the development of road transport was frustrated. As the economy changed, demand for railway services declined considerably and is now often too low for efficient railway operations. This is evidenced by the low intensity of use of the railway network: about 2.5 million Traffic Units/km of line in Bulgaria, compared to about 4.2 million in Poland, 3.3 million in Romania, and about 3.5 million on the large Western European railway networks (Table 9.3). In particular, a sizable proportion of BDZ's network (1,460 km, out of 4,290 km of lines) is made up of small branch lines serving mainly rural areas or single industries. It is on these lines that railway operations are the most inefficient.

Other services (other than those on branch lines) are also uneconomic and in fact contribute much more to BDZ's deficit. This is the case with most passenger services. On average, the cost of passenger service on BDZ was about 0.073 Leva/Passenger-km in 2000.[95] This compares with

---

[95] As reported by PADECO consultants on the basis of studies by the National Railway Institute. Given the absence of precise cost accounting at BDZ, this number and the cost estimates mentioned later in this paragraph are approximations. The cost of passenger service on low density routes is probably overestimated. The difference between the costs of bus and railway services on these routes is so wide, however, that the argument that bus services are far more economic remains valid.

TABLE 9.2: STATE SUPPORT TO BDZ

(MILLION LEVA)

	ACTUAL		ESTIMATE	FORECAST
	1999	2000	2001	2002
PSO Subsidy and other operating subsidies	79	77	76	61
Arrears (to State budget and social funds)	17	17	21.5	
Exemption from VAT and customs duties	33	19	7	6
Regional Investment Program (including from Road Fund)	38	49	38	30
National Investment Program	15	20	27	13
European Investment Bank (EIB), PHARE, and ISPA	17	31	62	139.5
Total	199	213	231.5	249.5
GDP (at current prices)	23,790	26,753	29,618	30,783
State Support as percent of GDP	0.84	0.80	0.78	0.81

Source: BDZ accounts.

a rough estimate of 0.040–0.050 Leva/Passenger-km for bus service (including a correction for road user charges). The road transport industry has developed impressively in Bulgaria in the past 10 years. Bus services, which use second-hand imported vehicles, take full advantage of the cheap and productive local labor, and are stimulated by a highly competitive environment, have proven far more efficient in general than railway services. Only long distance railway passenger services, which have an estimated cost broadly similar to that of bus services, could compete. In fact, passenger trains on branch lines (with an estimated cost of 0.28 Leva/Passenger-km) and the "regional" trains which link small towns located on the main lines (at a cost of 0.12 Leva/Passenger-km) have no economic rationale.[96] Given present economic and geographic circumstances, these services also do not have any significant environmental or other external benefits that would give them an advantage over bus services. Similarly, some rail freight services do not have a sound economic rationale. Indeed, many small freight stations have a volume of activity which is too small to justify their continued operation. Local freight trains serving these stations have a cost of operation probably far in excess of that of trucks.

In addition, BDZ has not reduced the supply of services as it should have if it was to match the decline in demand of the past years. Since 1998, passenger traffic has shrunk by 34 percent,

---

[96] Assuming, which is generally the case, that towns and villages are served by a practicable road.

TABLE 9.3: COMPARATIVE RAILWAY STATISTICS, 2000

	BULGARIA	POLAND	ROMANIA	WESTERN EUROPE
Use of railway network, million traffic units/km	2.5	4.2	3.3	3.5
Labor productivity, traffic units per employee	223,000	431,000	284,000	600,000
Average revenue per t/km, US$	0.019	0.023	0.022	n.a.
Average revenue per passenger/km, US$	0.008	0.018	0.010	n.a.

Source: BDZ, Polish and Romanian Railways, World Bank Railway Database.

from 4.7 to 3.1 billion Passenger-km, while the number of Train-km has declined by only 16 percent (from 29.8 to 25.1 million). As a result, there are fewer passengers per train. Similarly, freight traffic has contracted by 18 percent (from 6.2 to 5.1 billion Ton-km), while the number of freight Train-km has fallen by only 5 percent.

It is often argued that BDZ cannot fairly compete with truck and bus operators because it pays for its infrastructure, while the latter do not. This is largely incorrect and not a major issue. Truck and bus operators do pay for the cost of using the road through a special tax on diesel fuel which amounts to about US$0.093/liter,[97] somewhat above the amount recommended in the World Bank's 1998 paper on Commercial Management and Financing of Roads. And the true contribution of truck and bus operators is even higher, since the price of diesel fuel includes in Bulgaria, an additional excise tax amounting to about US$0.057/liter. On the contrary, truck and bus operators pay a relatively low annual registration tax of roughly US$100 per heavy truck and US$50 per bus, while the above paper recommends amounts more than 10 times higher. An increase in the annual registration tax would be warranted but would not significantly change the competitive position of rail transport.

Low Passenger Fares

Revenues from passenger services are, on average, only about 25 percent of costs. Cost recovery varies greatly, according to tentative estimates by the Railway Institute; it ranges from 52 percent for express trains which operate between large cities, to 17 percent for regional trains and 8 percent for trains on branch lines. This is due essentially to the very low level of standard fares, which are, for example, 0.023 Leva/Passenger-km, or about one third of the average cost of 0.073 Leva/Passenger-km for long distances in economy class on regular trains. These low fares are generally explained by the need to serve poor people. Indeed, incomes are low in Bulgaria and the cost of a family trip may quickly amount to a substantial share of the monthly salary of the main income earner. However, there is no evidence that rail users in Bulgaria are poorer than the average non-motorized population, so that the benefits of cheap railway transport appear not to be targeted. In any case, if cheap intercity transport was considered a basic need that the Government should provide, cost realities, as mentioned above, would also argue for these services to be provided by bus and not rail transport.[98] There is also no differentiation in the pricing structure between highly uneconomic services (such as those on branch lines or the regional trains) and those that are comparatively less costly. The same unit prices are applied all over the country.

Not only are normal fares low, in addition, a large number of passengers benefit from substantial discounts. Indeed, children, students and retirees, who account for close to 50 percent of the railway passengers, travel at half price. These benefits, which are also provided in other Central and Eastern European countries, are not valid instruments of social policy. Like the low level of standard fares, they are not targeted and benefit poor and non-poor people alike.

A comparison with other Central and Eastern European countries shows that effective passenger fares in Bulgaria are indeed low. In 2000, average revenue per passenger was US$0.008/Passenger-km in Bulgaria, 0.010 in Romania, 0.018 in Poland, and 0.023 in Croatia.

Low Labor Productivity

Although BDZ has considerably reduced labor throughout the 1990s, it still had about 36.600 employees in 2001, making it one of the largest employer in the country. At about 223,000 Traffic Units per employee, labor productivity is lower than in most Eastern European countries. In 2000,

---

[97] Taking into account that the value added tax on fuel is also levied on that special tax.

[98] BDZ also argues that low fares are necessary to maintain competition with bus services. This, however, is not a sound argument as, under normal circumstances, any commercial firm would leave a market rather than accumulate losses. In any case, in general, bus fares are still significantly over railway fares.

productivity was, for example, about 431,000 TU/employee in Poland and 284,000 TU/employee in Romania. It was generally around 600,000 TU/employee in Western Europe and often above 1,000,000 TU/employee in Latin America. As a result, labor costs are by far the largest cost item for BDZ. With about 40 percent of its total cost due to labor, BDZ is not taking advantage of the country's low wages.

Inadequate Incentive Structure

Ever since the economic transition began, the relationships between BDZ and the Bulgarian State have been similar to those found all over the world between states and most of their state-owned enterprises (SOEs). As shown by many studies,[99] these relationships do not provide an incentive structure that promotes efficient decision making by either state supervisory authorities or SOE managers. In the case of BDZ, most strategic decisions on railway services to be provided, passenger fares, labor reduction, senior staff appointments, and investments are taken directly or indirectly by the state in the context of the general political process. As a result, senior managers do not feel and are not held accountable for major actions, and state officials, confronted by difficult decisions that have short-term political costs but only long-term economic benefits, are led to focus on short-term fixes which address the structural issues facing BDZ at best partially.

Some important restructuring of BDZ has taken place nevertheless in the past years: labor has been reduced by about 37 percent since 1995; all non core businesses have been divested; and unit revenues have increased significantly. Yet, many decisions have been too limited in scope to resolve problems, and BDZ has not truly focused on its commercial imperatives. The issue of financial losses on branch lines, for example, have been known for many years but not addressed so far. Similarly, the fact that many passenger services, even on the main lines, are not economic is understood, but its consequences in terms of necessary reduction of services not analyzed. The deleterious effects of inadequate maintenance and renewal of assets on BDZ's long-term capability to provide railway service, and indeed to survive, has also not been addressed so far.

Interest has focused in recent years on the lack of consistency between the major social services that the State requires BDZ to provide and the compensation provided for these services. Operating subsidies provided by the State, about 77 million leva in 2000 and 76 million leva in 2001, are well below the losses on passenger services, which have roughly been estimated at 187 million leva in 2000 and 191 million leva in 2001.[100] However, if all forms of State support are taken into account, and if allowance is made for the hidden cost of deferred maintenance and rehabilitation, the State's contribution to the railway would not be so much below the losses on passenger services.[101] It is, therefore, not only the volume of support but also the way the support is provided which constitute key issues. Had the incentive structure allowed BDZ to operate as a commercial enterprise seeking profits and assuming risks, it is likely that it would have used funds differently, reducing labor and organizing operations more efficiently, in particular, and using the resulting savings to maintain better and replace its assets.

Inadequate Investment Planning

A particularly important aspect of the relationship between BDZ and the State is that BDZ is entirely dependent on the State for its investments. As shown in Table 9.1, BDZ's net cash generation from operations has not even been sufficient to cover its debt service in the past few years.

---

[99] For example, the World Bank's "Bureaucrats in Business", 1994.

[100] Interim Report by PADECO Consultants, December 2001.

[101] Total state support was 194 million leva in 2000 and 224.5 million leva in 2001 (as shown in Table 9.2) after deduction of the VAT/custom duties exemptions which are not factored in costs. This would compare to total losses of about 225 million in each of these two years if it is assumed that the cost of deferred maintenance related to passenger services is approximately 30–40 million leva per year.

BDZ, therefore, does not make any financial contribution to its investments. These investments are financed from the state budget and from foreign loans and grants. Loans are guaranteed by the State or, in the case of EIB loans, passed on to BDZ as grants. Investment decisions are, thus, taken in the context of the annual budget process. As a result, BDZ's management is not in a position to select the investments that would best serve its commercial strategy.

Also, BDZ does not have a multi-year business plan, as any sound commercial enterprise does, based on the likely availability of funds and on a sound assessment of the railway's remunerative markets and the needs for serving them. Nor does the state have a multi-year investment program for the sector. In this context, BDZ and the Ministry of Transport and Communications, behaving like most government departments, submit requests far in excess of what they are likely to obtain and with insufficient concern for the financial and economic benefits of those proposals. For example, the Ministry of Transport's list of investment projects for 2005, which, in fact, covers projects to be implemented until 2010, includes railway investments of about 5 billion leva, an amount that may be driven by high expectations of cheap EU funding but is out of proportion for a business with a value added only slightly above 300 million leva. And these projects cover only investments in infrastructure and not even investments in rolling stock and locomotives.

Given this planning/budgeting process, it is doubtful that the selection of investments is appropriate. The largest project to be implemented in the coming years (the rehabilitation and reconstruction of the railway line from Plovdiv to Svilengrad, close to the Turkish border—a major project with a cost of about 340 million Euros for only 151 km of double track) has an economic rate of return of only 6.3 percent in its middle scenario. By contrast, there are sections of the main 2,800 km railway network which have much more traffic and are badly deteriorated, and where rehabilitation would achieve higher rates of return. These are unlikely to be implemented in the coming years. In addition, the exclusive focus of the State on infrastructure investments creates an imbalance in BDZ's assets. As the track improves, BDZ's capacity to use it, in the absence of any investment in rolling stock and locomotives, and given their insufficient maintenance, is becoming poorer and poorer.

Long-term Consequences of the Present Situation

Financial projections with a 10 year horizon (2002–11) have been prepared for this report to assess the likely consequences of the present situation. The main assumptions for these projections (Base Case) are listed in Annex 9.1 (at the end of this chapter) and further elaborated below:

(a) **Passenger traffic.** It was assumed that passenger traffic would decline by 25 percent in the 2003–06 period, due to the loss of about half the full-fare passengers, and remain stable afterwards. This assumption, although not in line with BDZ's expectations, is rather optimistic since: (a) recent declines in passenger traffic have been greater (−13.5 percent annually on average since 1998); (b) bus services which are highly competitive, especially in terms of speed and convenience, are likely to attract full-fare passengers away from the railway; and (c) the experience of other Central and Eastern European countries shows that, in countries that have had a decline in GDP comparable to that of Bulgaria, railways have lost a higher share of passenger services in general than BDZ.

(b) **Freight traffic.** It was assumed that freight traffic would remain at the 2001 level until 2006, and then grow in line with GDP. Again, this is a relatively optimistic assumption, since freight traffic has declined, on average, by 6 percent since 1998 and the growth prospects of BDZ's main freight clients are limited (with a major uncertainty concerning the top client, the Kremikovski steel mill).

(c) **Revenues.** Passenger fares and freight tariffs are expected to remain at their 2002 levels. As the proportion of passengers benefiting from discounts would increase, average unit passenger revenues would, in fact, decrease. Non-operating revenues are assumed to remain at the 1999 level, which was substantially below the level in 2000 and 2001. Indeed, the exceptional revenues obtained from the sale of surplus assets in those years cannot be expected to be sustained.

(d) **Costs.** Labor is expected to remain at 33,000 employees, the level to be reached at the end of 2002. Salaries would stay at the 2002 level. Fuel, energy, and miscellaneous costs to move in line with total traffic. The cost of materials and external services is assumed to grow 10 percent from 2003 until 2006. The cost of materials then varies in proportion to traffic. Such an increase is felt necessary to stem the accumulation of deferred maintenance and avoid disruptions in operations.

(e) **Debt and working capital.** It was assumed that BDZ would move closer to the liquidity situation of a normal company. Arrears to suppliers would be paid, arrears to the Government would be cancelled, as these arrears were tantamount to an additional operating subsidy, and other debt service would be honored when due.

(f) **Investments.** It was assumed that the recent trend towards increased investments, which is fueled by the availability of funds from the European Union, would continue. The assumption is that there would be a major infrastructure project every three years in the next 10 years equivalent to the forthcoming Plovdiv-Svilengrad project. These projects would be for infrastructure, as under the current policy, and should be better focused on priorities. In addition, a program of rolling stock and locomotives replacement would be carried out, aimed just at maintaining the minimum transport capacity.

The results of the projections (Base Case) are summarized in Table 9.4. These show that, based on the present situation and, if no reform were to take place, BDZ's annual losses would most likely increase rapidly and remain at 170–180 million leva in the foreseeable future. As BDZ's net cash generation would remain negative even after factoring in a PSO subsidy of 60 million leva, as in recent years, the State would be compelled to provide an additional "contribution to solvency" of about 100 million leva annually just to ensure that BDZ continues to operate, pays its suppliers, and services its debt. The State's support to the railway sector from its own funds would reach about 218 million, or about 0.7 percent of GDP. If loans and grants from the European Union are taken into account, the total State support would reach about 413 million leva, or about 1.3 percent of GDP. Therefore, if present trends are allowed to continue, the railway sector risks becoming an unsustainable burden on the State.

Necessary Reforms
The main reforms that need to be implemented to stem the deterioration of the railway sector are outlined below.

Rationalization of Railway Network and Services
Uneconomic services need to be drastically reduced. This applies especially to services on branch lines, regional passenger trains serving small localities on the main lines, and low-volume freight trains. In general, whenever there is potential for alternative passenger bus service or truck transport, it is almost certain that road transport will be more efficient than these rail services, and that the railway has no role to play.[102] About 1,400 km of branch lines are candidates for closure. Consultants are presently helping the Government assess the viability of these lines. On this basis and taking into account the considerable amount of study done in past years on these lines, the Government needs to prepare a plan for the rationalization of the rail network and operations. If the Government has justified doubts that private bus operators will not provide a regular service

---

[102] Branch lines serving mines or local industries may be exceptions, but in these cases the full cost of service should be charged.

TABLE 9.4: BASE CASE FINANCIAL PERFORMANCE SUMMARY

(AMOUNT IN MILLION LEVA)

	2002	2003	2004	2005	2006	2007	2008	2009	2010	2011
Passenger-km (billion)	3.1	2.8	2.6	2.5	2.3	2.3	2.3	2.3	2.3	2.3
Ton-km (billion)	5.1	5.1	5.1	5.1	5.1	5.3	5.4	5.6	5.8	5.9
Total Traffic Unit (billion) (pkm + tkm)	8.2	8.0	7.8	7.6	7.4	7.6	7.7	7.9	8.1	8.2
Revenue (operating + non-operating)	415	357	351	345	340	347	355	363	371	379
Costs (incl. depreciation and fin. charges)	548	557	563	571	583	589	595	601	605	608
Net income (deficit)	(133)	(200)	(212)	(226)	(243)	(242)	(240)	(238)	(234)	(229)
Govt. PSO and operating subsidy	61	61	61	61	61	61	61	61	61	61
Net income (deficit), incl. effect of subsidy	(72)	(139)	(151)	(165)	(182)	(181)	(179)	(177)	(173)	(168)
Net cash generation from operations (incl. effect of subsidy)	38	(19)	(30)	(41)	(54)	(50)	(46)	(42)	(38)	(34)
Necessary Govt. contribution to solvency	0	75	104	90	102	100	95	90	86	71
Cash at the end of year	7	7	7	8	8	10	11	12	12	14
Working Ratio (excl. PSO subsidy) in percent	116	122	126	129	133	132	130	128	127	125
Debt Service Coverage Ratio	1.2	(0.5)	(0.9)	(1.3)	(1.7)	(1.6)	(1.5)	(1.4)	(1.3)	(1.8)
Current Ratio	1.0	1.1	1.5	1.6	1.6	1.7	1.8	1.9	2.0	2.1
Budget support (excl. EIB and other grants)	103	189	218	204	216	214	209	204	200	185
Total budget support (incl. EIB and other grants)	243	384	413	399	411	409	404	399	395	380

Source: Staff estimates.

to some isolated communities, it or even the railway operating company itself could organize the bus service under a franchise arrangement. If justified on social grounds, this bus service could be subsidized. This has been done frequently by Western European railways as part of line closure programs.

Some of the regular intercity trains on the main lines may also be reconsidered. Many provide transport on distances that are too short, with frequent stops, and too few passengers. They often cannot be an economic alternative to bus services. There is no social or commercial justification for maintaining these trains. Their termination and the closure of related facilities should be part of the rationalization plan.

Increases in Revenues

If uneconomic services are terminated, overall cost recovery will improve, as these services are the most egregious cases of services provided below costs. However, other measures can also be taken to increase revenues. First, discounts could be reduced. As explained above, there is no strong justification on equity grounds for such discounts. They are perceived as an entitlement by part of the population, however, and the reduction could therefore only be gradual. Second, there is some limited scope for increasing freight revenues. On average, freight tariffs are somewhat lower in Bulgaria than in Central and Eastern European countries.[104] If the full cost of maintenance were taken into account, freight services would also only break even and not return a profit. It seems, therefore, possible for BDZ to raise tariffs without losing market share. This should be done in the context of improvements in marketing strategy. Third, more generally, as BDZ reconsiders the commercial soundness of all its passenger services and retains only those for which it has a comparative advantage, it would be able to identify opportunities for increasing some of the passenger full-fares. This is dependent on the ability of the railway to invest and improve the quality of the services that it provides.

Reduction in Labor

Compared to most other Central and Eastern European countries, BDZ is overstaffed, as shown in Section B above. If the labor force were reduced by 25 percent, the resulting productivity, 271 thousand Traffic Unit/employee, would remain below today's productivity of the Romanian railway. If the labor force were reduced by 35 percent, the productivity, 343 thousand Traffic Unit/employee, would still be well below that of the Polish railway,[105] and about half that of many West European railways. As will be shown in Section E below, reduction of labor is the single most important measure that can be taken to redress the railway's financial situation. In some cases, labor retrenchment would require changes in technology at BDZ (for example, for track maintenance) and complementary investments to achieve it. A reduction of the labor force by 3,600 employees for both National Company Railway Infrastructure (NCRI) and BDZ EAD is already envisaged for 2002.

Changes in the Relationships Between the State and the Railway

A major transformation of the railway sector is underway as the November 2000 railway law is being implemented. As explained earlier in this chapter, this law mandates the institutional separation of the infrastructure and the railway operations, open entry to the rail transport market by competing operators, and the creation of a railway executive agency in the Ministry of Transport and Communications to license operators and ensure open track access.[106] Implementation of this law provides an opportunity to establish relationships between the State and the two new enterprises (NCRI and BDZ EAD) that are conducive to efficient decision making. The main desirable features of these new relationships are outlined below.

BDZ EAD, the railway operating enterprise, should be established in a way that guarantees that it will be independent from the State, motivated solely by commercial objectives, and not shielded from risks. For this purpose, corporate governance arrangements should include, in particular: (i) delegation of the State's ownership role to a supervision board that is autonomous and includes strong representation of the stakeholders and the business community; and (ii) measures to ensure that the enterprise is managed autonomously with a long-term perspective regarding its commercial, financial and human resources strategies, its operating practices, and its investments. BDZ EAD would also have the freedom to set tariffs solely on the basis of its commercial interests and without any explicit or implicit government pressure. Most important, government support would be provided only under the form of long-term contracts for public service obligation (PSO) which ensure full compensation to BDZ EAD for the social services that it is mandated by the State to provide.[107]

---

[104] In 2000, average revenue per Ton-km was US$0.019 in Bulgaria compared to US$0.022 in Romania, US$0.023 in Poland and US$0.028 in Croatia.

[105] Which, itself, has embarked on a major program with the assistance of the World Bank and EBRD to reduce labor by 25 percent.

[106] See footnote 97.

[107] PSO contracts should not be "cost plus". They should be based on a contractually agreed payment per unit of service provided, and include rewards and penalties for obligations performed or not performed.

NCRI will remain a state enterprise. To the largest extent possible, it would be isolated from political interference. For this purpose, it would have systems and procedures which ensure that decisions on maintenance and investment expenditures will be based on economic criteria (such as compliance with a minimum economic rate of return). It would also have a supervisory board that includes representatives from its stakeholders. Finally it would contract out as many of its activities as possible under transparent, competitive procedures which will need to be established.

Open entry in the railway sector and fair competition would also be promoted. For this purpose, licensing procedures and controls would be such that any willing and competent service supplier is allowed to enter the market and transaction costs remain low. This principle has already been established by Ordinance 42 (July 6, 2001) of the Ministry of Transport. The rules for track access would also be fair, defined precisely, and administered transparently by the new railway executive agency. Finally, the infrastructure fee would cover the full marginal cost of usage of the track and other infrastructure facilities, i.e., the cost of operation and maintenance and the cost of the wear and tear attributable to any specific user.[108]

Ultimately, once the railway market is established, the administrative and regulatory capability of the railway executive agency is developed, and the PSO contract system is in place, BDZ EAD would be privatized.

Formulation of Sound Investment Policies

Given the poor shape of BDZ's infrastructure and especially its locomotives and rolling stock, significant investments (probably of the order of 200 million leva per year) will be required in the future. Even if part of these investments are funded from European funds, resources are likely to be scarce. It is, therefore, essential to optimize the selection of these investments.

In the case of BDZ EAD, investment decisions need to be made without any state influence and in the context of a sound business plan. This plan would be based on a critical review of all present services, an analysis of the comparative advantage of the railway in the Bulgarian overall transport sector, the most cost effective ways for BDZ EAD to serve its markets, a commercial strategy, and a realistic assessment of the availability of funds. Investments need to achieve financial rates of return comparable to those of sound commercial enterprises. Many are likely to be in rehabilitation of existing assets, but there is also a great need for modernization and replacement of the rolling stock and locomotives. BDZ needs a business plan urgently. It should create a unit for its preparation.

As a state infrastructure enterprise, NCRI cannot have the overriding commercial perspective that BDZ EAD would have. However, it needs to assess with great care the appropriate level of service that the infrastructure could provide. The marginal benefits of higher standards may often not be worth their additional costs as is most likely the case with the major Plovdiv-Svilengrad project. This needs to be established jointly with BDZ EAD and other operators, if any. Methodologies for this, based on economic criteria. need to be developed. On this basis, expenditure needs on the entire main line network require review. Large rehabilitation and capacity improvement projects, like those currently planned, should also be submitted to a stringent economic analysis. As a result, NCRI should prepare a multi-year expenditure plan.

Three Alternative Reform Programs

Most of the measures presented in Section D have been discussed within Bulgaria in the past few years. However, the impact of these measures has not been assessed in a comprehensive way. In particular, it has not been established how strong these measures need to be for fully redressing

---

[108] The Government should resist the temptation of lowering the costs of passenger services by cross-subsidizing the infrastructure fee for passenger trains by a high fee on freight trains. Such a cross-subsidy would hide the true cost of passenger rail transport and distort decisions on which service to keep or terminate, and how much PSO compensation to provide.

the financial situation of the railway sector and limiting state support to an amount that does not pose a threat to macro stability. Nor has the specific effect of each measure been determined.

In order to shed light on these questions, financial projections for 2002–01 have been prepared under three alternative reform scenarios with increasing strength. The scenarios are the following:

(a) **Mild reform scenario**

- Labor: 15 percent reduction in 2003–04.
- Termination of 75 percent of services on branch lines.

(b) **Medium reform scenario**

- Labor: 19 percent reduction in 2003–04 (corresponding to 10 percent each year).
- Increase in freight tariff: 5 percent in 2003.
- Reduction in passenger fare discounts from 50 percent to 40 percent.
- Reduction in railway service as follows:
  - Termination of 100 percent services on branch lines.
  - Termination of 50 percent of regional trains.
  - Termination of 33 percent of local and "shunting" freight trains.

(c) **Strong reform scenario**

- Labor: 35 percent reduction in 2003–05.
- Increase in freight tariff: 5 percent in 2003.
- Reduction in passenger fare discounts from 50 percent to 25 percent.
  - Reduction in railway service as follows:
    - Termination of 100 percent services on branch lines.
    - Termination of 100 percent of regional trains.
    - Termination of 50 percent of "fast" trains.
    - Termination of 66 percent of local and "shunting" freight trains.

The results of the projections are summarized in Table 9.5. These show that the mild reform scenario, although it includes measures at present considered as relatively radical, would not address railway issues in a significant way. Net cash generation would still be negative in 2006 and the railway would require a 67 million leva additional contribution from the State to pay its suppliers and service its debt. State support would be equal to 0.5 percent of GDP from the State own funds and 1.1 percent of GDP including foreign loans and grants.

In the medium reform scenario, the railway has a positive net cash generation in 2006 and requires only an additional 35 million leva State contribution to service its debt. Yet, state support is still about 0.4 percent of GDP from the State's own funds (which is about the level in 2000–01) and 1 percent of GDP including foreign loans and grants. It is only in the long-term that the medium reform scenario achieves significant results. The additional state contribution becomes zero and requirements for state investment funds decrease significantly in 2011. State support from its own funds would then be down to 0.30 percent of GDP.

Only the strong reform scenario results in a turnaround in the financial performance of the railway. The net cash generation from operations is substantial and reaches 100 million leva in 2005. There is no need for any additional state contribution and the requirements for state investment funds become zero as early as 2005 (foreign loans and grants would still be needed, although in a decreasing manner in the outer years). Yet, in this scenario, the railway is still not a fully commercial sector, as its net income remains negative. Clearly, the strong reform scenario is the only one that provides a sustainable solution to the problems of the railway sector.

TABLE 9.5: ALTERNATIVE REFORM SCENARIOS: FINANCIAL PERFORMANCE: SUMMARY

(AMOUNT IN LEVA MILLION)

		2006				2011			
	2002	BASE CASE	MILD REFORM	MEDIUM REFORM	STRONG REFORM	BASE CASE	MILD REFORM	MEDIUM REFORM	STRONG REFORM
Passenger-km (billion)	3.1	2.3	2.3	2.2	2.0	2.3	2.3	2.2	2.0
Ton-km (billion)	5.1	5.1	5.1	5.1	5.1	5.9	5.9	5.9	5.9
Total Traffic Unit (billion) (pkm + tkm)	8.2	7.4	7.4	7.3	7.1	8.2	8.2	8.1	7.9
Revenue (operating + non-operating)	415	340	340	355	357	379	379	397	398
Costs (incl. depreciation and fin. charges)	548	583	548	531	450	608	572	554	470
Net income (deficit)	(133)	(243)	(208)	(176)	(93)	(229)	(193)	(157)	(72)
Govt. PSO and operating subsidy	61	61	61	61	61	61	61	61	61
Net income (deficit), Incl. effect of subsidy	(72)	(182)	(147)	(115)	(32)	(168)	(132)	(96)	(11)
Net cash generation from operations (incl. effect of subsidy)	38	(54)	(18)	13	97	(34)	1	36	122
Necessary Govt. contribution to solvency	0	102	67	35	0	71	36	0	0
Cash at the end of year	7	8	8	9	10	14	14	14	73
Working Ratio (excl. PSO subsidy) in percent	116	133	123	113	90	125	116	106	84
Debt Service Coverage Ratio	1.2	(1.7)	(0.6)	0.5	3.2	(1.8)	0.1	2.0	6.6
Current Ratio	1.0	1.6	1.7	1.7	1.8	2.1	2.2	2.2	3.5
Budget support Excl. EIB and other grants	103	216	181	149	65	185	150	114	28
Total budget support Incl. EIB and other grants	243	411	376	344	260	380	345	309	223

Source: World Bank staff estimates.

Interesting lessons can also be drawn from the analysis of the specific effect of each reform measure. As Table 9.6 shows, reduction in labor is by far the most important source of savings. Terminations of services on branch lines do not reduce non-personnel costs in a major way but are probably necessary to allow a major reduction in labor. When there is a broad set of reductions in services, as in the strong reform scenario, high savings in non-personnel costs can be achieved. Increases in freight revenues can have a relatively important impact. This highlights the need for the operating company to develop its marketing capability and set tariffs solely on a commercial basis. Reduction in fare discounts do not have a major impact on revenues. However, as the implied elasticity of demand results in a decrease in passenger demand when discounts are reduced, they may be complementary to the termination of uneconomic services.

TABLE 9.6: ESTIMATED REVENUES INCREASES AND COSTS SAVINGS DUE TO SPECIFIC REFORMS, 2006

(AMOUNT IN MILLION LEVA)

	MILD REFORM	MEDIUM REFORM	STRONG REFORM
1. Revenue Increases:			
(a) Increase in freight tariff 5 percent		13	13
(b) Reduction in passenger fare discounts			
from 50 percent to 40 percent		4	
from 50 percent to 25 percent			6
2. Costs Savings			
(a) Reduction of labor:			
by 15 percent	30		
by 19 percent		38	
by 35 percent			72
(b) Termination[109] of services on:			
75 percent branch lines	5		
100 percent branch lines		7	
50 percent regional lines		7	
33 percent local/shunting freight trains		3	
100 percent branch lines			7
100 percent regional lines			13
50 percent "fast" trains			32
66 percent local/shunting freight trains			5
Total effect on net income/cash flows	**35**	**72**	**148**

Source: World Bank staff estimates.

---

[109] The savings shown in this table are the savings in non-personnel costs.

Recommendations

The analysis carried out in Sections C and E above, however crude it may be, highlights the key issues in the railway sector. It shows that only a strong effort at reforming the railway will eventually put it on a sustainable financial path. Although some measures, especially labor reduction, are much more significant than others, a comprehensive package of reforms is necessary to address the issues. The following railway action plan (Table 9.7) provides the main elements of the package of reforms that are needed to modernize the railway sector.

TABLE 9.7: RAILWAY ACTION PLAN

IMMEDIATELY	WITHIN 18 MONTHS	WITHIN 36 MONTHS
• Establishment of new railway operating company as joint stock company, with a charter that establishes its commercial objectives and ensures its autonomous decision making. • Establishment of new railway infrastructure company as an independent public company, with a charter that requires expenditures to comply with minimum economic criteria and mandates contracting of works. • Preparation of sound plan for rationalization of rail network and operations.	• Agreement on a medium-term business plan for the railway operating company. • Increase in intercity passenger full fares to at least 80 percent of cost recovery level. • Issuance by the Ministry of Transport of regulations that: (i) ensure that any willing and competent service supplier may be licensed; (ii) provide fair and transparent rules for track access; and (iii) fix track access charges on the basis of full marginal cost recovery. • Adoption by the Railway infrastructure of sound systems and procedures for: (i) planning/budgeting expenditures; and (ii) contracting out maintenance activities. • Termination of major loss-making services that will not be subject to public service obligation (PSO). • Signing of contracts between the Government and the operating company for major non-commercial passenger services that will be subject to PSO. • Total reduction of labor force by 10 percent.	• Adoption of privatization plan for the railway operating company. • Granting freedom to the railway operating company to set passenger full fares. • Contracting out of 100 percent of track rehabilitation and 75 percent of track maintenance. • Termination of all loss-making services not subject to PSO and closure of all related facilities. • Signing of contracts for all non-commercial passenger services subject to PSO. • Total reduction in labor force by 10 percent.

Annex

Financial Projections and Sensitivity Analysis
Main Assumptions

The major assumptions underlying the financial projections (WB staff estimates) are described below.

Base Case

Freight traffic is expected to remain constant at the 2002 level until 2006, then grow as much as an estimated GDP growth of 3 percent per annum from 2007 to 2011.

Passenger traffic is expected to decline 7 percent per annum from 2003 until 2006, so that at the end of the first four-year period, passenger traffic would have diminished by 25 percent, corresponding to a 50 percent decline of full-fare passenger traffic.

Freight tariff. The unit revenue (leva per ton-kilometer) remains constant in real terms after the expected 2002 increase.

Passenger tariff. Passenger tariff remains constant after the expected 2002 increase. Yet, the unit revenue (leva per passenger-kilometer) will decrease in real terms as the proportion of discount-fare passenger traffic is expected to increase from 50 percent today to 67 percent at the end of 2006.

Non-operating revenue. From 2000 to 2002, BDZ had an extraordinary income, mainly from selling the surplus of motive power and rolling stock. The projections for non-operating revenues assume that the sale of surplus assets cannot continue, and thus non-operating revenues are kept constant at the 1999 level.

Government contribution. The state support is required to cover: (i) the deficit on services which the Government would like the railways to continue to provide under public service obligation contracts; (ii) infrastructure investments funded from the state budget as well as from EIB loans (borrowed by the Government) and other sources such as ISPA grants, which are expected to grow substantially in the future; and (iii) a new contribution to solvency which will be necessary to keep BDZ from going bankrupt.

Operating costs.
 (a) Labor. Total staff number remains at 33,000 from the end of 2002. No salary increase is assumed after 2002 increase.
 (b) Materials. The material cost will vary in proportion to traffic. In addition, an increase of 10 percent per annum is assumed in 2003–06 to avoid major bottlenecks.
 (c) External services. A 10 percent growth is assumed per annum in 2003–06. Then, the amount remains constant
 (d) Other costs (including fuel, electricity, miscellaneous): They are assumed to vary in proportion to traffic.

Depreciation. It will vary in proportion to fixed assets. With rapidly increasing infrastructure investment which has an average economic life of 40 years, average depreciation rates will decline gradually from 5.6 percent of gross fixed assets in 2002 to 3 percent in 2011.

Debt. Existing loans are serviced. Arrears to the State budget and social funds are cancelled in 2002 by offsetting the BDZ liabilities with a corresponding increase in its capital. Arrears to NEK and other suppliers are paid so that the payable/receivable situation becomes "normal" at the end of 2004. Arrears to personnel are paid in 2002.

Capital investment: Starting in 2003, the State grant for capital investment and the proceeds of EIB loans and external grants will be spent for capital investment in infrastructure. The State grant will be leva 25 million in 2002 and increase to 54 million in each year after 2002, the same as the average for 1999–2001. External funds will be leva 63 million in 2002, and increase to leva 195 million in each year after 2002, given the availability of funds from the European Union. Total infrastructure investment will increase from leva 120 million in 2002 to leva 244 million in 2003–11. New investment in motive power and rolling stock remains at leva 31 million in 2003–11.

Sensitivity Analysis

Three sensitivity scenarios have been analyzed. In each one, the main assumptions of the base case are carried over. In addition, the following reforms are assumed to take place.

Mild Reform Scenario

- Labor: 15 percent reduction in 2003–04.
- Termination of 75 percent of services on branch lines: impact on non-personnel operating costs: 2 percent reduction.[110]

Medium Reform Scenario

- Labor: 25 percent reduction in 2003–04.
- Increase in freight tariff: 5 percent in 2003.
- Reduction in passenger fare discounts: the special fare is increased from 50 percent to 60 percent of the standard full fare and, as a result, discount fare passenger traffic declines 5 percent.
- Reduction in railway service and resulting reduction of non-personnel operating costs: as follows:
  - Termination of 100 percent services on branch lines: −2.6 percent.
  - Termination of 50 percent of regional trains: −2.6 percent.
  - Termination of 33 percent of local and "shunting" freight trains: −1.1 percent.

Strong Reform Scenario

- Labor: 35 percent reduction in 2003–05.
- Increase in freight tariff: 5 percent in 2003.
- Reduction in passenger fare discounts: the special fare is increased from 50 percent to 75 percent of the standard full fare and, as a result, discount fare passenger traffic declines 20 percent.
- Reduction in service and resulting reduction of non-personnel operating costs: as follows:
  - Termination of 100 percent services on branch lines: −2.6 percent.
  - Termination of 100 percent of regional trains: −5.1 percent.
  - Termination of 50 percent of "fast" trains: −12.8 percent.
  - Termination of local and "shunting" freight trains: −2.1 percent

---

[110] The impact of service reductions on non-personnel operating costs (NPOC) was calculated in each scenario on the basis of the following assumptions: (i) NPOC were split about 80 percent for railway operations and 20 percent for infrastructure in 2001; (ii) NPOC for railway operations were split 60 percent for passenger trains and 40 percent for freight trains; and (iii) NPOC) per type of passenger or freight train are allocated based on the share of such train type in the total number of train-kilometers assuming conservatively in addition that NPOC for "small" trains (regional rains on main lines, trains on branch lines, commuter trains) are one-third of the NPOC for express and fast trains.

CHAPTER 10

THE ENERGY SECTOR AND STATE SUPPORT[111]

The Sector's Complex Challenges

Like other sectors providing vital infrastructure services to underpin economic growth and poverty alleviation, Bulgaria's energy sector will continue to rely on public financial support during its transition to a commercialized, well-regulated, market-based system. Unlike some of the other infrastructure sectors, the energy sector can be fully commercialized. Furthermore, under an appropriate legal and regulatory framework, providers of energy services can become net contributors to the state budget,[112] and privatization of sector assets and services could generate significant funds with which to reduce public debt or boost public investment. More important for the next few years of Bulgaria's economic growth and social betterment will be the Government's ability to improve access to efficient infrastructure and energy services in a fiscally and environmentally sustainable manner, while continuing to phase out price subsidies on which households still rely heavily.

Like other transition countries in Eastern and Central Europe, over the next 5–10 years Bulgaria will have to invest several billion dollars in the rehabilitation, replacement and expansion of its energy infrastructure to meet domestic demand efficiently and reliably, meet EU environmental and nuclear safety requirements, and compensate for the last 10 years of under-investment. Unlike other transition countries, Bulgaria's transition faces the following characteristics:

- its historically heavy reliance on costly electricity and polluting solid fuels (coal briquettes) to meet its energy needs;
- the inherited high level subsidy of household electricity and district heating prices (and structural impediments to commercializing the latter)—which only recently has started to decline;
- the virtual absence of a low-pressure natural gas distribution system to allow consumers the benefit of gas as an efficient and clean alternative energy resource;
- the fact that except for environmentally-polluting lignite, the country does not have economical energy resources; and

---

[111] The Bulgarian Government's revised Energy Strategy adopted in July 2002, and some important reforms undertaken in the first half of 2002 take into account some of the findings and recommendations of this Chapter.

[112] In 2001, the electricity and gas sub-sectors were net contributors to the budget—however, both sub-sectors are still dependent on state guarantees for capital investments.

- the country's wish to maintain its growing electricity exports (US$100-150 million annually for the last two years), particularly to Turkey, which have proven to be economically, socially, financially and geo-politically important during the last few years.[113]

Since the bulk of Bulgaria's electricity (about 80 percent) is generated from nuclear fuel and indigenous, low-quality lignite, disproportionate reliance on electricity will be costly, particularly as the country strives to meet the nuclear safety and environmental compliance requirements for accession to the European Union. Consequently, in crafting the country's energy strategy and the composition and phasing of public financial support, policy-makers will need to be guided by the goal of:

- ensuring efficient, secure, safe and clean energy supply at the least cost to Bulgarian consumers and economy;

while bearing in mind the objectives of:

- acting as a dominant energy supplier in the region;
- minimizing dependence on imported energy; and
- meeting international environmental and nuclear safety commitments.

Achieving any of these objectives will require significant capital expenditures and entail associated capital risks. While such risks may be mitigated by including capital costs in end-user energy prices, income constraints will require investments to be carefully sequenced to ensure that they remain affordable. Since the prices of all infrastructure services (water, electricity, coal, district heating, transportation, etc.) will have to be adjusted to their cost-recovery levels more-or-less simultaneously, and the high level of public debt will require a greater reliance on non-subsidized private capital, improperly sequenced investments and market reforms will erode industrial competitiveness and consumer welfare. If households are forced to use costly electricity or polluting coal for heating, because more cost-effective district heating services are not modernized or efficient gas-based systems not developed, the poverty impact and loss of national competitiveness will be considerable. Expenditures on services such as heating, water and transportation are relatively inelastic and already capture a sizeable part of household income; heating bills alone consume about 20 percent of the average pensioner's annual income, and constitute the second largest expenditure category after food. Enabling customers to better manage and reduce these expenditures through more efficient consumption and supply, even as prices are adjusted to their cost-recovery levels, will be important for alleviating poverty and freeing up income for other expenditures, savings and investment.

Over the past three to four years, the authorities have implemented important reforms in the energy sector, including an unbundling of vertically integrated utilities to enhance regulation and prepare the sector for competition, creation of a regulatory authority for tariff-setting and licensing, tariff adjustments towards full cost recovery levels, reduction of fiscal subsidies to cover operating costs, and moving forward privatization in the energy sector to enable much needed new investment. While the country has taken, and continues to take, important steps to bring energy prices to full cost recovery (thereby reducing budgetary transfers, and real resource costs due to the price distortion), energy prices for households still require significant adjustment to cover costs. Assuming that Bulgaria has surplus power generation capacity and a significant potential for energy efficiency measures and low-cost demand management, a sound approach going forward would be to sequence investments and reforms in a way that minimizes fiscal risk and mitigates adverse effects

---

[113] Electricity exports from *existing* plants have helped Bulgaria's balance of payments, defrayed the sector's social and economic costs resulting from declining domestic demand, optimized system efficiency, and funded routine maintenance and repair. They have also enabled Bulgaria's neighbors to benefit from competitively priced and reliable electricity supply during a period of high oil and natural gas prices.

on consumer welfare. This chapter estimates the magnitude of the major forms of public financial support for energy services and, for the transition to full commercialization, and it offers a policy and market framework which would better target state support for public objectives such as poverty alleviation, economic competitiveness, energy security and sound environmental performance.

Magnitude and Forms of State Support

At present, households are the only consumers which benefit from subsidized energy prices.[114] While household electricity prices have started to gradually adjust towards full cost recovery, these have the highest subsidy content (about US$18–20/mwh), compared with the long-run average cost of supplying low-voltage consumers, followed by natural gas (about US$12/mwh) and district heating (about US$7/mwh). The cash-costs of electricity supply to households are cross-subsidized by non-household consumers, while costs of district heating services (provided in the 21 highest density cities and serving about 22 percent of the population) are subsidized by the state budget.[115] Until recently natural gas prices for households were cross-subsidized by other consumers: a single price was maintained for all consumer categories, including the higher cost household segment.[116] Recently, prices are starting to be adjusted according to their corresponding costs. Nevertheless, there are few households with access to natural gas, in part because distorted energy prices and a restrictive market structure have prevented the development of a low pressure gas system in Bulgaria. Prices of petroleum products were liberalized several years back. Coal briquette prices for non-household customers were set at cost-recovery levels in 1999; household prices were increased gradually and are expected to reach cost-recovery levels in 2002.[117] However, all coal prices remain administered, as all the major mines and the only briquette plant are state owned and government controlled.

Recently, there has been important progress in the energy reforms discussed in this chapter—including electricity and heating price adjustments, approval of tariff restructuring schedules, and implementation of cost-based tariffs for gas used by households. In mid-2002, the State Energy Regulatory Commission (SERC) adopted an electricity tariff adjustment schedule that envisages bringing household electricity prices to full cost recovery in a period of three years (2002–04).

The SERC reached that conclusion after taking into account the Bulgarian Energy Strategy, the ordinance mechanisms to adjust prices and tariffs, the estimates of tariff adjustments towards full cost recovery, and to ensure a stable regulatory framework. The SERC adopted a price adjustment of 20-15-10 percent for each of the three consecutive years starting in 2002, which if fully implemented would bring electricity prices to full cost recovery by end-2004. To protect the poor from the impact of the price adjustments, the Government supplemented this price reform with two mechanisms: (i) expanding the winter energy subsidy program which supplements the winter income of low-income families; and (ii) by adopting a two-tier price system whereby a subsidized tariff will be maintained for a life-line level of consumption until 2005, and a higher tariff is applied to consumption above this level. Implementation of these and other energy reforms remain central to the modernization of the energy sector.

With state ownership or control over all major energy assets, virtually all capital investment in the sector requires state support. Budget funds and state-guaranteed loans have been used to rehabilitate

---

[114] Subsidy here is defined as the difference between average cost of supply and average tariff for a particular customer category. Consequently, the estimation of supplier subsidies (difference between costs and tariff revenues) is somewhat uncertain, as accounting costs do not adequately reflect the costs of proper maintenance or asset replacement, nor the efficiency gains possible through modern technology and management systems.

[115] Fourteen of 21 district heating companies received state subsidies in 2001.

[116] A single price is applied to low cost large consumers as well as to the higher cost household consumers.

[117] Coal briquette prices were adjusted in early 2002 in line with the Energy Strategy of these reaching full cost recovery by end-2002.

TABLE 10.1: FORMS OF STATE SUPPORT AND FISCAL IMPLICATIONS FOR ENERGY SERVICES

	DIRECT FISCAL IMPACT	CONTINGENT FISCAL IMPACT
Explicit Support	• Under-pricing of district heating (DH) to households (difference between cost and tariff is covered by the budget); • Support for partially or completely liquidating non-viable coal mines, their technical safety, and clearance of arrears to National Social Security Institute; • Winter energy benefits program for low income and vulnerable people; • Re-investment in gas infrastructure of Government's natural gas transit fee. [118]	• State-guaranteed debt for power sector enterprises (IBRD, EBRD, EIB) and for safety enhancement of Kozloduy nuclear units 5 and 6, (Euratom, Citibank, RosEximBank) district heating pilot metering and demand management (IBRD)—Debt being serviced by sector enterprises; • Long-term (15 year) power purchase agreements (PPAs) between independent power plants Maritsa East 1 and 3 and NEK (the state guarantees NEK's performance obligations); • Commitment to cover civil damages up to SDR$15M resulting from nuclear accident and SDR$2.5M for nuclear accidents during transport technological operations with nuclear fuel.
Implicit Support	• Accumulated and expected public investment needs to sustain delivery of public services and meet key requirements for accession to the EU (develop low pressure gas system, improve efficiency and accountability of DH services, ensure safe closure of Kozloduy units 1–4,[119] and ensure technical efficiency of non-privatized part of the power sector); • Future recurrent costs of public investment projects.	• Take-or-pay gas contract between state-owned Bulgargaz and Russia's Gazprom; • Long-term (1998-2008) power sales agreements between NEK & Turkey's TEAS (and associated obligations to use part of revenues to construct Gorna-Arda hydropower cascade and Maritsa highway); • Environmental commitments for still unknown damage, and nuclear/toxic waste; • Clean up of enterprise arrears and liabilities; • Default of state/municipally funded entities on payment of energy bills; • "Bailout" of public or private suppliers of energy/ infrastructure services which have a significant "public goods" dimension (in the event of financial failure).

Source: World Bank.

power sector assets (including improving the safety of the Kozloduy nuclear power plant), carry out critical repairs in the DH sector and improve metering and demand management, and expand the capacity of the gas transit system.[120] The various forms of explicit and implicit state support which have direct and contingent implications for the budget are summarized in Table 10.1. A quantitative estimation of the various forms of fiscal or quasi-fiscal support for energy services is provided in the tables and text that follow.

---

[118] This practice was discontinued in 2002.

[119] Units 1 and 2 are planned for closure by the end of 2002. By that time the discussions for the future of Units 3 and 4 are expected to be completed.

[120] The recently concluded contracts with strategic private investors to rehabilitate the Maritsa East 3 thermal power plant and to construct a new plant at Maritsa East 1 are the first projects of any significant size for which financing would not involve a sovereign guarantee. The state would, however, have to guarantee the performance of the state-owned National Electricity Company with regard to the long-term power purchase agreements it has signed with the two power plants.

Explicit Subsidies (Non-Capital Investment Related)

District heating subsidies are provided to cover the operating costs of DH companies which are not covered by tariffs.[121] Commercial customer tariffs are set to cover reasonable supply costs, plus a profit margin; budget-dependent entities are charged at cost, and tariffs for households are set at estimated affordability levels. Cost structures vary for each DH company, depending on the fuel used, losses in transmission and distribution, and whether heat production also results in electricity production. All households consumers serviced by 14 district heating companies based in large urban areas across the country are charged the same tariff, while tariffs for non-household customers reflect the supply cost of the DH company serving them. In companies which have combined heat and power production facilities, revenues from electricity sales are used to defray some costs of heat supply. However, pricing and dispatch rules and practices for combined heat and power (CHP) plants need to be strengthened to allow operators to predict better the revenues from electricity sales. With most customers metered at the building level, heat supply costs can now be audited better; as a result, customer bills reflect actual heat consumed within a building. Yet, the obstacles to full commercialization, followed by privatization, of this service are significant. They include:

- Delays in modernizing this service to be more responsive to changing customer incomes and divergent heating/comfort preferences. Bulgaria's DH systems do not allow consumers at the building or apartment level to decide when and how much heat to consume. While this flexibility is not present and may not be important in many DH systems in OECD countries where utility bills consume a small percentage of household income, it is vital in countries such as Bulgaria where heating bills are the second highest expenditure after food for the average household. A change in supplier mindset and management, and comprehensive technical modernization are needed to give customers more choice in their comfort, consumption and corresponding expenditure levels.
- Wide income differences among residents (DH customers) within the same apartment building, which make it even more necessary for service providers to facilitate consumption flexibility while tariffs are adjusted to cover costs for an efficient service.
- Societal reluctance to organize apartment owners within multi-apartment buildings into a legal body (condominium or other home-owner association) to be the contracting party for all communal services (including district heating), with rules and technical means to allocate these costs fairly among building residents.
- Technical difficulty of disconnecting individual apartments for non-payment or to prevent them from enjoying the benefits of this communal service if they opt not to subscribe;
- However, district heating systems are introducing meter devices in blocks and apartments which will enable every customer to decide individually when and how much heat to use. Targets in this direction are 72 percent of the buildings by end October 2002; and 85 percent of the system by end-2002; and
- Poor payment discipline by state-dependent organizations (state and municipal buildings, schools, hospitals, etc.), which constitute the second largest customer group after households, and which are difficult to disconnect because of the high social and political costs.

The Government's District Heating Strategy (2000) and revisions to the Energy and Energy Efficiency Act made in October 2001 are addressing the need to modernize DH services and balance the rights and obligations of suppliers and customers; however, challenges to full commercialization remain significant. The Government expects that a quick adjustment of tariffs to their cost-recovery levels will be sufficient to commercialize DH services. However, experience over the

---

[121] The COM approves the price of district heating, applied only to subsidized district heating companies, following a proposal by the Ministry of Energy and Energy Resources.

last few years has shown that without modernization and ultimate recourse to disconnection for non-payment, tariff adjustments result in higher non-payment and an erosion in the customer base because of the perceived inefficiency and unfairness of the service.

Gas Supply. The Bulgargaz Financial Rehabilitation Plan approved by the Government in 1999 resulted in a re-capitalization of the company and a reduction in accounts payable and receivable. About BGN 630 million of the company's debt to the Government (for tax arrears and loans) was partly converted into state equity and partly off-set against receivables from select state-owned enterprises (mainly DH companies). However, with financially weak district heating companies accounting for over 45 percent of Bulgargaz' sales (and gas costs accounting for about 70 percent of total DH costs), the company's fortunes remain inextricably linked with the recovery of the DH business in Bulgaria.

Coal Mines. Uneconomic coal mines are being either partially closed and the companies liquidated, while viable mines are in the process of being privatized, with subsidies increasingly targeted towards facilitating these outcomes.

Coal Briquettes. Briquettes made from the indigenous high-sulfur lignite constitute between 30–40 percent of household energy consumption, almost equal to electricity. While price subsidies for non-household customers were eliminated in end-1999, the only briquette plant in the country was merged with a thermal power plant (Maritsa East-1)—the plant's electricity sales cross-subsidized household briquette prices. However, as of early 2002, household briquette prices were reportedly on average higher than estimated average production costs, thus eliminating this cross-subsidy.

On the **consumer side**, the budget also funds a **"Winter Energy Benefits Program"** to supplement the winter income of low-income families, typically living in households which are eligible for Guaranteed Minimum Income benefits (see Chapter 8). This benefit, provided for five winter months from November to April, is now provided to about 600,000 families (or about 25 percent of total households covering about 15 percent of the total population). Until 2002, the bulk of these households (about 95 percent) were in areas not served by the district heating companies and relied mainly on coal and/or electricity for their heating needs. In 2002, the eligibility of families in areas served by DH companies is expected to increase to about 17 percent of the total families covered by this benefit program.

As is evident from Table 10.2, budget subsidies for service providers have been steadily declining since 1998, while those for vulnerable consumers have been increasing after a big decline between 1998 and 1999. For district heating, the biggest recipient of annual budget transfers, the ratio of subsidy to billed sales dropped from 50.7 percent in 1998 to 16.3 percent in 2000 and 12.7 percent in 2001.

Quasi-Fiscal Subsidies

Quasi-fiscal subsidies include:

- operating losses (before any bad-debt provisioning) of the state-owned district heating companies which are not covered by explicit subsidies;[122] and
- non-payment (or delayed payment) by budget-dependent entities (schools, hospitals, municipal and state buildings, etc.) and households, and by the energy entities to the tax authorities. Non-payment is most pronounced for district heating services, with DH companies, in turn, not paying their gas bills to Bulgargaz.

---

[122] Electricity, gas and most major coal mines are profitable.

TABLE 10.2: EXPLICIT FISCAL SUBSIDIES

(EXCLUDING CAPITAL INVESTMENT)

TYPE OF ENERGY SERVICE	SUBSIDIES, MILLION BGN					
	1997	1998	1999	2000	2001	2002 (PLAN)
1 District Heating	65.11	183.03	60.48	63.65	50.00	37.00
2 Coal Mines	4.95	21.96	70.85	15.99	5.00	3.00
3 Coal Briquette Plant	20.94	48.50	24.28	4.36	—	—
4 Gas (Bulgargaz Debt Write-off)	—	—	370.00	—	—	—
5 Winter Energy Subsidy Program[a]		147.60	61.60	66.40	74.50	110.60
TOTAL		401.09	587.21	150.40	129.50	150.60
GDP		22,421	23,790	26,753	29,618	30,783
Subsidies as percent of GDP		1.79	2.47	0.56	0.44	0.49

[a] Budget allocation is made towards the end of each year for that 5-month (November-March) heating season. The above figures assume that two-fifths of the budget is for the year in which it is allocated and three-fifths for the following year (January-March).

Note: Non-payment by state and municipally-funded entities are typically cleared by the budget at year-end or in the following year (by increasing budget allocation for heating bills).

Source: Ministry of Energy and Energy Resources.

Part of the operating losses are a result of state tolerance of inefficient operation (including high levels of energy losses in electricity and heat transmission and distribution) while a part of it is a reluctance to support investment and adjust tariffs to better reflect service costs. Only recently has the Government started to take steps to address these problems. Bulgaria would need to maintain the reform momentum until energy tariffs reach full cost recovery.

With respect to non-payment, while the budget usually ends up paying for budget-dependent entities (usually with an off-set between receivables, arrears for gas and the gas received from Gazprom for transit fee payment), collection from households remains difficult due to legal barriers and technical difficulty to disconnect individual apartments in a multi-apartment building. Privatization of the largest commercial consumers has significantly reduced non-payment from this customer segment.

Operating losses (after subsidy provision) are most significant in the district heating subsector. DH company losses rose from around BGN 2.6 million in 1999 to 30.6 million in 2000, largely due to the increases in natural gas prices which are not passed through into tariffs or subsidized by the budget. Non-payments for district heating amounted to BGN 135.5 million in 2000, or about 7 percent of sales, and are estimated at BGN 179.5 million in 2001, with households and budget-funded organizations being the biggest non-payers. Quasi-fiscal subsidies resulting from excess losses and non-payments for DH services amount to 0.3 percent of GDP in 2000. Excess loss estimates are not available for 2001.

Consumer Subsidies with Limited Impact on the State Budget
One major form of consumer subsidy in Bulgaria is the below-cost price of electricity for household customers (covered by higher-than-cost prices paid by all other customers). Non-payment for electricity is not a serious problem in Bulgaria, particularly after privatization of the largest enterprises during 1998–2000. It should be noted that while average electricity tariffs are sufficient to

TABLE 10.3: HOUSEHOLD ELECTRICITY SUBSIDIES

(CROSS-SUBSIDIZED BY OTHER CONSUMERS)

	1998	1999	2000	2001 (EST)	2002 (PLAN)
Household Electricity Supply, '000 mwh	10,602	10,116	11,001	10,017	10,183
Average Tariff, BGN/mwh (net of VAT)	44.72	53.60	62.80	63.54	70.60
Average Tariff, US$/mwh (net of VAT)	24.17	29.61	31.72	30.84	33.94
Est. "cash" cost of LV supply, BGN/mwh[a]	59.2	62.45	71.28	74.16	74.88
Implicit Subsidy to Households, m BGN[b]	153.49	89.48	93.29	106.38	43.58

[a] Costs estimated based on average generation cost of US$/mwh 20–22 for generation, 3.0 for transmission/dispatch and 9.0–10.0 for low voltage (LV) distribution. Subsidy content is considerably higher if long-run average cost of LV (household) supply is used. This cost is estimated to be about US$50–60/mwh net of VAT (BGN 105–125/mwh) based on an average generation cost of US$32–35/mwh, and at least US$3 and US$15–20 per mwh for transmission and distribution respectively.

[b] The implicit subsidy is based on the estimated cash cost of LV supply. If the long-run average cost of LV (household) supply is used, the implicit subsidy would be considerably higher.

Source: Tariff development (NEK). Household electricity supply (Energy-Environment Review).

cover cash operating costs, they do not adequately contribute to the sector least-cost investment and environmental improvement program.

This high level of cross-subsidization of household electricity supply (see Table 10.3), compounded by technical and institutional barriers for households to control consumption of district heat (and the correspondence DH bills), and the inconvenience and environmental unattractiveness of coal briquettes, have resulted in excessive and uneconomic use of electricity for cooking and heating.[123] While the total energy consumed by households is in line with other countries with similar climatic and economic conditions, at 1,257 kwh per capita or 3,549 kwh per household (average annual consumption in 1999), Bulgaria is among countries with a high level of household electricity consumption. This consumption can be compared with substantially lower household consumption (per capita) in Romania (352 kwh), Lithuania (471 kwh), Turkey (608 kwh), Estonia (923 kwh) and Slovak Republic (1,030 kwh). The high usage of electricity by Bulgarian households reflects the dependence on electricity for heating and will be particularly challenging to overcome in the transition to a market economy.

State Investment Support—Contingent Liabilities

The power and gas subsectors, and to a lesser extent the DH subsector, have been beneficiaries of state support for their capital investment programs. The National Electricity Company and DH companies have received state-guaranteed loans, and the state has provided "comfort" to the private sponsors of the Maritsa East 1 (new) and 3 (rehabilitation) power plants, undertaking to guarantee the performance of NEK in accordance with contracts signed with the plants. These two projects have the major advantage of being privately sponsored and financed by reputable international investors. However, the contracts require NEK to take or pay for the contracted capacity at negotiated prices and leave the bulk of market risks (demand, price and payment, including for

---

[123] Net fuel conversion efficiency (after auxiliary uses) is about 25–30 percent for the bulk of Bulgaria's power plants; another 15–20 percent of this is "lost" in transmission/distribution to end-users, resulting in a very inefficient (and fuel intensive) means of heating and cooking. District heating, particularly if produced by combined heat and power plants with over 80 percent conversion efficiency, and other fuels such as gas, would be far more efficient and clean modes of cooking and space heating.

TABLE 10.4: STATE-GUARANTEED SUPPORT FOR THE POWER AND GAS SECTORS

PURPOSE/PROJECT	YEAR CON-TRACTED	CREDITOR OR SPONSOR	LOAN/PRO-JECT AMT, mUS$	BALANCE DUE ON 1/1/02, mUS$	EST. ANNUAL PAYMENTS AMOUNT, mUS$	START YEAR	END YEAR
State Guaranteed Loans							
1 Energy (I)—Power Generation and System Management	1993	IBRD	78.30	50.30	$7.20	1997	2010
2 Maritsa East 2, Block 8—Environmental Improvement[a]	1993	EIB	40.54	34.50	$7.39	1997	2007
3 Maritsa East 2, Block 8—Environ. Improvement[b]	1993	EBRD	40.00	21.89	$5.05	1997	2007
4 Kozloduy—Modernization of Units 5 and 6[c]	2001	Several	400.00	400.00	$45.31	2001	2020
5 District Heating Metering (Pilot)	1998	IBRD	15.00	15.00	$1.70	2000	2012
Explicit Contingent Fiscal Liability			573.84	521.70	66.65		
1 Maritsa East 1—New 2x335 (670) MW plant[d]	2001	AES	900.00*		211.29	2005	2020
2 Maritsa East 3—Rehab of 4×210 (840) MW plant[e]	2001	Entergy	440.00*		176.60	2003	2020
Implicit Contingent Fiscal Liability			1,340.00		387.89		
TOTAL					454.54		

Estimates not available of reinvestment of gas transit fees into Bulgargaz' investment program.

* Estimated project costs (including contingencies and financing cost).

[a] EUR 45 million at 1 US$ = 1.11 EUR.

[b] EUR 40 million at 1 US$ = 1.11 EUR.

[c] Amortization based on an estimated loan amount of $400 million, an assumed interest rate of 7.5 percent and 15 year maturity. Actual loan amount is $368.5 million.

[d] Payment begins after construction (3 years) at $45/mwh and 80 percent net plant and capacity factor.

[e] Payment for each unit begins after rehab (12–18 mos) at $30/mwh (80 percent net plant/capacity factor).

Source: SAEER for State Guaranteed Loans 1 to 3. Rest World Bank estimates.

exports) with NEK. It should also be noted, that the existing legal and regulatory framework does not allow private investors and consumers of electricity to assume any significant market risks, thus expressly leaving a significant portion of investment risks with the Government. While some opening of the domestic electricity market is envisaged, the framework requires the Government to prescribe power generation projects and establishes NEK as the only entity allowed to import and export electricity.

In the case of Bulgargaz, its investment program 1999–2001 to expand transit to Turkey, Greece and Macedonia, estimated to cost US$300–400 million, was financed by the budget which reinvests transit fees (actually, proceeds from gas received from Gazprom for payment of transit fees),[124] and by a loan from Russia's Gazprom.

---

[124] It is not clear whether this financing is provided as state equity or loan. However, this practice has reportedly been discontinued in 2002.

Available estimates of state support for capital investment are shown in Table 10.4.

In addition to the contingent liabilities associated with the power purchase agreements and state-guaranteed loans assumed by state-owned power enterprises, the gas contract between Russia's Gazprom and the state-owned gas monopoly Bulgargaz signed in 1998 involves an implicit state guarantee of Bulgargaz' obligations. The contract ensures sufficient supply to meet Bulgaria's needs; however, the following elements of the contract could potentially impose costly obligations on the country: (i) fixed annual volume ceilings until 2010, set when demand forecasts were more optimistic than actual market absorption, and with a requirement to take-or-pay for a high proportion of the ceiling amount; (ii) the roll-over period for non-taken gas is only five years; (iii) the volumes contracted are over-and-above volumes received from transit fees; (iv) Gazprom does not allow the re-export of volumes contracted by Bulgargaz or volumes received for transit fees; and (v) the contract price is indexed to international oil prices (specifically to gas oil and heavy fuel oil). While it is difficult to predict the flexibility with which this gas contract can be re-negotiated, declining demand over the last few years and high prices suggest that the contract poses a significant fiscal risk if it is enforced. A similar outcome is possible with regard to the contracting of electricity from the planned new Maritsa East 1 power plant.

Conclusion on Current Situation

As is evident from the preceding analysis, the operational and investment efficiency of energy sector enterprises have played, and will continue to play, a major role in shaping Bulgaria's fiscal situation, its economic competitiveness, and the well-being of its people. The country has taken important steps over the last three years to reduce the operating subsidies granted to district heating and coal entities, adjust tariffs, increase the transparency of sector operations (through unbundling of NEK), and amend the legal framework to facilitate the commercialization of energy services. There has been an overall reduction in subsidies (both direct and quasi-fiscal). Going forward, reforms in the energy sector should continue to aim at reversing the following trends:

- an increase in demand for economically costly electricity[125] for heating purposes, particularly by households, substituting coal and district heating, the household prices of which now have a lower subsidy content than electricity;
- focusing government attention on building new independent power plants to meet electricity demand (with demand distorted by high relative subsidies), rather than on developing policies to promote the rational and efficient use of energy; and
- an erosion in consumer welfare, particularly of the poor who rely more extensively on coal and district heating, the prices of which were without commensurate actions to improve supply quality and end-use efficiency.

In parallel, further delays in liberalizing investment decisions and allowing consumers (particularly large industries) and investors to take a great share of investment and supply risks (and rewards), will mean that the contingent public risk associated with energy services will remain high. Table 10.4 illustrates the magnitude of the contingent liability associated with state guarantees (or other forms of state support). However, it also follows that further reform in these areas have potentially a very high pay-off.

Investment Requirements

The Government has been taking important steps to reduce the fiscal and quasi-fiscal burden associated with the provision of energy services by advancing the commercialization of these services.

---

[125] In contrast to administrative or accounting costs, economic costs take into account the opportunity costs and benefits of the use of resources and therefore economic costs provide a much better metric to inform public policy.

The key challenge ahead will be to completely phase out subsidies related to covering operating costs of service providers (while further strengthening social support to low income and vulnerable consumer groups), eliminate price distortions represented by cross-subsidies between customer groups (particularly in favor of household electricity customers), and manage the capital investment program to minimize explicit state liabilities while ensuring efficient, safe and secure energy services for the country.

Experience to date suggests that full commercialization will be difficult in the case of district heating (see above), and will need to be attempted in a balanced manner for all services in order to prevent a distortion of demand, as experienced in the case of electricity. While the aggressive removal of price subsidies for coal briquettes is laudable, the heavy subsidization of household electricity (an energy source used most by the wealthy) and delays in modernizing the district heating systems through low-cost investments and institutional reforms, could be interpreted as having a pro-rich rather than a pro-poor bias.

Optimizing the investment program will be particularly challenging. While the Government rightly intends to maximize the use of private capital, quantifying and managing public risk will be important. Studies and anecdotal information indicate the following investment requirements in the sector over the 2001-15 period (recognizing that they are based on changeable assumptions of demand growth and capital costs):

Power Sector (US$1.7–3.4 billion). Work done by the World Bank and the Bulgarian authorities in preparation of the Energy-Environment Review (2001) estimated the rehabilitation of power generation plants to cost US$934, and the rehabilitation of transmission and distribution—US$150–200 million, with rehabilitation to be carried out between 2001 and 2006. The estimated cost of investments in new power plants ranged from about US$660 million (in the case of no electricity exports) to US$2.3 billion (assuming maximum exports), with *base case* investments (mid-level exports) estimated at US$1.7 billion and the first new plant being required by 2006.

Gas Sector (US$0.3–1.5 billion). The expansion of gas transit capacity to Turkey, Greece and Macedonia (US$300–400 million) which is helping to develop a low-pressure gas system in Bulgaria was completed in 2002. Other major investments will be directed to the development of a low-pressure gas system. These investments are expected to be taken mainly by the private sector and a small investment of some US$50 million by Bulgargaz. While the World Bank has not made any estimates of these investment costs, they could well be in excess of US$1.0 billion.

District Heating Sector. (US$220 million, excluding investment in heat generation sources). Background work done in preparation of the Government's District Heating Strategy (2000) estimated that investments of about US$220 million over five years were needed to modernize and rehabilitate the transmission and distribution systems in Sofia, Pernik and several of the largest DH systems, accounting for 80 percent of the national DH consumption.

Additional investments (not estimated) will be needed to rehabilitate some of the coal mines, and consumers will need to invest in systems to regulate better district heat consumption and utilize natural gas once it is supplied.

During the transition phase, while price distortions and legal/regulatory impediments to liberalizing the energy market are being removed, the state will need to strengthen its analytical and planning capacity to ensure that vital investments, whether publicly or privately financed, are made to support clear and well-justified public objectives. State support for such investments will need to weighed against the possible loss in economic growth or consumer welfare due to a deterioration in service quality. Planning capacity, and corresponding regulatory capacity, will be of even greater importance once Bulgaria's creditworthiness improves to a point where access to credit for infrastructure investment is less constrained.

Priorities

Separate Policy-Making, Economic Regulation and Ownership (or Operational) Functions. This has been achieved to a considerable degree, though with some delay, through the October 2001 amendments to the Energy and Energy Efficiency Act. Consolidation of all regulatory functions in the State Energy Regulatory Commission and improvement of its stature and competence should contribute to a better balancing of consumer and supplier long-term interests.

Facilitate Consumer Choice for More Efficient and Clean Space Heating. In high population density areas, where the necessary infrastructure is already installed, district heating is the least cost and environmentally cleanest means of space and water heating. However, as discussed earlier, some serious impediments need to be overcome and the system modernized before it can be successfully commercialized. The investments cited above, supported with legal and institutional changes, would provide consumers with the means to control their heating expenditures and allow operating subsidies to be completely phased out in 4–5 years. They would also permit recipients of targeted income subsidies to use these subsidies more cost-effectively. Indeed, if distorted energy prices and lack of a suitable heating strategy for high-population density areas (served by district heating) result in a collapse of the major district heating systems (with over 5,000 MW equivalent of connected load), the impact on electricity distribution networks could be damaging and the need for investment in new power generation capacity, the costs of which would need to be passed on to consumers, would be prohibitive.

In areas not served by district heating, the development of low-pressure natural gas services should be a priority. Consumers in these areas typically use either costly electricity (even at subsidized prices, electricity is costly) or polluting coal. The extensive use of coal has been identified as a major source of local pollution and respiratory ailments. Coal usage would have to be phased out to meet EU environmental standards. Bulgaria could boost both its competitiveness and social welfare through the efficient use of its energy resources.

Although extensive electricity use for heating may have been sustainable with the low costs of nuclear fuel and indigenous lignite (on which Bulgaria relies most), and the depreciated asset base, this high dependence will not be affordable if Bulgaria is to meet EU environmental requirements and reflect the costs of new investment in electricity tariffs. In the second half of the current decade, the average electricity price for households is expected to rise to its economic cost of US$50–60/mwh—more than twice the economic cost of low-pressure natural gas and district heating. Assuming five winter months and an average heat requirement of 1.0 mwh heat equivalent per month, households relying on district heating and gas would spend about US$125/season on heating (about 5 percent of annual household income), while those relying on electricity would spend more than twice that amount or sacrifice comfort.

Replace Price Subsidies with Better Targeted Income Supplements for Low-Income and Vulnerable Households, Particularly for Winter Heating. With the modernization of DH services and expanding access to gas, income supplements should be linked to a reasonable amount of energy for heating, lighting and cooking services. The cash provided for each service should be linked to the price of the most efficient and readily available form of energy for that service: district heating or gas for heating, coal, gas or LPG for cooking, and electricity for lighting. Capital costs of key equipment or connection costs could also be subsidized.

In providing heating subsidies in areas served by district heating where wealthy and poor typically live in the same building, the social protection program should be designed to mitigate social tensions, particularly since the entire building could be subject to disconnection if the entire heating bill is not paid. The creation of home-owner associations and the channeling of subsidies for low-income residents through this association may be an effective means of allowing buildings to avail themselves of relatively low-cost district heating services or to develop alternative building-level heating options.

Accelerate Electricity Price Adjustments to Eliminate Distortions. Household surveys suggest that low income and vulnerable households do not use electricity for heating purposes; only higher income groups do. Consequently, there appears to be limited justification for gradualism in the adjustment of household electricity prices to their cost-recovery levels. As an interim solution, a subsidized tariff could be considered for a life-line level of 30–50 kwh/month in summer and 50–100 kwh/month in winter, or the present low night-time (off-peak) tariff maintained.[126] This would, of course, need to be supported with appropriate metering and billing mechanisms.

Accelerate Cost-Effective Rehabilitation of Existing Assets, Ideally Through Proper Privatization. While appropriate regulations are being put in place, it may be necessary to consider suitable contracts, with sovereign guarantees if necessary, to attract qualified investors to improve energy services. In areas such as the transmission/distribution of district heat, where major legal and regulatory reforms are still needed and contractual arrangements are more complex, investments could be initiated through the state budget and sovereign loans (see District Heating above).

Defer Costly Investments in New Power and Heat Generation Capacity Until Regulatory Reforms are More Advanced and Investors Can Assume a Larger Share of the Market Risks.[127] Given the high level of uncertainty associated with demand projections at this stage of transition to a market economy, the available surplus capacity, the "lumpy" nature of investments in power plants, and the high risk premium which private capital is likely to demand at the present time, it would be more prudent to direct investment capital towards areas of highest return. These include rehabilitation of existing assets to improve their efficiency, reliability and safety, and measures to reduce the high dependence on electricity for heating and cooking.

Require private investors to assume the bulk of market risks associated with their investments in new power capacity for export, and quickly create the legal and regulatory framework to allow such risk sharing. This is particularly important because over 55 percent of investment in new capacity being considered by NEK is associated with projected export demand. Under the present market structure, only NEK can export (and import) electricity and, therefore, must assume all the market risks (and rewards) of the export markets. These risks and rewards are best assumed by the private sector.

Privatize Electricity and Gas Distribution. Privatization of electricity and gas distribution to strategic investors has important potential benefits including eliminating high level of technical and non-technical losses (accounting for more than 20 percent of electricity in some distribution companies), and providing generators and other suppliers with creditworthy customers. Potential benefits of privatization of gas distribution also include clean and competitive alternatives to coal briquettes and electricity.

Limit State-Owned NEK's Long-Term Power Purchase Contracts. In order not to constrain the emergence of a competitive electricity market, NEK (the transmission/dispatch company) should consider long-term power purchase agreements (PPAs) only for essential investments to ensure reliable supply over the next 4–5 years. Currently, only about 40 percent of projected demand will be available to competitive suppliers and that includes the electricity generated by the nuclear plant and the long-term PPAs for the Maritsa East 1 (670 MW) new plant and Maritsa East 3 (860 MW) rehabilitation.

---

[126] In mid-2002, the Government introduced a subsidized tariff for a life-line level of consumption as well as implementing tariff adjustments aimed at reaching full cost recovery levels by end-2004.

[127] This and the following recommendations are based on the findings of the Bank's Energy-Environment Review for Bulgaria (June 29, 2001).

Liberalize Investment Decisions Related to Supplying Industry and Large Commercial Consumers.
As with the export market, the Government should allow industrial and large commercial customers of gas and electricity to contract the bulk of their supply directly from private power producers and gas suppliers, including from abroad. In addition to boosting competition and increasing efficiency, this will mitigate the Government's contingent liabilities associated with all supply in Bulgaria being handled by NEK. Limit the Government's role to one of "authorization" for the construction of new power plants which do not sell their electricity in the regulated part of the electricity market.

Direct Privatization Proceeds Towards Social and Other Strategic Objectives.   Design the power and DH privatization strategy so as to strike an optimal balance between cash proceeds from asset sale, end-use tariffs, investment obligations placed on the new owner,[128] and debts to be serviced by the privatized company. To maximize privatization proceeds, privatize generating plants after clear market rules have been adopted, giving generators the ability to improve efficiency and capture domestic and foreign markets. Use revenues from privatization to retire sovereign debt and invest in areas where social welfare can be significantly improved (such as by reducing heating bills through more efficient energy services) but where private investment would not be affordable under the present legal and regulatory environment.

---

[128] Ideally, instead of investment requirements, the privatized entity should be required to meet specific service quality standards over a reasonable time period.

REFERENCES

The word "processed" describes informally reproduced works that may not be commonly available through libraries.

Burnside, A. Craig. 2002. "Fiscal sustainability in Bulgaria." World Bank, Europe and Central Asia Region, Washington, D.C. Processed.

Commission of European Communities. *2001 Regular Report On Bulgaria's Progress Towards Accession*, Brussels, 13.11.2001, SEC(2001) 1744, p. 96.

Crochet, Jean-Jacques. 2002. "The State Railway—Fiscal Burden and Options for Reform." World Bank, Europe and Central Asia Region, Washington, D.C. Processed.

Jack, William G. 2002. "Health in Transition." World Bank, Europe and Central Asia Region, Washington, D.C. Processed.

Mertaugh, Michael. 2002. "Education—The Demographic Challenge." World Bank, Europe and Central Asia Region, Washington, D.C. Processed.

Ringold, Dena. 2000. *Roma and the Transition in Central and Eastern Europe: Trends and Challenges*. World Bank, Washington, D.C.

Ringold, Dena and Esperanza Lasagabaster. 2002. "Social Protection: Issues and Recommendations." World Bank, Europe and Central Asia Region, Washington, D.C. Processed.

Ross, Kenneth and Rosalind Levačić, eds. 1999. *Needs-Based Resource Allocation in Education via Formula Funding of Schools*. Paris: International Institute for Education Planning, UNESCO.

Tesliuc, Cornelia.2002. "Social Protection and Poverty Reduction in Bulgaria." World Bank, Europe and Central Asia Region, Washington, D.C. Processed.

Tommasi Daniel. 2002. "Is Bulgaria Ready for MTEF and Outcome Budgeting." World Bank, Europe and Central Asia Region, Washington, D.C. Processed.

Bulgaria, Council of Ministers. 2001. *The Governance Program of the Government of the Republic of Bulgaria*, 2001–2005. Sofia.

World Bank. 1994. *Bureaucrats in Business*. Washington, D.C.

World Bank. 2000a. *Anticorruption in Transition: A Contribution to the Policy Debate*. World Bank, Europe and Central Asia Region, Washington, D.C. Processed.

World Bank. 2000b. *Managing Fiscal Risk in Bulgaria*. Policy Research Working Paper No. 2282. Washington, D.C.

World Bank. 2001. *Bulgaria: The Dual Challenge of Transition and Accession*. Europe and Central Asia Region. Washington, D.C.

World Bank. 2002a. "Expenditure Policies Towards EU Accession." World Bank, Europe and Central Asia Region, Washington, D.C. Processed.

World Bank. 2002b. "Measuring Governance in South East Europe." World Bank, Europe and Central Asia Region, Washington, D.C. Processed.

World Bank. Forthcoming. *Poverty Assessment Update*. World Bank, Europe and Central Asia Region, Washington, D.C.

Zaheer, Salman. 2002. "Energy—A Complex Restructuring: Fiscal, Social and Market Interactions." World Bank, Europe and Central Asia Region, Washington, D.C. Processed.

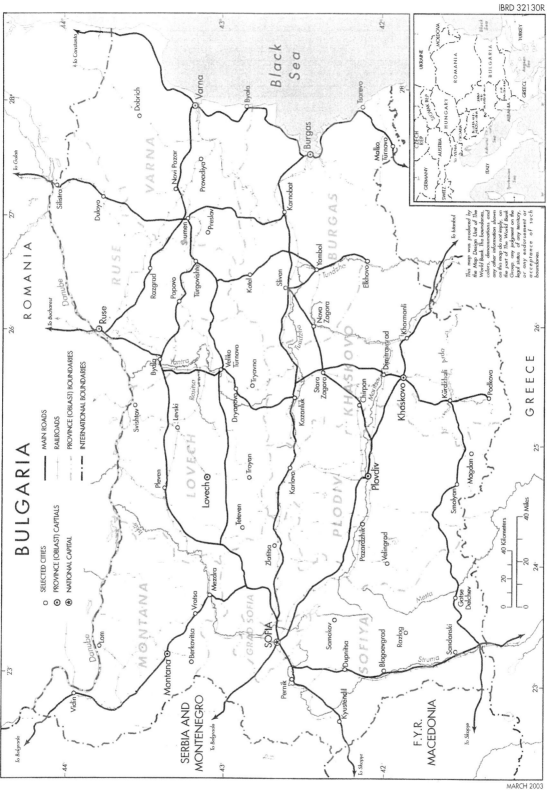

BULGARIA

Legend:
- ○ SELECTED CITIES
- ⊙ PROVINCE (OBLAST) CAPITALS
- ⊛ NATIONAL CAPITAL
- —— MAIN ROADS
- ┼┼┼ RAILROADS
- ·················· PROVINCE (OBLAST) BOUNDARIES
- ─·─·─ INTERNATIONAL BOUNDARIES

IBRD 32130R

MARCH 2003

This map was produced by the Map Design Unit of The World Bank. The boundaries, colors, denominations and any other information shown on this map do not imply, on the part of The World Bank Group, any judgment on the legal status of any territory, or any endorsement or acceptance of such boundaries.

ROMANIA

SERBIA AND MONTENEGRO

F.Y.R. MACEDONIA

GREECE

Black Sea

Provinces: VARNA, RUSE, BURGAS, MONTANA, LOVECH, GRAD SOFIA, PLODIV, KHASKOVO, SOFIYA

Cities: Dobrich, Varna, Byala, Tsarevo, Burgas, Malko Tŭrnovo, Novi Pazar, Provadiya, Silistra, Dulovo, Preslav, Shumen, Karnobat, Razgrad, Popovo, Tŭrgovishte, Kotel, Sliven, Yambol, Elkhovo, Ruse, Byala, Veliko Tŭrnovo, Tryavna, Nova Zagora, Kharmanli, Svishtov, Levski, Dryanovo, Stara Zagora, Chirpan, Dimitrovgrad, Kŭrdzhali, Podkova, Pleven, Troyan, Karlovo, Kazanlŭk, Khaskovo, Teteven, Zlatitsa, Plovdiv, Pazardzhik, Magdan, Smolyan, Mezdra, Vratsa, Berkovitsa, Montana, Samokov, Dupnitsa, Velingrad, Razlog, Blagoevgrad, Gotse Delchev, Sandanski, Vidin, Lom, Pernik, Kyustendil

Rivers: Danube, Yantra, Rositsa, Tundzha, Maritsa, Mesta, Struma

To Constanța, To Galați, To Bucharest, To Istanbul, To Belgrade, To Skopje

40 Miles / 40 Kilometers

Inset map: UKRAINE, MOLDOVA, ROMANIA, BULGARIA, TURKEY, GREECE, ALBANIA, ITALY, HUNGARY, AUSTRIA, SLOVAK REP., CZECH REP., GERMANY, SWITZ., Black Sea